On the Holy Spirit *with* Letters to Amphilochius

Saint Basil of Caesarea

On the Holy Spirit

with

Letters to Amphilochius

DOUBLE VOLUME EDITION

Saint Basil of Caesarea

FROM VOLUME 8 OF THE SECOND SERIES OF
THE NICENE & POST-NICENE FATHERS

On the Holy Spirit *with* Letters to Amphilochius
DOUBLE VOLUME EDITION
Saint Basil of Caesarea
© 2018 Paterikon Publications

Some illustrations were retrieved from the *Orthodox Arts Journal*
© 2017 Orthodox Arts Journal

All rights reserved. No part of this publication may be reproduced, stored in a retrieval system, or transmitted in any form or by any means—electronic, mechanical, photocopy, recording, or any other—without the prior written permission of the publisher. The only exception is brief quotations in printed reviews.

ISBN 978-1985634558

PATERIKON PUBLICATIONS
Brookline, MA 02445

info@paterikonpublications.com

TABLE *of* CONTENTS

NOTE FROM THE PUBLISHER 7

SECTION ONE: *On the Holy Spirit*

    Preface 11

    Text 13

SECTION TWO: *Letters to Amphilochius*

    LETTER 150 – In the name of Heraclidas 143

    LETTER 161 – On his consecration as Bishop 146

    LETTER 176 148

    LETTER 188 – Concerning the Canons (I-XVI) 149

    LETTER 199 – Concerning the Canons (XVII-L) 162

    LETTER 200 172

    LETTER 201 173

    LETTER 202 174

    LETTER 217 – Concerning the Canons (LI-LXXXIV) 174

    LETTER 218 185

    LETTER 231 186

    LETTER 232 188

    LETTER 233 – In reply to certain questions 189

    LETTER 234 – In an answer to another question 191

    LETTER 235 – In an answer to another question 193

    LETTER 236 196

    LETTER 248 203

NOTE FROM THE PUBLISHER

THE INTENT OF this publication was dual-fold: to offer a curated double volume of related texts, and to do so in a manner that is pleasing to the eye of the reader. While we have maintained the extant introductory remarks and footnotes of the original editions, a few updates have been made to the formatting, namely, Psalm numbering according to the LXX, and other biblical references notated in Arabic rather than Roman numerals.

Blame for any remaining formatting errors belong solely on our shoulders, and for those we ask forgiveness.

Paterikon Publications
Feast of the Life-Giving Spring
April 13, 2018

SECTION ONE
On the Holy Spirit
by Saint Basil of Caesarea

TRANSLATED WITH NOTES BY
The Rev. Blomfield Jackson, M.A.
Vicar of Saint Bartholomew's, Moor Lane, and Fellow of King's College, London

SAINT BASIL OF CAESAREA

PREFACE TO THE BOOK OF SAINT BASIL
On the Holy Spirit

THE HERESY OF ARIUS lowered the dignity of the Holy Ghost as well as that of the Son. He taught that the Three Persons of the Holy Trinity are wholly unlike one another both in essence and in glory. "There is a triad, not in equal glories;" "one more glorious than the other in their glories to an infinite degree." So says the *Thalia*, quoted in Ath. de Syn. § 15. But the Nicene definition, while it was precise in regard to the Son, left the doctrine of the Holy Ghost comparatively open, (Πιστεύομεν εἰς τὸ Ἅγιον Πνεῦμα,) not from hesitation or doubt, but because this side of Arian speculation was not prominent. (Cf. Basil, Letters cxxv. and ccxxvi. and Dr. Swete in D.C.B. iii. 121.) It was the expulsion of Macedonius from the see of Constantinople in 360 which brought "Macedonianism" to a head. He was put there by Arians as an Arian. Theodoret (Ecc. Hist. ii. 5) explains how disagreement arose. He was an upholder, if not the author, of the watchword ὁμοιούσιον (Soc. ii. 45) (but many supporters of the ὁμοιούσιον (*e.g.*, Eustathius of Sebasteia) shrank from calling the Holy Ghost a creature. So the Pneumatomachi began to be clearly marked off. The various creeds of the Arians and semi-Arians did not directly attack the Godhead of the Holy Ghost, though they did not accept the doctrine of the essential unity of the Three Persons. (Cf. Hahn, *Bibliothek der Symbole*, pp. 148–174, quoted by Swete.) But their individual teaching went far beyond their confessions. The Catholic theologians were roused to the danger, and on the return of Athanasius from his third exile, a council was held at Alexandria which resulted in the first formal ecclesiastical condemnation of the depravers of the Holy Ghost, in the *Tomus ad Antiochenos* (*q.v.* with the preface on p. 481 of Ath. in the edition of this series. Cf. also Ath.

ad Serap. i. 2, 10). In the next ten years the Pneumatomachi, Macedonians, or Marathonians, so called from Marathonius, bishop of Nicomedia, whose support to the party was perhaps rather pecuniary than intellectual (Nicephorus H.E. ix. 47), made head, and were largely identified with the Homoiousians. In 374 was published the *Ancoratus* of St. Epiphanius, bishop of Salamis in Cyprus, written in 373, and containing two creeds (*vide* Heurtley de F. et Symb. pp. 14–18), the former of which is nearly identical with the Confession of Constantinople. It expresses belief in τὸ Πνεῦμα τὸ Ἅγιον, Κύριον, καὶ Ζωοποιὸν, τὸ ἐκ τοῦ Πατρὸς ἐκπορευόμενον, τὸ σὺν Πατρὶ καὶ Υἱῷ συμπροσκυνοί μενον καὶ συνδοξαζόμενον, τὸ λαλῆσαν διὰ τῶν προφητῶν. It is in this same year, 374, that Amphilochius, the first cousin of Gregory of Nazianzus and friend and spiritual son of Basil, paid the first of his annual autumn visits to Cæsarea (Bishop Lightfoot, D.C.B. i. 105) and there urged St. Basil to clear up all doubt as to the true doctrine of the Holy Spirit by writing a treatise on the subject. St. Basil complied, and, on the completion of the work, had it engrossed on parchment (Letter ccxxxi.) and sent it to Amphilochius, to whom he dedicated it.

CHAPTER ONE

Prefatory remarks on the need of exact investigation of the most minute portions of theology.

YOUR DESIRE FOR INFORMATION, my right well-beloved and most deeply respected brother Amphilochius, I highly commend, and not less your industrious energy. I have been exceedingly delighted at the care and watchfulness shown in the expression of your opinion that of all the terms concerning God in every mode of speech, not one ought to be left without exact investigation. You have turned to good account your reading of the exhortation of the Lord, "Everyone that asketh receiveth, and he that seeketh findeth,"[1] and by your diligence in asking might, I ween, stir even the most reluctant to give you a share of what they possess. And this in you yet further moves my admiration, that you do not, according to the manners of the most part of the men of our time, propose your questions by way of mere test, but with the honest desire to arrive at the actual truth. There is no lack in these days of captious listeners and questioners; but to find a character desirous of information, and seeking the truth as a remedy for ignorance, is very difficult. Just as in the hunter's snare, or in the soldier's ambush, the trick is generally ingeniously concealed, so it is with the inquiries of the majority of the questioners who advance arguments, not so much with the view of getting any good out of them, as in order that, in the event of their failing to elicit answers which chime in with their own desires, they may seem to have fair ground for controversy.

If "To the fool on his asking for wisdom, wisdom shall be reckoned,"[2] at how high a price shall we value "the wise hearer" who is

---
[1] Luke 11:10.
[2] Prov. 17:28 (LXX).

quoted by the Prophet in the same verse with "the admirable counsellor"?[3] It is right, I ween, to hold him worthy of all approbation, and to urge him on to further progress, sharing his enthusiasm, and in all things toiling at his side as he presses onwards to perfection. To count the terms used in theology as of primary importance, and to endeavor to trace out the hidden meaning in every phrase and in every syllable, is a characteristic wanting in those who are idle in the pursuit of true religion, but distinguishing all who get knowledge of "the mark" "of our calling;"[4] for what is set before us is, so far as is possible with human nature, to be made like unto God. Now without knowledge there can be no making like; and knowledge is not got without lessons. The beginning of teaching is speech, and syllables and words are parts of speech. It follows then that to investigate syllables is not to shoot wide of the mark, nor, because the questions raised are what might seem to some insignificant, are they on that account to be held unworthy of heed. Truth is always a quarry hard to hunt, and therefore we must look everywhere for its tracks. The acquisition of true religion is just like that of crafts; both grow bit by bit; apprentices must despise nothing. If a man despises the first elements as small and insignificant, he will never reach the perfection of wisdom.

Yea and Nay are but two syllables, yet there is often involved in these little words at once the best of all good things, Truth, and that beyond which wickedness cannot go, a Lie. But why mention Yea and Nay? Before now, a martyr bearing witness for Christ has been judged to have paid in full the claim of true religion by merely nodding his head.[5] If, then, this be so, what term in theology is so small but that the effect of its weight in the scales according as it be right-

---

[3] Is. 3:3 (LXX).

[4] Phil. 3:14.

[5] *i.e.*, confessed or denied himself a Christian. The Benedictine Editors and their followers seem to have missed the force of the original, both grammatically and historically, in referring it to the time when St. Basil is writing; ἤδη ἐκρίθη does not mean "at the present day is judged," but "ere now has been judged." And in A.D. 374 there was no persecution of Christians such as seems to be referred to, although Valens tried to crush the Catholics.

ly or wrongly used is not great? Of the law we are told "not one jot nor one tittle shall pass away;"[6] how then could it be safe for us to leave even the least unnoticed? The very points which you yourself have sought to have thoroughly sifted by us are at the same time both small and great. Their use is the matter of a moment, and peradventure they are therefore made of small account; but, when we reckon the force of their meaning, they are great. They may be likened to the mustard plant which, though it be the least of shrub-seeds, yet when properly cultivated and the forces latent in its germs unfolded, rises to its own sufficient height.

If anyone laughs when he sees our subtlety, to use the Psalmist's[7] words, about syllables, let him know that he reaps laughter's fruitless fruit; and let us, neither giving in to men's reproaches, nor yet vanquished by their disparagement, continue our investigation. So far, indeed, am I from feeling ashamed of these things because they are small, that, even if I could attain to ever so minute a fraction of their dignity, I should both congratulate myself on having won high honor, and should tell my brother and fellow-investigator that no small gain had accrued to him therefrom.

While, then, I am aware that the controversy contained in little words is a very great one, in hope of the prize I do not shrink from toil, with the conviction that the discussion will both prove profitable to myself, and that my hearers will be rewarded with no small benefit. Wherefore now with the help, if I may so say, of the Holy Spirit Himself, I will approach the exposition of the subject, and, if you will, that I may be put in the way of the discussion, I will for a moment revert to the origin of the question before us.

Lately when praying with the people, and using the full doxology to God the Father in both forms, at one time "*with* the Son *together with* the Holy Ghost," and at another "*through* the Son *in* the Holy

---

[6] Matt. 5:18.
[7] Ps. 118:85 (LXX). "The lawless have described subtleties for me, but not according to thy law, O Lord;" for A.V. & R.V., "The proud have digged pits for me which are not after thy law." The word ἀδολεσχία is used in a bad sense to mean garrulity; in a good sense, keenness, subtlety.

Ghost," I was attacked by some of those present on the ground that I was introducing novel and at the same time mutually contradictory terms.[8] You, however, chiefly with the view of benefiting them, or, if they are wholly incurable, for the security of such as may fall in with them, have expressed the opinion that some clear instruction ought to be published concerning the force underlying the syllables employed. I will therefore write as concisely as possible, in the endeavor to lay down some admitted principle for the discussion.

CHAPTER TWO

The origin of the heretics' close observation of syllables.

THE PETTY EXACTITUDE OF these men about syllables and words is not, as might be supposed, simple and straightforward; nor is the mischief to which it tends a small one. There is involved a deep and covert design against true religion. Their pertinacious contention is to show that the mention of Father, Son, and Holy Ghost is unlike, as though they will thence find it easy to demonstrate that there is a variation in nature. They have an old sophism, invented by Aetius, the champion of this heresy, in one of whose Letters there is passage to the effect that things naturally unlike are expressed in unlike terms, and, conversely, that things expressed in unlike terms are naturally unlike. In proof of this statement he drags in the words of the Apostle, "One God and Father of whom are all things...and one Lord Jesus Christ by whom are all things."[9] "Whatever, then," he goes on, "is the relation of these terms to one another, such will be the

---

[8] It is impossible to convey in English the precise force of the prepositions used. "*With*" represents μετά, of which the original meaning is "amid;" "*together* with," σύν, of which the original meaning is "at the same time as." The Latin of the Benedictine edition translates the first by "*cum*," and the second by "*una cum.*" "*Through*" stands for διά, which, with the genitive, is used of the instrument; "*in*" for ἐν, "*in*," but also commonly used of the instrument or means. In the well-known passage in 1 Cor. 8:6, A.V. renders δι' οὗ τὰ πάντα by "*through* whom are all things;" R.V., by "*by* whom."

[9] 1 Cor. 8:6.

relation of the natures indicated by them; and as the term 'of whom' is unlike the term 'by whom,' so is the Father unlike the Son."[10] On this heresy depends the idle subtlety of these men about the phrases in question. They accordingly assign to God the Father, as though it

---

[10] The story as told by Theodoret (Ecc. Hist. ii. 23) is as follows: "Constantius, on his return from the west, passed some time at Constantinople" (*i.e.* in 360, when the synod at Constantinople was held, shortly after that of the Isaurian Seleucia, "substance" and "hypostasis" being declared inadmissible terms, and the Son pronounced like the Father according to the Scriptures). The Emperor was urged that "Eudoxius should be convicted of blasphemy and lawlessness. Constantius however...replied that a decision must first be come to on matters concerning the faith, and that afterwards the case of Eudoxius should be enquired into. Basilius (of Ancyra), relying on his former intimacy, ventured boldly to object to the Emperor that he was attacking the apostolic decrees; but Constantius took this ill, and told Basilius to hold his tongue, for to you, said he, the disturbance of the churches is due. When Basilius was silenced, Eustathius (of Sebasteia) intervened and said, Since, sir, you wish a decision to be come to on what concerns the faith, consider the blasphemies uttered against the Only Begotten by Eudoxius; and, as he spoke, he produced the exposition of faith, wherein, besides many other impieties, were found the following expressions: Things that are spoken of in unlike terms are unlike in substance; there is one God the Father of Whom are all things, and one Lord Jesus Christ by Whom are all things. Now the term 'of Whom' is unlike the term 'by Whom;' so the Son is unlike God the Father. Constantius ordered this exposition of the faith to be read, and was displeased with the blasphemy which it involved. He therefore asked Eudoxius if he had drawn it up. Eudoxius instantly repudiated the authorship, and said that it was written by Aetius. Now Aetius...at the present time was associated with Eunomius and Eudoxius, and, as he found Eudoxius to be, like himself, a sybarite in luxury as well as a heretic in faith, he chose Antioch as the most congenial place of abode, and both he and Eunomius were fast fixtures at the couches of Eudoxius....The Emperor had been told all this, and now ordered Aetius to be brought before him. On his appearance, Constantius showed him the document in question, and proceeded to enquire if he was the author of its language. Aetius, totally ignorant of what had taken place, and unaware of the drift of the enquiry, expected that he should win praise by confession, and owned that he was the author of the phrases in question. Then the Emperor perceived the greatness of his iniquity, and forthwith condemned him to exile and to be deported to a place in Phrygia." St. Basil accompanied Eustathius and his namesake to Constantinople on this occasion, being then only in deacon's orders. (Philost. iv. 12.) Basil of Ancyra and Eustathius in their turn suffered banishment. Basil, the deacon, returned to the Cappadocian Cæsarea.

were His distinctive portion and lot, the phrase "of Whom;" to God the Son they confine the phrase "by Whom;" to the Holy Spirit that of "in Whom," and say that this use of the syllables is never interchanged, in order that, as I have already said, the variation of language may indicate the variation of nature.[11] Verily it is sufficiently obvious that in their quibbling about the words they are endeavoring to maintain the force of their impious argument.

By the term "*of* whom" they wish to indicate the Creator; by the term "*through* whom," the subordinate agent[12] or instrument;[13] by the term "*in* whom," or "*in* which," they mean to show the time or place. The object of all this is that the Creator of the universe[14] may be regarded as of no higher dignity than an instrument, and that the Holy Spirit may appear to be adding to existing things nothing more than the contribution derived from place or time.

CHAPTER THREE

The systematic discussion of syllables is derived from heathen philosophy.

THEY HAVE, HOWEVER, BEEN led into this error by their close study of heathen writers, who have respectively applied the terms "*of* whom" and "*through* whom" to things which are by

---

[11] Cf. the form of the Arian Creed as given by Eunomius in his Ἀπολογία (Migne, xxx. 840. "We believe in one God, Father Almighty, of whom are all things; and in one only begotten Son of God, God the word, our Lord Jesus Christ, through whom are all things; and in one Holy Ghost, the Comforter, in whom distribution of all grace in proportion as may be most expedient is made to each of the Saints."

[12] Cf. Eunomius, Liber. Apol. § 27, where of the Son he says ὑπουργός.

[13] On the word ὄργανον, a tool, as used of the Word of God, cf. Nestorius in Marius Merc. Migne, p. 761 & Cyr. Alex. Ep. 1. Migne, x. 37. "The creature did not give birth to the uncreated, but gave birth to man, organ of Godhead." Cf. Thomasius, Christ. Dog. i. 336.

Mr. Johnston quotes Philo (de Cher. § 35; i. 162. n.) as speaking of ὄργανον δὲ λόγον Θεοῦ δι' οὗ κατεσκευάσθη (*sc.* ὁ κόσμος).

[14] Here of course the Son is meant.

nature distinct. These writers suppose that by the term "*of* whom" or "*of* which" the matter is indicated, while the term "*through* whom" or "*through* which"[15] represents the instrument, or, generally speaking, subordinate agency.[16] Or rather—for there seems no reason why we should not take up their whole argument, and briefly expose at once its incompatibility with the truth and its inconsistency with their own teaching—the students of vain philosophy, while expounding the manifold nature of cause and distinguishing its peculiar significations, define some causes as principal,[17] some as cooperative or con-causal, while others are of the character of "*sine qua non*," or indispensable.[18]

---

[15] The ambiguity of gender in ἐξ οὗ and δι' οὗ can only be expressed by giving the alternatives in English.

[16] There are four causes or varieties of cause:
1. The essence or quiddity (Form): τὸ τί ἦν εἶναι.
2. The necessitating conditions (Matter): τὸ τίνων ὄντων ἀνάγκη τοῦτ' εἶναι.
3. The proximate mover or stimulator of change (Efficient): ἡ τί πρῶτον ἐκίνησε.
4. That for the sake of which (Final Cause or End): τὸ τίνος ἕνεκα. Grote's *Aristotle*, I. 354.

The four Aristotelian causes are thus: 1. Formal. 2. Material. 3. Efficient. 4. Final. cf. Arist. Analyt. Post. II. xi., Metaph. I. iii., and Phys. II. iii. The six causes of Basil may be referred to the four of Aristotle as follows:

Aristotle.
1. τὸ τί ἦν εἶναι
2. τὸ ἐξ οὗ γίνεταί τι
3. ἡ ἀρχὴ τῆς μεταβολῆς ἡ πρώτη
4. τὸ οὗ ἕνεκα

Basil.
1. καθ' ὅ: *i.e.*, the form or idea *according to which* a thing is made.
2. ἐξ οὗ: *i.e.*, the matter *out of which* it is made.
3. ὑφ' οὗ: *i.e.*, the agent, using means.
δι' οὗ: *i.e.* the means.
4. δι' ὅ: *i.e.*, the end.
εν ᾧ, or *sine quâ non*, applying to all.

[17] προκαταρκτική. Cf. Plut. 2, 1056. B.D. προκαταρκτικὴ αἰτία ἡ εἱμαρμένη.

[18] Cf. Clem. Alex. Strom. viii. 9. "Of causes some are principal, some preservative, some coöperative, some indispensable; *e.g.* of education the principal cause is the father; the preservative, the schoolmaster; the coöperative, the disposition of the pupil; the indispensable, time."

For every one of these they have a distinct and peculiar use of terms, so that the maker is indicated in a different way from the instrument. For the maker they think the proper expression is "*by* whom," maintaining that the bench is produced "*by*" the carpenter; and for the instrument "through which," in that it is produced "through" or by means of adze and gimlet and the rest. Similarly, they appropriate "*of* which" to the material, in that the thing made is "of" wood, while "according to which" shows the design, or pattern put before the craftsman. For he either first makes a mental sketch, and so brings his fancy to bear upon what he is about, or else he looks at a pattern previously put before him, and arranges his work accordingly. The phrase "*on account of* which" they wish to be confined to the end or purpose, the bench, as they say, being produced for, or on account of, the use of man. "*In* which" is supposed to indicate time and place. When was it produced? In this time. And where? In this place. And though place and time contribute nothing to what is being produced, yet without these the production of anything is impossible, for efficient agents must have both place and time. It is these careful distinctions, derived from unpractical philosophy and vain delusion,[19] which our opponents have first studied and admired, and then transferred to the simple and unsophisticated doctrine of the Spirit, to the belittling of God the Word, and the setting at naught of the Divine Spirit. Even the phrase set apart by non-Christian writers for the case of lifeless instruments[20] or of manual service of the meanest kind, I mean the expression "*through* or *by means of* which," they do not shrink from transferring to the Lord of all, and Christians feel no

---

[19] ἐκ τῆς ματαιότητος καὶ κενῆς ἀπάτης.
Cf. ματαιότης ματαιοτήτων, "vanity of vanities," Ecc. 1:2 (LXX). In Arist. Eth. i. 2, a desire is said to be κενὴ καὶ ματαία, which goes into infinity—everything being desired for the sake of something else—i.e., κενη, void, like a desire for the moon, and ματαία, unpractical, like a desire for the empire of China. In the text ματαιότης seems to mean heathen philosophy, a vain delusion as distinguished from Christian philosophy.

[20] ἄψυχα ὄργανα. A slave, according to Aristotle, Eth. Nich. viii. 7, 6, is ἔμψυχον ὄργανον.

CHAPTER FOUR

That there is no distinction in the scriptural use of these syllables.

WE ACKNOWLEDGE THAT THE word of truth has in many places made use of these expressions; yet we absolutely deny that the freedom of the Spirit is in bondage to the pettiness of Paganism. On the contrary, we maintain that Scripture varies its expressions as occasion requires, according to the circumstances of the case. For instance, the phrase "*of* which" does not always and absolutely, as they suppose, indicate the material,[21] but it is more in accordance with the usage of Scripture to apply this term in the case of the Supreme Cause, as in the words "One God, of whom are all things,"[22] and again, "All things of God."[23] The word of truth has, however, frequently used this term in the case of the material, as when it says "Thou shalt make an ark of incorruptible wood;"[24] and "Thou shalt make the candlestick of pure gold;"[25] and "The first man is

---

[21] ὕλη=Lat. *materies*, from the same root as *mater*, whence Eng. *material* and *matter*. (ὕλη, ὕλFα, is the same word as sylva=wood. With *materies* cf. Madeira, from the Portuguese "*madera*"=timber.) "The word ὕλη in Plato bears the same signification as in ordinary speech: it means wood, timber, and sometimes generally material. The later philosophic application of the word to signify the abstract conception of material substratum is expressed by Plato, so far as he has that concept at all, in other ways." Ed. Zeller. *Plato and the older Academy*, ii. 296. Similarly Basil uses ὕλη. As a technical philosophic term for abstract matter, it is first used by Aristotle.

[22] 1 Cor. 8:6.

[23] 1 Cor. 11:12.

[24] Ex. 25:10 (LXX). A.V. "shittim." R.V. "acacia." St. Ambrose (*de Spiritu Sancto*, ii. 9) seems, say the Benedictine Editors, to have here misunderstood St. Basil's argument. St. Basil is accusing the Pneumatomachi not of tracing all things to God as the material "of which," but of unduly limiting the use of the term "of which" to the Father alone.

[25] Ex. 25:31.

of the earth, earthy;"[26] and "Thou art formed out of clay as I am."[27] But these men, to the end, as we have already remarked, that they may establish the difference of nature, have laid down the law that this phrase befits the Father alone. This distinction they have originally derived from heathen authorities, but here they have shown no faithful accuracy of limitation. To the Son they have in conformity with the teaching of their masters given the title of instrument, and to the Spirit that of place, for they say *in* the Spirit, and *through* the Son. But when they apply "of whom" to God they no longer follow heathen example, but "go over, as they say, to apostolic usage, as it is said, "But of him are ye in Christ Jesus,"[28] and "All things of God."[29] What, then, is the result of this systematic discussion? There is one nature of Cause; another of Instrument; another of Place. So the Son is by nature distinct from the Father, as the tool from the craftsman; and the Spirit is distinct in so far as place or time is distinguished from the nature of tools or from that of them that handle them.

CHAPTER FIVE

That "through whom" is said also in the case of the Father, and "of whom" in the case of the Son and of the Spirit.

AFTER THUS DESCRIBING THE outcome of our adversaries' arguments, we shall now proceed to show, as we have proposed, that the Father does not first take "of whom" and then abandon "through whom" to the Son; and that there is no truth in these men's ruling that the Son refuses to admit the Holy Spirit to a share in "of whom" or in "through whom," according to the limitation of their new-fangled allotment of phrases. "There is one God and Father of whom are all things, and one Lord Jesus Christ through whom are all things."[30]

---

[26] 1 Cor. 15:47.
[27] Job 33:6 (LXX).
[28] 1 Cor. 1:30.
[29] 1 Cor. 11:12.
[30] 1 Cor. 8:6.

Yes; but these are the words of a writer not laying down a rule, but carefully distinguishing the hypostases.[31]

The object of the apostle in thus writing was not to introduce the diversity of nature, but to exhibit the notion of Father and of Son as unconfounded. That the phrases are not opposed to one another and do not, like squadrons in war marshalled one against another, bring the natures to which they are applied into mutual conflict, is perfectly plain from the passage in question. The blessed Paul brings both phrases to bear upon one and the same subject, in the words "of him and through him and to him are all things."[32] That this plainly refers to the Lord will be admitted even by a reader paying but small attention to the meaning of the words. The apostle has just quoted from the prophecy of Isaiah, "Who hath known the mind of the Lord, or who hath been his counsellor,"[33] and then goes on, "For of him and from him and to him are all things." That the prophet is speaking about God the Word, the Maker of all creation, may be learnt from what immediately precedes: "Who hath measured the waters in the hollow of his hand, and meted out heaven with the span, and comprehended the dust of the earth in a measure, and weighed the mountains in scales, and the hills in a balance? Who hath directed the Spirit of the Lord, or being his counsellor hath taught him?"[34] Now the word "who" in this passage does not mean absolute impossibility, but rarity, as in the passage "Who will rise up for me against the evil doers?"[35] and

---

[31] If Catholic Theology does not owe to St. Basil the distinction between the connotations of οὐσία and ὑπόστασις which soon prevailed over the identification obtaining at the time of the Nicene Council, at all events his is the first and most famous assertion and defense of it. At Nicæa, in 325, to have spoken of St. Paul as "distinguishing the hypostases" would have been held impious. Some forty-five years later St. Basil writes to his brother, Gregory of Nyssa (Ep. xxxviii.), in fear lest Gregory should fall into the error of failing to distinguish between hypostasis and ousia, between person and essence. Cf. Theodoret Dial. i. 7, and my note on his Ecc. Hist. i. 3.

[32] Rom. 11:36.
[33] Rom. 11:34, and Is. 40:13.
[34] Is. 40:12, 13.
[35] Ps. 93:16 (LXX).

"What man is he that desireth life?"[36] and "Who shall ascend into the hill of the Lord?"[37] So is it in the passage in question, "Who hath directed [LXX, known] the Spirit of the Lord, or being his counsellor hath known him?" "For the Father loveth the Son and showeth him all things."[38] This is He who holds the earth, and hath grasped it with His hand, who brought all things to order and adornment, who poised[39] the hills in their places, and measured the waters, and gave to all things in the universe their proper rank, who encompasseth the whole of heaven with but a small portion of His power, which, in a figure, the prophet calls a span. Well then did the apostle add "Of him and through him and to him are all things."[40] For of Him, to all things that are, comes the cause of their being, according to the will of God the Father. Through Him all things have their continuance[41] and constitution,[42] for He created all things, and metes out to each severally what is necessary for its health and preservation. Wherefore to Him all things are turned, looking with irresistible longing and unspeakable affection to "the author"[43] and maintainer "of" their "life," as it is written "The eyes of all wait upon thee,"[44] and again, "These wait all upon thee,"[45] and "Thou openest thine hand, and satisfiest the desire of every living thing."[46]

But if our adversaries oppose this our interpretation, what argument will save them from being caught in their own trap?

For if they will not grant that the three expressions "of him" and "through him" and "to him" are spoken of the Lord, they cannot but be applied to God the Father. Then without question their rule will fall

---

[36] Ps. 33:12 (LXX).
[37] Ps. 23:3 (LXX).
[38] John 5:20.
[39] ἰσορροπία. Cf. Plat. Phæd. 109, A.
[40] Rom. 11:38.
[41] διαμονή. Cf. Arist. de Sp. i. 1.
[42] Cf. Col. 1:16, 17.
[43] Acts 3:15.
[44] Ps. 44:15 (LXX).
[45] Ps. 103:27 (LXX).
[46] Ps. 144:16 (LXX).

through, for we find not only "of whom," but also "through whom" applied to the Father. And if this latter phrase indicates nothing derogatory, why in the world should it be confined, as though conveying the sense of inferiority, to the Son? If it always and everywhere implies ministry, let them tell us to what superior the God of glory[47] and Father of the Christ is subordinate.

They are thus overthrown by their own selves, while our position will be on both sides made sure. Suppose it proved that the passage refers to the Son, "of whom" will be found applicable to the Son. Suppose on the other hand it be insisted that the prophet's words relate to God, then it will be granted that "through whom" is properly used of God, and both phrases have equal value, in that both are used with equal force of God. Under either alternative both terms, being employed of one and the same Person, will be shown to be equivalent. But let us revert to our subject.

In his Epistle to the Ephesians the apostle says, "But speaking the truth in love, may grow up into him in all things, which is the head, even Christ; from whom the whole body fitly joined together and compacted by that which every joint supplieth, according to the effectual working in the measure of every part, maketh increase of the body."[48]

And again, in the Epistle to the Colossians, to them that have not the knowledge of the Only Begotten, there is mention of him that holdeth "the head," that is, Christ, "from which all the body by joints and bands having nourishment ministered increaseth with the increase of God."[49] And that Christ is the head of the Church we have learned in another passage, when the apostle says "gave him to be the head over all things to the Church,"[50] and "of his fullness have all we received."[51] And the Lord Himself says "He shall take of mine, and

---

[47] Ps. 28:3 (LXX); Acts 7:2.
[48] Eph. 4:15, 16.
[49] Col. 2:19.
[50] Eph. 1:22.
[51] John 1:16.

shall show it unto you."[52] In a word, the diligent reader will perceive that "of whom" is used in diverse manners.[53] For instance, the Lord says, "I perceive that virtue is gone out of me."[54] Similarly, we have frequently observed "of whom" used of the Spirit. "He that soweth to the spirit," it is said, "shall of the spirit reap life everlasting."[55] John too writes, "Hereby we know that he abideth in us by (ἐκ) the spirit which he hath given us."[56] "That which is conceived in her," says the angel, "is of the Holy Ghost,"[57] and the Lord says, "that which is born of the spirit is spirit."[58] Such then is the case so far.

It must now be pointed out that the phrase "through whom" is admitted by Scripture in the case of the Father and of the Son and of the Holy Ghost alike. It would indeed be tedious to bring forward evidence of this in the case of the Son, not only because it is perfectly well known, but because this very point is made by our opponents. We now show that "through whom" is used also in the case of the Father. "God is faithful," it is said, "by whom (δι' οὗ) ye were called unto the fellowship of his Son,"[59] and "Paul an apostle of Jesus Christ by (διά) the will of God;" and again, "Wherefore thou art no more a servant, but a son; and if a son, then an heir through God."[60] And "like as Christ was raised up from the dead by (διά) the glory of God the Father."[61] Isaiah, moreover, says, "Woe unto them that make deep

---

[52] 1 John 16:15.

[53] πολύτροποι. Cf. the cognate adverb in Heb. 1:1.

[54] "ἐξ ἐμοῦ " The reading in St. Luke (8:46) is ἀπ' ἐμοῦ. In the parallel passage, Mark 5:30, the words are, "Jesus knowing in himself that virtue had gone out of him," ἐξ αὐτοῦ which D. inserts in Luke 8:45.

[55] Gal. 6:8.

[56] 1 John 3:24.

[57] Matt. 1:20.

[58] John 3:6.

[59] 1 Cor. 1:9.

[60] Gal. 4:7. A.V. reads "an heir of God through Christ;" so ℵCD. R.V. with the copy used by Basil agrees with A.B.

[61] Rom. 6:4. It is pointed out by the Rev. C.F.H. Johnston in his edition of the *De Spiritu* that among quotations from the New Testament on the point in question, St. Basil has omitted Heb. 2:10, "It became him for whom (δι' ὅν) are all things and through whom (δι' οὗ) are all things," "where the Father is described as being the final Cause and efficient Cause of all things."

counsel and not through the Lord;"[62] and many proofs of the use of this phrase in the case of the Spirit might be adduced. "God hath revealed him to us," it is said, "by (διά) the spirit;"[63] and in another place, "That good thing which was committed unto thee keep by (διά) the Holy Ghost;"[64] and again, "To one is given by (διά) the spirit the word of wisdom."[65]

In the same manner, it may also be said of the word "in," that Scripture admits its use in the case of God the Father. In the Old Testament, it is said through (ἐν) God we shall do valiantly,[66] and, "My praise shall be continually of (ἐν) thee;"[67] and again, "In thy name will I rejoice."[68] In Paul we read, "In God who created all things,"[69] and, "Paul and Silvanus and Timotheus unto the church of the Thessalonians in God our Father;"[70] and "if now at length I might have a prosperous journey by (ἐν) the will of God to come to you;"[71] and, "Thou makest thy boast of God."[72] Instances are indeed too numerous to reckon; but what we want is not so much to exhibit an abundance of evidence as to prove that the conclusions of our opponents are unsound. I shall, therefore, omit any proof of this usage in the case of our Lord and of the Holy Ghost, in that it is notorious. But I cannot forbear to remark that "the wise hearer" will find sufficient proof of the proposition before him by following the method of contraries. For if the difference of language indicates, as we are told, that the nature has been changed, then let identity of language compel our adversaries to confess with shame that the essence is unchanged.

---

[62] Is. 29:15 (LXX).
[63] 1 Cor. 2:10.
[64] 2 Tim. 1:14
[65] 1 Cor. 12:8.
[66] Ps. 107:13 (LXX).
[67] Ps. 70:6 (LXX).
[68] For "shall they rejoice," Ps. 88:16 (LXX).
[69] Eph. 3:9.
[70] 2 Thess. 1:1.
[71] Rom. 1:10.
[72] Rom. 2:17.

And it is not only in the case of the theology that the use of the terms varies,[73] but whenever one of the terms takes the meaning of the other we find them frequently transferred from the one subject to the other. As, for instance, Adam says, "I have gotten a man *through* God,"[74] meaning to say the same as from God; and in another passage "Moses commanded...Israel through the word of the Lord,"[75] and, again, "Is not the interpretation through God?"[76] Joseph, discoursing about dreams to the prisoners, instead of saying *"from God"* says plainly *"through* God." Inversely Paul uses the term *"from* whom" instead of *"through* whom," when he says "made from a woman" (A.V., "of" instead of *"through* a woman").[77] And this he has plainly distinguished in another passage, where he says that it is proper to a woman to be made of the man, and to a man to be made through the woman, in the words "For as the woman is from [A.V., of] the man, even so is the man also through [A.V., by] the woman."[78] Nevertheless in the passage in question the apostle, while illustrating the variety of usage, at the same time corrects *obiter* the error of those who supposed that the body of the Lord was a spiritual body,[79] and, to show that the God-bearing[80] flesh was

---

[73] According to patristic usage the word "theology" is concerned with all that relates to the divine and eternal nature of Christ, as distinguished from the οἰκονομία, which relates to the incarnation, and consequent redemption of mankind. Cf. Bishop Lightfoot's *Apostolic Fathers*, Part II. Vol. ii. p. 75, and Newman's *Arians*, Chapter I. Section iii.

[74] Gen. 4:1 (LXX). A.V. renders "*she* conceived and bare Cain and said," and here St. Basil has been accused of quoting from memory. But in the Greek of the LXX, the subject to εἶπεν is not expressed, and a possible construction of the sentence is to refer it to Adam. In his work *adv. Eunom.* ii. 20, St. Basil again refers the exclamation to Adam.

[75] Num. 36:5 (LXX).

[76] Gen. 40:8 (LXX).

[77] Gal. 4:4.

[78] 1 Cor. 11:12.

[79] The allusion is to the Docetæ. Cf. Luke 24:39.

[80] The note of the Benedictine Editors remarks that the French theologian Fronton du Duc (Ducæus) accuses Theodoret (on Cyril's Anath. vii.) of misquoting St. Basil as writing here "God-bearing man" instead of "God bearing flesh," a term of different signification and less open as a Nestorian interpretation. "God-bearing," θεοφόρος, was an epithet applied to mere men, as, for instance, St. Ignatius. So Clement of Alexandria, I. Strom. p. 318, and Greg-

formed out of the common lump[81] of human nature, gave precedence to the more emphatic preposition.

The phrase "through a woman" would be likely to give rise to the suspicion of mere transit in the generation, while the phrase "of the woman" would satisfactorily indicate that the nature was shared by the mother and the offspring. The apostle was in no wise contradicting himself, but he showed that the words can without difficulty be interchanged. Since, therefore, the term "from whom" is transferred to the identical subjects in the case of which "through whom" is decided to be properly used, with what consistency can these phrases be invariably distinguished one from the other, in order that fault may be falsely found with true religion?

CHAPTER SIX

Issue joined with those who assert that the Son is not with the Father, but after the Father. Also concerning the equal glory.

OUR OPPONENTS, WHILE THEY thus artfully and perversely encounter our argument, cannot even have recourse to the plea of ignorance. It is obvious that they are annoyed with us for completing the doxology to the Only Begotten together with the Father, and for not separating the Holy Spirit from the Son. On this account they style us innovators, revolutionizers, phrase-coiners, and every other possible name of insult. But so far am I from being irritated at their abuse, that, were it not for the fact that their loss causes me "heaviness and continual sorrow,"[82] I could almost have said that I was grateful to them for the blasphemy, as though they were agents for providing me with blessing. For "blessed are ye," it is said, "when men shall revile you for my sake."[83] The grounds of their indignation

---

ory of Nazianzus, Or. xxxvii. p. 609. St. Basil does use the expression Jesus Christ ἄνθρωπον Θεόν in Hom. on Ps. 48 (LXX).

[81] φύραμα. Cf. Rom. 9:21.
[82] Cf. Rom. 9:2.
[83] Matt. 5:11.

are these: The Son, according to them, is not together with the Father, but after the Father. Hence it follows that glory should be ascribed to the Father "*through* him," but not "*with* him;" inasmuch as "*with* him" expresses equality of dignity, while "*through* him" denotes subordination. They further assert that the Spirit is not to be ranked along with the Father and the Son, but under the Son and the Father; not coordinated, but subordinated; not connumerated, but subnumerated.[84]

With technical terminology of this kind they pervert the simplicity and artlessness of the faith, and thus by their ingenuity, suffering no one else to remain in ignorance, they cut off from themselves the plea that ignorance might demand.

Let us first ask them this question: In what sense do they say that the Son is "after the Father;" later in time, or in order, or in dignity? But in time no one is so devoid of sense as to assert that the Maker of the ages[85] holds a second place, when no interval intervenes in the natural conjunction of the Father with the Son.[86] And indeed so far as our conception of human relations goes,[87] it is impossible to think of the Son as being later than the Father, not only from the fact that Father and Son are mutually conceived of in accordance with the relationship subsisting between them, but because posteriority in time is predicated of subjects separated by a less interval from the present, and priority of subjects farther off. For instance, what happened in Noah's time is prior to what happened to the men of Sodom, inasmuch as Noah is more remote from our own day; and, again, the events of the history of the men of Sodom are posterior, because they seem in a sense to approach nearer to our own day. But, in addition to its being a breach of true religion, is it not really the most extreme folly to measure the existence of the life which transcends all time and all the ages by its distance from the present? Is it not as though

---

[84] ὑποτάσσω. Cf. 1 Cor. 15:27, and *inf.* cf. chapter xvii. ὑποτεταγμένος is applied to the Son in the Macrostich or Lengthy Creed, brought by Eudoxius of Germanicia to Milan in 344. *Vide* Soc. ii. 19.

[85] ποιητὴς τῶν αἰώνων.

[86] Yet the great watchword of the Arians was ἦν ποτε ὅτε οὐκ ἦν.

[87] τῇ ἐννοίᾳ τῶν ἀνθρωπίνων is here the reading of five MSS. The Benedictines prefer τῶν ἀνθρώπων, with the sense of "in human thought."

God the Father could be compared with, and be made superior to, God the Son, who exists before the ages, precisely in the same way in which things liable to beginning and corruption are described as prior to one another?

The superior remoteness of the Father is really inconceivable, in that thought and intelligence are wholly impotent to go beyond the generation of the Lord; and St. John has admirably confined the conception within circumscribed boundaries by two words, "In the *beginning was* the Word." For thought cannot travel outside "was," nor imagination[88] beyond "*beginning*." Let your thought travel ever so far backward you cannot get beyond the "*was*," and however you may strain and strive to see what is beyond the Son, you will find it impossible to get further than the "*beginning*." True religion, therefore, thus teaches us to think of the Son together with the Father.

If they really conceive of a kind of degradation of the Son in relation to the Father, as though He were in a lower place, so that the Father sits above, and the Son is thrust off to the next seat below, let them confess what they mean. We shall have no more to say. A plain statement of the view will at once expose its absurdity. They who refuse to allow that the Father pervades all things do not so much as maintain the logical sequence of thought in their argument. The faith of the sound is that God fills all things;[89] but they who divide their up and down between the Father and the Son do not remember even the word of the Prophet: "If I climb up into heaven thou art there; if I go down to hell thou art there also."[90] Now, to omit all proof of the ignorance of those who predicate place of incorporeal things, what excuse can be found for their attack upon Scripture, shameless as

---

[88] Φαντασία is the philosophic term for imagination or presentation, the mental faculty by which the object made apparent, φάντασμα, becomes apparent, φαίνεται. Aristotle, *de An*. III. iii. 20 defines it as "a movement of the mind generated by sensation." Fancy, which is derived from φαντασία (φαίνω, BHA=shine) has acquired a slightly different meaning in some usages of modern speech.

[89] Eph. 4:10.

[90] Ps. 138:7 (LXX).

their antagonism is, in the passages "Sit thou on my right hand"[91] and "Sat down on the right hand of the majesty of God"?[92] The expression "right hand" does not, as they contend, indicate the lower place, but equality of relation; it is not understood physically, in which case there might be something sinister about God,[93] but Scripture puts before us the magnificence of the dignity of the Son by the use of dignified language indicating the seat of honor. It is left then for our opponents to allege that this expression signifies inferiority of rank. Let them learn that "Christ is the power of God and wisdom of God,"[94] and that "He is the image of the invisible God"[95] and "brightness of his glory,"[96] and that "Him hath God the Father sealed,"[97] by engraving Himself on Him.[98]

Now are we to call these passages, and others like them, throughout the whole of Holy Scripture, proofs of humiliation, or rather public proclamations of the majesty of the Only Begotten, and of the equality of His glory with the Father? We ask them to listen to the Lord Himself, distinctly setting forth the equal dignity of His glory

---

[91] Ps. 109:1 (LXX).

[92] Heb. 1:3, with the variation of "of God" for "on high."

[93] I know of no better way of conveying the sense of the original σκαῖος than by thus introducing the Latin *sinister*, which has the double meaning of left and ill-omened. It is to the credit of the unsuperstitious character of English speaking people that while the Greek σκαῖος and ἀριστερός, the Latin *sinister* and *lævus*, the French *gauche*, and the German link, all have the meaning of awkward and unlucky as well as simply on the left hand, the English *left* (though probably derived from lift=weak) has lost all connotation but the local one.

[94] 1 Cor. 1:24.

[95] Col. 1:15.

[96] Heb. 1:3.

[97] John 6:27.

[98] The more obvious interpretation of ἐσφράγισεν in John 6:27, would be sealed with a mark of approval, as in the miracle just performed. Cf. Bengel, "*sigillo id quod genuinum est commendatur, et omne quod non genuinum est excluditur.*" But St. Basil explains "sealed" by "stamped with the image of His Person," an interpretation which Alfred rejects. St. Basil at the end of Chapter xxvi. of this work, calls our Lord the χαρακτὴρ καὶ ἰσότυπος σφραγίς, *i.e.*, "express image and seal graven to the like" of the Father. St. Athanasius (Ep. i. *ad Serap.* xxiii.) writes, "The seal has the form of Christ the sealer, and in this the sealed participate, being formed according to it." Cf. Gal. 4:19, and 2 Pet. 1:4.

with the Father, in His words, "He that hath seen me hath seen the Father;"[99] and again, "When the Son cometh in the glory of his Father;"[100] that they "should honor the Son even as they honor the Father;"[101] and, "We beheld his glory, the glory as of the only begotten of the Father;"[102] and "the only begotten God which is in the bosom of the Father."[103] Of all these passages they take no account, and then assign to the Son the place set apart for His foes. A father's bosom is a fit and becoming seat for a son, but the place of the footstool is for them that have to be forced to fall.[104]

We have only touched cursorily on these proofs, because our object is to pass on to other points. You at your leisure can put together the items of the evidence, and then contemplate the height of the glory and the preeminence of the power of the Only Begotten. However, to the well-disposed hearer, even these are not insignificant, unless the terms "right hand" and "bosom" be accepted in a physical and derogatory sense, so as at once to circumscribe God in local limits, and invent form, mold, and bodily position, all of which are totally distinct from the idea of the absolute, the infinite, and the incorporeal. There is moreover, the fact that what is derogatory in the idea of it is the same in the case both of the Father and the Son; so that whoever repeats these arguments does not take away the dignity of the Son, but does incur the charge of blaspheming the Father; for whatever audacity a man be guilty of against the Son he cannot but transfer to the Father. If he assigns to the Father the upper place by way of prece-

---

[99] John 14:9.

[100] Mark 8:38.

[101] John 5:23.

[102] John 1:14.

[103] John 1:18. "Only begotten God" is here the reading of five MSS. of Basil. The words are wanting in one codex. In Chapter viii. of this work St. Basil distinctly quotes Scripture as calling the Son "only begotten God." (Chapter viii. Section 17.) But in Chapter xi. Section 27, where he has been alleged to quote John 1:18, with the reading "Only begotten Son" (*e.g.*, Alford), the MS. authority for his text is in favor of "Only begotten God." *OC* is the reading of ℵ.B.C. TC of A. On the comparative weight of the textual and patristic evidence *vide* Bp. Westcott *in loc*.

[104] Cf. Ps. 109:1 (LXX).

dence, and asserts that the only begotten Son sits below, he will find that to the creature of his imagination attach all the consequent conditions of body. And if these are the imaginations of drunken delusion and frenzied insanity, can it be consistent with true religion for men taught by the Lord himself that "He that honoreth not the Son honoreth not the Father"[105] to refuse to worship and glorify with the Father him who in nature, in glory, and in dignity is conjoined with him? What shall we say? What just defense shall we have in the day of the awful universal judgment of all-creation, if, when the Lord clearly announces that He will come "in the glory of his Father;"[106] when Stephen beheld Jesus standing at the right hand of God;[107] when Paul testified in the spirit concerning Christ "that he is at the right hand of God;"[108] when the Father says, "Sit thou on my right hand;"[109] when the Holy Spirit bears witness that he has sat down on "the right hand of the majesty"[110] of God; we attempt to degrade him who shares the honor and the throne, from his condition of equality, to a lower state?[111] Standing and sitting, I apprehend, indicate the fixity and entire stability of the nature, as Baruch, when he wishes to exhibit the immutability and immobility of the Divine mode of existence, says, "For thou sittest forever and we perish utterly."[112] Moreover, the place on the right hand indicates in my judgment equality of honor. Rash, then, is the attempt to deprive the Son of participation in the doxology, as though worthy only to be ranked in a lower place of honor.

---

[105] John 5:23.
[106] Matt. 16:27.
[107] Acts 7:55.
[108] Rom. 8:34.
[109] Ps. 109:1 (LXX).
[110] Heb. 8:1.
[111] Mr. Johnston well points out that these five testimonies are not cited fortuitously, but "in an order which carries the reader from the future second coming, through the present session at the right hand, back to the ascension in the past."
[112] Baruch 3:3 (LXX).

CHAPTER SEVEN

Against those who assert that it is not proper for "with whom" to be said of the Son, and that the proper phrase is "through whom."

BUT THEIR CONTENTION IS that to use the phrase "with him" is altogether strange and unusual, while "through him" is at once most familiar in Holy Scripture, and very common in the language of the brotherhood.[113] What is our answer to this? We say, Blessed are the ears that have not heard you and the hearts that have been kept from the wounds of your words. To you, on the other hand, who are lovers of Christ,[114] I say that the Church recognizes both uses, and deprecates neither as subversive of the other. For whenever we are contemplating the majesty of the nature of the Only Begotten, and the excellence of His dignity, we bear witness that the glory is *with* the Father; while on the other hand, whenever we bethink us of His bestowal[115] on us of good gifts, and of our access[116] to, and admission into, the household of God,[117] we confess that this grace is effected for us *through* Him and *by*[118] Him.

It follows that the one phrase "with whom" is the proper one to be used in the ascription of glory, while the other, *"through* whom," is especially appropriate in giving of thanks. It is also quite untrue to allege that the phrase *"with* whom" is unfamiliar in the usage of the devout. All those whose soundness of character leads them to hold the dignity of antiquity to be more honorable than mere new-fangled novelty, and who have preserved the tradition of their fathers[119] un-

---

[113] The word ἀδελφότης is in the New Testament peculiar to St. Peter (1 Peter 2:17, and v. 9); it occurs in the Epistle of St. Clement to the Corinthians, Chap. ii.

[114] Φιλόχριστοι. The word is not common, but occurs in inscriptions. Cf. Anth. Pal. I. x. 13. ὀρθὴν πίστιν ἔχουσα φιλοχρίστοιο μενοινῆς.

[115] χορηγία. Cf. the use of the cognate verb in 1 Pet. 4:11. ἐξ ἰσχύος ἧς χορηγεῖ ὁ θεός.

[116] προσαγωγή. Cf. Eph. 2:18.

[117] οἰκείωσιν πρὸς τὸν Θεόν. Cf. οἰκεῖοι τοῦ Θεοῦ in Eph. 2:19.

[118] ἐν.

[119] Cf. Gal. 1:14.

adulterated, alike in town and in country, have employed this phrase. It is, on the contrary, they who are surfeited with the familiar and the customary, and arrogantly assail the old as stale, who welcome innovation, just as in dress your lovers of display always prefer some utter novelty to what is generally worn. So you may even still see that the language of country folk preserves the ancient fashion, while of these, our cunning experts[120] in logomachy, the language bears the brand of the new philosophy.

What our fathers said, the same say we, that the glory of the Father and of the Son is common; wherefore we offer the doxology to the Father *with* the Son. But we do not rest only on the fact that such is the tradition of the Fathers; for they too followed the sense of Scripture, and started from the evidence which, a few sentences back, I deduced from Scripture and laid before you. For "the brightness" is always thought of with "the glory,"[121] "the image" with the archetype,[122] and the Son always and everywhere together with the Father; nor does even the close connection of the names, much less the nature of the things, admit of separation.

---

[120] The verb, ἐντρίβομαι, appears to be used by St. Basil, if he wrote ἐντετριμμένων in the sense of to be ἐντριβής or versed in a thing (cf. Soph. Ant. 177)—a sense not illustrated by classical usage. But the reading of the Moscow MS. (μ) ἐντεθραμμένων, "trained in," "nurtured in," is *per se* much more probable. The idea of the country folk preserving the good old traditions shows the change of circumstances in St. Basil's day from those of the 2d c., when the "pagani" or villagers were mostly still heathen, and the last to adopt the novelty of Christianity. Cf. Pliny's Letter to Trajan (Ep. 96), "*neque civitates tantum sed vicos etiam atque agros superstitionis istius contagio pervagata est.*"

[121] Heb. 1:1. Cf. Aug. *Ep.* ii. ad Serap.: "The Father is Light, and the Son brightness and true light."

[122] 2 Cor. 4:4.

CHAPTER EIGHT

In how many ways "Through whom" is used; and in what sense "with whom" is more suitable. Explanation of how the Son receives a commandment, and how He is sent.

WHEN, THEN, THE apostle "thanks God through Jesus Christ,"[123] and again says that "through Him" we have "received grace and apostleship for obedience to the faith among all nations,"[124] or "through Him have access unto this grace wherein we stand and rejoice,"[125] he sets forth the boons conferred on us by the Son, at one time making the grace of the good gifts pass through from the Father to us, and at another bringing us to the Father through Himself. For by saying "through whom we have received grace and apostleship,"[126] he declares the supply of the good gifts to proceed from that source; and again, in saying "through whom we have had access,"[127] he sets forth our acceptance and being made "of the household of God"[128] through Christ. Is then the confession of the grace wrought by Him to usward a detraction from His glory? Is it not truer to say that the recital of His benefits is a proper argument for glorifying Him? It is on this account that we have not found Scripture describing the Lord to us by one name, nor even by such terms alone as are indicative of His godhead and majesty. At one time, it uses terms descriptive of His nature, for it recognizes the "name which is above every name,"[129] the name of

---

[123] Rom. 1:8.
[124] Rom. 1:5.
[125] Rom. 5:2.
[126] Rom. 1:5.
[127] Rom. 5:2.
[128] Cf. Eph. 2:19.
[129] Phil. 2:9.

Son,[130] and speaks of true Son,[131] and only begotten God,[132] and Power of God,[133] and Wisdom,[134] and Word.[135] Then again, on account of the divers manners[136] wherein grace is given to us, which, because of the riches of His goodness,[137] according to his manifold[138] wisdom, he bestows on them that need, Scripture designates Him by innumerable other titles, calling Him Shepherd,[139] King,[140] Physician,[141] Bridegroom,[142] Way,[143] Door,[144] Fountain,[145] Bread,[146] Axe,[147] and Rock.[148] And these titles do not set forth His nature, but, as I have remarked, the variety of the effectual working which, out of His tender-heartedness to His own creation, according to the peculiar necessity of each, He bestows upon them that need. Them that have fled for refuge to His ruling care, and through patient endurance have mended their wayward ways,[149] He calls "sheep," and confesses Himself to be, to

---

[130] Two MSS., those in the B. Museum and at Vienna, read here Ιησοῦ. In Ep. 210. 4, St. Basil writes that the name above every name is αὐτὸ τὸ καλεῖσθαι αὐτὸν Υιον τοῦ Θεοῦ.

[131] Cf. Matt. 14:33, and 27:54.

[132] John 1:18.

[133] 1 Cor. 1:24, and possibly Rom. 1:16, if with D. we read gospel of *Christ*.

[134] 1 Cor. 1:24.

[135] *e.g.*, John 1:1. Cf. Ps. 116:20 (LXX); Wisdom 9:1, 18:15; Ecclesiasticus 43:20.

[136] Τὸ πολύτροπον. Cf. Heb. 1:1.

[137] Τὸν πλοῦτον τῆς ἀγαθότητος. Cf. Rom. 2:4, τοῦ πλούτου τῆς χρηστότητος.

[138] Eph. 3:10.

[139] *e.g.*, John 10:12.

[140] *e.g.*, Matt. 21:5.

[141] *e.g.*, Matt. 9:12.

[142] *e.g.*, Matt. 9:15.

[143] *e.g.*, John 14:6.

[144] *e.g.*, John 10:9.

[145] Cf. Rev. 21:6.

[146] *e.g.*, John 6:21.

[147] Cf. Matt. 3:10.

[148] *e.g.*, 1 Cor. 10:4.

[149] I translate here the reading of the Parisian Codex called by the Benedictine Editors *Regius Secundus*, τὸ εὐμετάβολον κατωρθωκότας. The harder reading, τὸ εὐμετάδοτον, which may be rendered "have perfected their readiness to distribute," has the best manuscript authority, but it is barely intelligible; and the Benedictine Editors are quite right in calling attention to the fact that the point in question here is not the readiness of the flock to distribute (Cf. 1 Tim.

them that hear His voice and refuse to give heed to strange teaching, a "shepherd." For "my sheep," He says, "hear my voice." To them that have now reached a higher stage and stand in need of righteous royalty,[150] He is a King. And in that, through the straightway of His commandments, He leads men to good actions, and again because He safely shuts in all who through faith in Him betake themselves for shelter to the blessing of the higher wisdom,[151] He is a Door.

So He says, "By me if any man enter in, he shall go in and out and shall find pasture."[152] Again, because to the faithful He is a defense strong, unshaken, and harder to break than any bulwark, He is a Rock. Among these titles, it is when He is styled Door, or Way, that the phrase "through Him" is very appropriate and plain. As, however, God and Son, He is glorified with and together with[153] the Father, in that "at, the name of Jesus every knee should bow, of things in heaven, and things in earth, and things under the earth; and that every tongue should confess that Jesus Christ is Lord, to the glory of God the Father."[154] Wherefore we use both terms, expressing by the one His own proper dignity, and by the other His grace to usward.

For "through Him" comes every succor to our souls, and it is in accordance with each kind of care that an appropriate title has been devised. So, when He presents to Himself the blameless soul, not

---

6:18), but their patient following of their Master. The Benedictine Editors boldly propose to introduce a word of no authority τὸ ἀμετάβολον, rendering *qui per patientiam animam immutabilem præbuerunt*. The reading adopted above is supported by a passage in *Ep.* 244, where St. Basil is speaking of the waywardness of Eustathius, and seems to fit in best with the application of the passage to the words of our Lord, "have fled for refuge to his ruling care," corresponding with "the sheep follow him, for they know his voice" (St. John 10:4), and "have mended their wayward ways," with "a stranger will they not follow," v. 5. Mr. Johnston, in his valuable note, compares Origen's teaching on the Names of our Lord.

[150] So three MSS. Others repeat ἐπιστασία, translated "ruling care" above. ἔννομος is used by Plato for "lawful" and "law-abiding." (Legg. 921 C. and Rep. 424 E.) In 1 Cor. 9:21, A.V. renders "under the law."

[151] Τὸ τῆς γνώσεως ἀγαθόν: possibly "the good of knowledge of him."

[152] John 10:9.

[153] Cf. note from Ch. 1, on μετά and σύν.

[154] Phil. 2:10, 11.

having spot or wrinkle,[155] like a pure maiden, He is called Bridegroom, but whenever He receives one in sore plight from the devil's evil strokes, healing it in the heavy infirmity of its sins, He is named Physician. And shall this His care for us degrade to meanness our thoughts of Him? Or, on the contrary, shall it smite us with amazement at once at the mighty power and love to man[156] of the Savior, in that He both endured to suffer with us[157] in our infirmities, and was able to come down to our weakness? For not heaven and earth and the great seas, not the creatures that live in the water and on dry land, not plants, and stars, and air, and seasons, not the vast variety in the order of the universe,[158] so well sets forth the excellency of His might as that God, being incomprehensible, should have been able, impassibly, through flesh, to have come into close conflict with death, to the end that by His own suffering He might give us the boon of freedom from suffering.[159] The apostle, it is true, says, "In all these things we are more than conquerors through him that loved

---

[155] Eph. 5:29.

[156] φιλανθρωπία occurs twice in the N.T. (Acts 28: 2, and Titus 3:4) and is in the former passage rendered by A.V. "*kindness,*" in the latter by "love to man." The φιλανθρωπία of the Maltese barbarians corresponds with the lower classical sense of kindliness and courtesy. The love of God in Christ to man introduces practically a new connotation to the word and its cognates.

[157] Or to sympathize with our infirmities.

[158] ποικίλη διακόσμησις. διακόσμησις was the technical term of the Pythagorean philosophy for the orderly arrangement of the universe (Cf. Arist. *Metaph*. I. v. 2. "ἡ ὅλη διακόσμησις); Pythagoras being credited with the first application of the wordκόσμος to the universe. (Plut. 2, 886 c.) So *mundus*in Latin, whence Augustine's oxymoron, "*O munde immunde!*" On the scriptural use of κόσμος andαἰών vide Archbp. Trench's *New Testament Synonyms*, p. 204.

[159] In Hom. on Ps. 64 (LXX) Section 5, St. Basil describes the power of God the Word being most distinctly shown in the œconomy of the incarnation and His descent to the lowliness and the infirmity of the manhood. Cf. Ath. *on the Incarnation*, sect. 54, "He was made man that we might be made God; and He manifested Himself by a body that we might receive the idea of the unseen Father; and He endured the insolence of men that we might inherit immortality. For while He Himself was in no way injured, being impassible and incorruptible and the very Word and God, men who were suffering, and for whose sakes He endured all this, He maintained and preserved in His own impassibility."

us."[160] But in a phrase of this kind there is no suggestion of any lowly and subordinate ministry,[161] but rather of the succor rendered "in the power of his might."[162] For He Himself has bound the strong man and spoiled his goods,[163] that is, us men, whom our enemy had abused in every evil activity, and made "vessels meet for the Master's use"[164] us who have been perfected for every work through the making ready of that part of us which is in our own control.[165] Thus we have had our approach to the Father through Him, being translated from "the power of darkness to be partakers of the inheritance of the saints in light."[166] We must not, however, regard the œconomy[167] through the Son as a compulsory and subordinate ministration resulting from the low estate of a slave, but rather the voluntary solicitude working effectually for His own creation in goodness and in pity, according to the will of God the Father. For we shall be consistent with true religion if in all that was and is from time to time perfected by Him, we both bear witness to the perfection of His power, and in no case put it asunder from the Father's will. For instance, whenever the Lord is called the Way, we are carried on to a higher meaning, and not to

---

[160] Rom. 8:37.

[161] ὑπηρεσία. Lit. "under-rowing." The cognate ὑπηρέτης is the word used in Acts 26:16, in the words of the Savior to St. Paul, "to make thee a minister," and in 1 Cor. 4:1, "Let a man so account of us as of the ministers of Christ."

[162] Eph. 6:10.

[163] Cf. Matt. 12:29.

[164] 2 Tim. 2:21.

[165] This passage is difficult to render alike from the variety of readings and the obscurity of each. I have endeavored to represent the force of the Greek ἐκ τῆς ἑτοιμασίας τοῦ ἐφ' ἡμῖν, understanding by "τὸ ἐφ' ἡμῖν," practically, "our free will." Cf. the enumeration of what is ἐφ' ἡμῖν, within our own control, in the *Enchiridion* of Epicetus, Chap. I. "Within our own control are impulse, desire, inclination." On Is. 6:8, "Here am I; send me," St. Basil writes, "He did not add 'I will go;' for the acceptance of the message is within our control (ἐφ' ἡμῖν), but to be made capable of going is of Him that gives the grace, of the enabling God." The Benedictine translation of the text is "*per liberi arbitrii nostri præparationem.*" But other readings are (i) τῆς ἑτοιμασίας αὐτοῦ, "the preparation which is in our own control;" (ii) τῆς ἑτοιμασίας αὐτοῦ, "His preparation;" and (iii) the Syriac represented by "*arbitrio suo.*"

[166] Col. 1:12, 13.

[167] Cf. note in Ch. 5.

that which is derived from the vulgar sense of the word. We understand by Way that advance[168] to perfection which is made stage by stage, and in regular order, through the works of righteousness and "the illumination of knowledge;"[169] ever longing after what is before, and reaching forth unto those things which remain,[170] until we shall have reached the blessed end, the knowledge of God, which the Lord through Himself bestows on them that have trusted in Him. For our Lord is an essentially good Way, where erring and straying are unknown, to that which is essentially good, to the Father. For "no one," He says, "cometh to the Father but ["by" A.V.] through me."[171] Such is our way up to God "through the Son."

It will follow that we should next in order point out the character of the provision of blessings bestowed on us by the Father "through him." Inasmuch as all created nature, both this visible world and all that is conceived of in the mind, cannot hold together without the care and providence of God, the Creator Word, the Only begotten God, apportioning His succor according to the measure of the needs of each, distributes mercies various and manifold on account of the many kinds and characters of the recipients of His bounty, but appropriate to the necessities of individual requirements. Those that are confined in the darkness of ignorance He enlightens: for this reason He is true Light.[172] Portioning requital in accordance with the desert of deeds, He judges: for this reason He is righteous Judge.[173] "For the Father judgeth no man, but hath committed all judgment to the Son."[174] Those that have lapsed from the lofty height of life into sin He raises from their fall: for this reason He is Resurrection.[175] Effectually working by the touch of His power and the will of His goodness He does all things. He shep-

---

[168] προκοπή: Cf. Luke 2:52, where it is said that our Lord προέκοπτε, *i.e.*, "continued to cut His way forward."

[169] 1 Cor. 4:6, R.V. marg.

[170] There seems to be here a recollection, though not a quotation, of Phil. 3:13.

[171] John 14:6.

[172] John 1:9.

[173] 2 Tim. 4:8.

[174] John 5:22.

[175] John 11:25.

herds; He enlightens; He nourishes; He heals; He guides; He raises up; He calls into being things that were not; He upholds what has been created. Thus, the good things that come from God reach us "through the Son," who works in each case with greater speed than speech can utter. For not lightnings, not light's course in air, is so swift; not eyes' sharp turn, not the movements of our very thought. Nay, by the divine energy is each one of these in speed further surpassed than is the slowest of all living creatures outdone in motion by birds, or even winds, or the rush of the heavenly bodies: or, not to mention these, by our very thought itself. For what extent of time is needed by Him who "upholds all things by the word of His power,"[176] and works not by bodily agency, nor requires the help of hands to form and fashion, but holds in obedient following and unforced consent the nature of all things that are? So as Judith says, "Thou hast thought, and what things thou didst determine were ready at hand."[177] On the other hand, and lest we should ever be drawn away by the greatness of the works wrought to imagine that the Lord is without beginning,[178] what

---

[176] Heb. 1:3.

[177] Judith 9:5 and 6.

[178] ἄναρχος. This word is used in two senses by the Fathers. (i) In the sense of ἀΐδιος or eternal, it is applied (a) to the Trinity in unity. e.g., Quæst. Misc. v. 442 (Migne Ath. iv. 783), attributed to Athanasius, κοινὸν ἡ οὐσία· κοινὸν τὸ ἄναρχον. (b) To the Son. e.g., Greg. Naz. Orat. xxix. 490, ἐὰν τὴν ἀπὸ χρόνου νοῇς ἀρχὴν καὶ ἄναρχος ὁ υἱός, οὐκ ἄρχεται γὰρ ἀπὸ χρόνου ὁ χρόνων δεσπότης. (ii) In the sense of ἀναίτιος, "causeless," "originis principio carens," it is applied to the Father alone, and not to the Son. So Gregory of Nazianzus, in the oration quoted above, ὁ υἱός, ἐὰν ὡς αἴτιον τὸν πατέρα λαμβάνῃς, οὐκ ἄναρχος, "the Son, if you understand the Father as cause, is not without beginning." ἀρχὴ γὰρ υἱοῦ πατὴρ ὡς αἴτιος. "For the Father, as cause, is Beginning of the Son." But, though the Son in this sense was not ἄναρχος, He was said to be begotten ἀνάρχως. So Greg. Naz. (Hom. xxxvii. 590) τὸ ἴδιον ὄνομα τοῦ ἀνάρχως γεννηθέντος, υἱός. Cf. the Letter of Alexander of Alexandria to Alexander of Constantinople. Theod. Ecc. Hist. i. 3. τὴν ἄναρχον αὐτῷ παρὰ τοῦ πατρὸς γέννησιν ἀνατί θεντας. Cf. Hooker, Ecc. Pol. v. 54. "By the gift of eternal generation Christ hath received of the Father one and in number the self-same substance which the Father hath of himself unreceived from any other. For every *beginning is a father* unto that which cometh of it; and *every offspring is a son* unto that out of which it groweth. Seeing, therefore, the Father alone is originally that Deity which Christ originally is not (for Christ is God by being of God, light by issuing out of light), it

saith the Self-Existent?[179] "I live through [by, A.V.] the Father,"[180] and the power of God; "The Son hath power [can, A.V.] to do nothing of himself."[181] And the self-complete Wisdom? I received "a commandment what I should say and what I should speak."[182] Through all these words He is guiding us to the knowledge of the Father, and referring our wonder at all that is brought into existence to Him, to the end that "through Him" we may know the Father. For the Father is not regarded from the difference of the operations, by the exhibition of a separate and peculiar energy; for whatsoever things He sees the Father doing, "these also doeth the Son likewise;"[183] but He enjoys our wonder at all that comes to pass out of the glory which comes to Him from the Only Begotten, rejoicing in the Doer Himself as well as in the greatness of the deeds, and exalted by all who acknowledge Him as Father of our Lord Jesus Christ, "through whom [by whom, A.V.] are all things, and for whom are all things."[184] Wherefore, saith the Lord, "All mine are thine,"[185] as though the sovereignty over created things were conferred on Him, and "Thine are mine," as though the creating Cause came thence to Him. We are not to suppose that He used assistance in His action, or yet was entrusted with the ministry of each individual work by detailed commission, a condition distinctly menial and quite inadequate to the divine dignity. Rather was the Word full of His Father's excellences; He shines forth from the Father, and does all things

---

followeth hereupon that whatsoever Christ hath common unto him with his heavenly Father, the same of necessity must be *given* him, but naturally and eternally given." So Hillary *De Trin.* xii. 21. "*Ubi auctor eternus est, ibi et nativatis æternitas est: quia sicut nativitas ab auctore est, ita et ab æterno auctore æterna nativitas est.*" And Augustine *De Trin.* v. 15, "*Naturam præstat filio sine initio generatio.*"

[179] ἡ αὐτοζωή.
[180] John 6:57.
[181] John 5:19.
[182] John 12:49.
[183] John 5:19.
[184] Heb. 2:10. Cf. Rom. 11:36, to which the reading of two manuscripts more distinctly assimilates the citation. The majority of commentators refer Heb. 2:10, to the Father, but Theodoret understands it of the Son, and the argument of St. Basil necessitates the same application.
[185] John 17:10.

according to the likeness of Him that begat Him. For if in essence He is without variation, so also is He without variation in power.[186] And of those whose power is equal, the operation also is in all ways equal. And Christ is the power of God, and the wisdom of God.[187] And so "all things are made through [by, A.V.] him,"[188] and "all things were created through [by, A.V.] him and for him,"[189] not in the discharge of any slavish service, but in the fulfilment of the Father's will as Creator.

When then He says, "I have not spoken of myself,"[190] and again, "As the Father said unto me, so I speak,"[191] and "The word which ye hear is not mine, but [the Father's] which sent me,"[192] and in another place, "As the Father gave me commandment, even so I do,"[193] it is not because He lacks deliberate purpose or power of initiation, nor yet because He has to wait for the preconcerted key-note, that he employs language of this kind. His object is to make it plain that His own will is connected in indissoluble union with the Father. Do not then let us understand by what is called a "commandment" a peremptory mandate delivered by organs of speech, and giving orders to the Son, as to a subordinate, concerning what He ought to do. Let us rather, in a sense befitting the Godhead, perceive a transmission of will, like the reflection of an object in a mirror, passing without note of time from Father to Son. "For the Father loveth the Son and showeth him all things,"[194] so that "all things that the Father hath" belong to the Son, not gradually accruing to Him little by little, but with Him all together and at once. Among men, the workman who has been thoroughly taught his craft, and, through long training, has sure and

---

[186] ἀπαραλλάκτως ἔχει. Cf. James 1:17. παρ' ᾧ οὐκ ἔνι παραλλαγή. The word ἀπαράλλακτος was at first used by the Catholic bishops at Nicæa, as implying ὁμοούσιος. Vide Athan. De Decretis, § 20, in Wace and Schaff's ed., p. 163.
[187] 1 Cor. 1:24.
[188] John 1:3.
[189] Col. 1:16.
[190] John 12:49.
[191] John 12:50.
[192] John 14:24.
[193] John 14:31.
[194] John 5:20.

established experience in it, is able, in accordance with the scientific methods which now he has in store, to work for the future by himself. And are we to suppose that the wisdom of God, the Maker of all creation, He who is eternally perfect, who is wise, without a teacher, the Power of God, "in whom are hid all the treasures of wisdom and knowledge,"[195] needs piecemeal instruction to mark out the manner and measure of His operations? I presume that in the vanity of your calculations, you mean to open a school; you will make the one take His seat in the teacher's place, and the other stand by in a scholar's ignorance, gradually learning wisdom and advancing to perfection, by lessons given Him bit by bit. Hence, if you have sense to abide by what logically follows, you will find the Son being eternally taught, nor yet ever able to reach the end of perfection, inasmuch as the wisdom of the Father is infinite, and the end of the infinite is beyond apprehension. It results that whoever refuses to grant that the Son has all things from the beginning will never grant that He will reach perfection. But I am ashamed at the degraded conception to which, by the course of the argument, I have been brought down. Let us therefore revert to the loftier themes of our discussion.

"He that hath seen me hath seen the Father;[196] not the express image, nor yet the form, for the divine nature does not admit of combination; but the goodness of the will, which, being concurrent with the essence, is beheld as like and equal, or rather the same, in the Father as in the Son.[197]

---

[195] Col. 2:3, A.V. cf. the amendment of R.V., "all the treasures of wisdom and knowledge hidden," and Bp. Lightfoot on St. Paul's use of the gnostic term ἀπόκρυφος.

[196] John 14:9.

[197] The argument appears to be not that Christ is not the "express image," or impress of the Father, as He is described in Heb. 1:3, or form, as in Phil. 2:6, but that this is not the sense in which our Lord's words in St. John 14:9, must be understood to describe "seeing the Father." Χαρακτὴρ and μορφὴ are equivalent to ἡ θεία φύσις, and μορφή is used by St. Basil as it is used by St. Paul—coinciding with, if not following, the usage of the older Greek philosophy—to mean essential attributes which the Divine Word had before the incarnation (Cf. Eustathius in *Theod. Dial.* II. [Wace and Schaff Ed., p. 203]; "the express image made man,"—ὁ τῷ πνεύματι σωματοποιηθεὶς ἄνθρωπος χαρακτήρ.)

What then is meant by "became subject"?[198] What by "delivered him up for us all"?[199] It is meant that the Son has it of the Father that He works in goodness on behalf of men. But you must hear too the words, "Christ hath redeemed us from the curse of the law;"[200] and "while we were yet sinners, Christ died for us."[201]

Give careful heed, too, to the words of the Lord, and note how, whenever He instructs us about His Father, He is in the habit of using terms of personal authority, saying, "I will; be thou clean;"[202] and "Peace, be still;"[203] and "But I say unto you;"[204] and "Thou dumb and deaf spirit, I charge thee;"[205] and all other expressions of the same kind, in order that by these we may recognize our Master and Maker, and by the former may be taught the Father of our Master and Creator.[206] Thus on all sides is demonstrated the true doctrine that the fact that the Father creates through the Son neither constitutes the creation of the Father imperfect nor exhibits the active energy of the Son as feeble, but indicates the unity of the will; so the expression "through whom" contains a confession of an antecedent Cause, and is not adopted in objection to the efficient Cause.

The divine nature does not admit of *combination*, in the sense of *confusion* (Cf. the protests of Theodoret in his Dialogues against the confusion of the Godhead and manhood in the Christ), with the human nature in our Lord, and remains invisible. On the word χαρακτήρ vide Suicer, and on μορφήArchbp. Trench's *New Testament Synonyms* and Bp. Lightfoot on Philippians 2:6.

[198] Phil. 2:8.
[199] Rom. 8:32.
[200] Gal. 3:13.
[201] Rom. 5:8.
[202] Matt. 8:3.
[203] Mark 4:39.
[204] Matt. 5:22, etc.
[205] Mark 9:25.

[206] There is a difficulty in following the argument in the foregoing quotations. F. Combefis, the French Dominican editor of Basil, would boldly interpose a "not," and read 'whenever he does *not* instruct us concerning the Father.' But there is no MS. authority for this violent remedy. The Benedictine Editors say all is plain if we render "*postquam nos de patre erudivit.*" But the Greek will not admit of this.

CHAPTER NINE

Definitive conceptions about the Spirit which conform to the teaching of the Scriptures.

LET US NOW INVESTIGATE what are our common conceptions concerning the Spirit, as well those which have been gathered by us from Holy Scripture concerning It as those which we have received from the unwritten tradition of the Fathers. First of all we ask, who on hearing the titles of the Spirit is not lifted up in soul, who does not raise his conception to the supreme nature? It is called "Spirit of God,"[207] "Spirit of truth which proceedeth from the Father,"[208] "right Spirit,"[209] "a leading Spirit."[210] Its[211] proper and peculiar title is "Holy Spirit;" which is a name especially appropriate to everything that is incorporeal, purely immaterial, and indivisible. So our Lord, when teaching the woman who thought God to be an object of local worship that the incorporeal is incomprehensible, said "God is a spirit."[212] On our hearing, then, of a spirit, it is impossible to form the idea of a nature circumscribed, subject to change and variation, or at all like the creature. We are compelled to advance in our conceptions to the highest, and to think of an intelligent essence, in power infinite, in magnitude unlimited, unmeasured by times or ages, generous of Its good gifts, to whom turn all things needing sanctification, after whom reach all things that live in virtue, as being watered by Its inspiration and helped on toward their natural and proper end; perfecting all other things, but Itself in nothing lacking; living not as needing restoration, but as Supplier of life; not growing by additions; but straightway full, self-established, omnipresent, origin of

---

[207] Matt. 12:28, etc.
[208] John 15:26.
[209] Ps. 50:10 (LXX).
[210] Ps. 50:12 (LXX). R.V. and A.V., "free spirit."
[211] It will be remembered that in the Nicene Creed "the Lord and Giver of life" is τὸ κύριον τὸ ζωοποιόν In A.V. we have both *he* (John 15:26, ἐκεῖνος) and *it* (Rom. 8:16, αὐτὸ τὸ πνεῦμα).
[212] John 4:24.

sanctification, light perceptible to the mind, supplying, as it were, through Itself, illumination to every faculty in the search for truth; by nature unapproachable, apprehended by reason of goodness, filling all things with Its power,[213] but communicated only to the worthy; not shared in one measure, but distributing Its energy according to "the proportion of faith;"[214] in essence simple, in powers various, wholly present in each and being wholly everywhere; impassively divided, shared without loss of ceasing to be entire, after the likeness of the sunbeam, whose kindly light falls on him who enjoys it as though it shone for him alone, yet illumines land and sea and mingles with the air. So, too, is the Spirit to everyone who receives it, as though given to him alone, and yet It sends forth grace sufficient and full for all mankind, and is enjoyed by all who share It, according to the capacity, not of Its power, but of their nature.

Now the Spirit is not brought into intimate association with the soul by local approximation. How indeed could there be a corporeal approach to the incorporeal? This association results from the withdrawal of the passions which, coming afterwards gradually on the soul from its friendship to the flesh, have alienated it from its close relationship with God. Only then after a man is purified from the shame whose stain he took through his wickedness, and has come back again to his natural beauty, and as it were cleaning the Royal Image and restoring its ancient form, only thus is it possible for him to draw near to the Paraclete.[215] And He, like the sun, will by the aid of thy purified eye show thee in Himself the image of the invisible, and in the blessed spectacle of the image thou shalt behold the unspeakable beauty of the archetype.[216] Through His aid hearts are lifted

---

[213] Cf. Wisdom 1:7.

[214] Rom. 12:6.

[215] Cf. Theodoret, *Dial.* i. p. 164, Schaff and Wace's ed. "Sin is not of nature, but of corrupt will." So the ninth article of the English Church describes it as not the nature, but the "fault and corruption of the nature, of every man." On the figure of the restored picture Cf. Ath. *de Incar.* § 14, and Theod. *Dial.* ii. p. 183.

[216] Cf. Ep. 236. "Our mind enlightened by the Spirit, looks toward the Son, and in Him, as in an image, contemplates the Father." There seems at first sight some confusion in the text between the "Royal Image" in us and Christ as the

up, the weak are held by the hand, and they who are advancing are brought to perfection.[217] Shining upon those that are cleansed from every spot, He makes them spiritual by fellowship with Himself. Just as when a sunbeam falls on bright and transparent bodies, they themselves become brilliant too, and shed forth a fresh brightness from themselves, so souls wherein the Spirit dwells, illuminated by the Spirit, themselves become spiritual, and send forth their grace to others. Hence comes foreknowledge of the future, understanding of mysteries, apprehension of what is hidden, distribution of good gifts, the heavenly citizenship, a place in the chorus of angels, joy without end, abiding in God, the being made like to God, and, highest of all, the being made God.[218] Such, then, to instance a few out of many, are the conceptions concerning the Holy Spirit, which we have been taught to hold concerning His greatness, His dignity, and His operations, by the oracles[219] of the Spirit themselves.

---

image of God; but it is in proportion as we are like Christ that we see God in Christ. It is the "pure in heart" who "see God."

[217] "*Proficientes perficiuntur.*" Ben. Ed.

[218] Θεὸν γενεσθαι. The thought has its most famous expression in Ath. *de Incar.* § 54. He was made man that we might be made God—Θεοποιηθῶμεν. Cf. *De Decretis*, § 14, and other passages of Ath. Irenæus (*Adv. Hær.* iv. 38 [lxxv.]) writes "*non ab initio dii facti sumus, sed primo quidem homines, tunc demum dii.*" "*Secundum enim benignitatem suam bene dedit bonum, et similes sibi suæ potestatis homines fecit;*" and Origen (*contra Celsum*, iii. 28), "That the human nature by fellowship with the more divine might be made divine, not in Jesus only, but also in all those who with faith take up the life which Jesus taught;" and Greg. Naz. *Or.* xxx. § 14, "Till by the power of the incarnation he make me God." In Basil *adv. Eunom.* ii. 4. we have, "They who are perfect in virtue are deemed worthy of the title of God." Cf. 2 Pet. 1:4: "That ye might be partakers of the divine nature."

[219] ὑπ' αὐτῶν τῶν λογίων τοῦ πνεύματος. St. Basil is as unconscious as other early Fathers of the limitation of the word λόγια to "discourses." *Vide* Salmon's *Int. to the N.T. Ed.* iv. p. 95.

CHAPTER TEN

Against those who say that it is not right to rank the Holy Spirit with the Father and the Son.

BUT WE MUST PROCEED to attack our opponents, in the endeavor to confute those "oppositions" advanced against us which are derived from "knowledge falsely so-called."[220]

It is not permissible, they assert, for the Holy Spirit to be ranked with the Father and Son, on account of the difference of His nature and the inferiority of His dignity. Against them it is right to reply in the words of the apostles, "We ought to obey God rather than men."[221]

For if our Lord, when enjoining the baptism of salvation, charged His disciples to baptize all nations in the name "of the Father and of the Son and of the Holy Ghost,"[222] not disdaining fellowship with Him, and these men allege that we must not rank Him with the Father and the Son, is it not clear that they openly withstand the commandment of God? If they deny that coordination of this kind is declaratory of any fellowship and conjunction, let them tell us why it behooves us to hold this opinion, and what more intimate mode of

---

[220] 1 Tim. 6:20. The intellectual championship of Basil was chiefly asserted in the vindication of the consubstantiality of the Spirit, against the Arians and Semi-Arians, of whom Euonomius and Macedonius were leaders, the latter giving his name to the party who were unsound on the third Person of the Trinity, and were Macedonians as well as Pneumatomachi. But even among the maintainers of the Nicene confession there was much less clear apprehension of the nature and work of the Spirit than of the Son. Even so late as 380, the year after St. Basil's death, Gregory of Nazianzus, *Orat.* xxxi. *de Spiritu Sancto*, Cap. 5, wrote "of the wise on our side some held it to be an energy, some a creature, some God. Others, from respect, they say, to Holy Scripture, which lays down no law on the subject, neither worship nor dishonor the Holy Spirit." Cf. Schaff's *Hist. of Christian Ch.* III. Period, Sec. 128. In Letter cxxv. of St. Basil will be found a summary of the heresies with which he credited the Arians, submitted to Eusthathius of Sebaste in 373, shortly before the composition of the present treatise for Amphilochius.

[221] Acts 5:29.
[222] Matt. 28:19.

conjunction[223] they have.

If the Lord did not indeed conjoin the Spirit with the Father and Himself in baptism, do not[224] let them lay the blame of conjunction upon us, for we neither hold nor say anything different. If on the contrary the Spirit is there conjoined with the Father and the Son, and no one is so shameless as to say anything else, then let them not lay blame on us for following the words of Scripture.

But all the apparatus of war has been got ready against us; every intellectual missile is aimed at us; and now blasphemers' tongues shoot and hit and hit again, yet harder than Stephen of old was smitten by the killers of the Christ.[225] And do not let them succeed in concealing the fact that, while an attack on us serves for a pretext for the war, the real aim of these proceedings is higher. It is against us, they say, that they are preparing their engines and their snares; against us that they are shouting to one another, according to each one's strength or cunning, to come on. But the object of attack is faith. The one aim of the whole band of opponents and enemies of "sound

---

[223] The word used is συνάφεια, a crucial word in the controversy concerning the union of the divine and human natures in our Lord, Cf. the third Anathema of Cyril against Nestorius and the use of this word, and Theodoret's counter statement (Theod. pp. 25, 27). Theodore of Mopsuestia had preferred συνάφεια to ἕνωσις; Andrew of Samosata saw no difference between them. Athanasius (de Sent. Dionys. § 17) employs it for the mutual relationship of the Persons in the Holy Trinity: "προκαταρκτικὸν γάρ ἐστι τῆς συναφείας τὸ ὄνομα."

[224] μηδέ. The note of the Ben. Eds. is, "this reading, followed by Erasmus, stirs the wrath of Combefis, who would read, as is found in four MSS., τότε ἡμῖν, 'then let them lay the blame on us.' But he is quite unfair to Erasmus, who has more clearly apprehended the drift of the argument. Basil brings his opponents to the dilemma that the words 'In the name of the Father and of the Son and of the Holy Ghost' either do or do not assert a conjunction with the Father and the Son. If not, Basil ought not to be found fault with on the score of 'conjunction,' for he abides by the words of Scripture, and conjunction no more follows from his words than from those of our Lord. If they do, he cannot be found fault with for following the words of Scripture. The attentive reader will see this to be the meaning of Basil, and the received reading ought to be retained."

[225] Χριστοφόνοι. The compound occurs in Ps. Ignat. ad Philad. vi.

doctrine"[226] is to shake down the foundation of the faith of Christ by levelling apostolic tradition with the ground, and utterly destroying it. So like the debtors—of course *bona fide* debtors—they clamor for written proof, and reject as worthless the unwritten tradition of the Fathers.[227] But we will not slacken in our defense of the truth. We will not cowardly abandon the cause. The Lord has delivered to us as a necessary and saving doctrine that the Holy Spirit is to be ranked with the Father. Our opponents think differently, and see fit to divide and rend[228] asunder, and relegate Him to the nature of a ministering spirit. Is it not then indisputable that they make their own blasphemy more authoritative than the law prescribed by the Lord? Come, then, set aside mere contention. Let us consider the points before us, as follows:

Whence is it that we are Christians? Through our faith, would be the universal answer. And in what way are we saved? Plainly because we were regenerate through the grace given in our baptism. How else could we be? And after recognizing that this salvation is established through the Father and the Son and the Holy Ghost, shall we fling away "that form of doctrine"[229] which we received? Would it not rather be ground for great groaning if we are found now further off from our salvation "than when we first believed,"[230] and deny now what we then received? Whether a man have departed this life without baptism, or have received a baptism lacking in some of the requirements of the tradition, his loss is equal.[231] And whoever does not always and

---

[226] 1 Tim. 1:10.

[227] Mr. Johnston sees here a reference to the parable of the unjust steward, and appositely quotes Greg. Naz. *Orat.* xxxi, § 3, on the heretics' use of Scripture, "They find a cloak for their impiety in their affection for Scripture." The Arians at Nicæa objected to the ὁμοούσιον as unscriptural.

[228] Cf. Ep. cxx. 5.

[229] Rom. 6:17.

[230] Rom. 13:11, R.V.

[231] The question is whether the baptism has been solemnized, according to the divine command, in the name of the Father, and of the Son, and of the Holy Ghost. St. Cyprian in his controversy with Stephen, Bp. of Rome, represented the sterner view that heretical baptism was invalid. But, with some exceptions in the East, the position ultimately prevailed that baptism with water, and *in*

everywhere keep to and hold fast as a sure protection the confession which we recorded at our first admission, when, being delivered "from the idols," we came "to the living God,"[232] constitutes himself a "stranger" from the "promises"[233] of God, fighting against his own handwriting,[234] which he put on record when he professed the faith. For if to me my baptism was the beginning of life, and that day of regeneration the first of days, it is plain that the utterance uttered in the grace of adoption was the most honorable of all. Can I then, perverted by these men's seductive words, abandon the tradition which guided me to the light, which bestowed on me the boon of the knowledge of God, whereby I, so long a foe by reason of sin, was made a child of God? But, for myself, I pray that with this confession I may depart hence to the Lord, and them I charge to preserve the faith secure until the day of Christ, and to keep the Spirit undivided from the Father and the Son, preserving, both in the confession of faith and in the doxology, the doctrine taught them at their baptism.

---

the prescribed words, by whomsoever administered, was valid. So St. Augustine, "*Si evangelicus verbis in nomine Patris et Filii et Spiritus Sancti Marcion baptismum consecrabat, integrum erat Sacramentum, quamvis ejus fides sub eisdem verbis aliud opinantis quam catholica veritas docet non esset integra.*" (*Cont. Petil. de unico bapt.* § 3.) So the VIII. Canon of Arles (314), "*De Afris, quod propria lege sua utuntur ut rebaptizent, placuit, ut, si ad ecclesiam aliquis de hæresi venerit, interrogent eum symbolum; et si perviderint eum in Patre, et Filio et Spiritu Sancto, esse baptizatum, manus ei tantum imponantur, ut accipiat spiritum sanctum. Quod si interrogatus non responderit hanc Trinitatem, baptizetur.*" So the VII. Canon of Constantinople (381) by which the Eunomians who only baptized with one immersion, and the Montanists, here called Phrygians, and the Sabellians, who taught the doctrine of the Fatherhood of the Son, were counted as heathen. *Vide* Bright's notes on the *Canons of the Councils*, p. 106. Socrates, v. 24, describes how the Eunomi-Eutychians baptized not in the name of the Trinity, but into the death of Christ.

[232] 1 Thess. 1:9.

[233] Eph. 2:12.

[234] The word χειρόγραφον, more common in Latin than in Greek, is used generally for a bond. Cf. Juv. *Sat.* xvi. 41, "*Debitor aut sumptos pergit non reddere nummos, vana supervacui dicens chirographa ligni.*" On the use of the word, *vide* Bp. Lightfoot on Col. 2:14. The names of the catechumens were registered, and the Renunciation and Profession of Faith (*Interrogationes et Responsa*; ἐπερωτήσεις καὶ ἀποκρίσεις) may have been signed.

CHAPTER ELEVEN

That they who deny the Spirit are transgressors.

"WHO HATH WOE? WHO hath sorrow?"[235] For whom is distress and darkness? For whom eternal doom? Is it not for the transgressors? For them that deny the faith? And what is the proof of their denial? Is it not that they have set at naught their own confessions? And when and what did they confess? Belief in the Father and in the Son and in the Holy Ghost, when they renounced the devil and his angels, and uttered those saving words. What fit title then for them has been discovered, for the children of light to use? Are they not addressed as transgressors, as having violated the covenant of their salvation? What am I to call the denial of God? What the denial of Christ? What but transgressions? And to him who denies the Spirit, what title do you wish me to apply? Must it not be the same, inasmuch as he has broken his covenant with God? And when the confession of faith in Him secures the blessing of true religion. and its denial subjects men to the doom of godlessness, is it not a fearful thing for them to set the confession at naught, not through fear of fire, or sword, or cross, or scourge, or wheel, or rack, but merely led astray by the sophistry and seductions of the pneumatomachi? I testify to every man who is confessing Christ and denying God, that Christ will profit him nothing;[236] to every man that calls upon God but rejects the Son, that his faith is vain;[237] to every man that sets aside the Spirit, that his faith in the Father and the Son will be useless, for he cannot even hold it without the presence of the Spirit. For he who does not believe the Spirit does not believe in the Son, and he who has not believed in the Son does not believe in the Father. For none "can say that Jesus is the Lord but by the Holy Ghost,"[238] and "No man hath seen God at any time, but the only begot-

---
[235] Prov. 23:29.
[236] Cf. Gal. 5:2.
[237] Cf. 1 Cor. 15:17.
[238] 1 Cor. 12:3.

ten God which is in the bosom of the Father, he hath declared him."[239]

Such a one hath neither part nor lot in the true worship; for it is impossible to worship the Son, save by the Holy Ghost; impossible to call upon the Father, save by the Spirit of adoption.

CHAPTER TWELVE

Against those who assert that the baptism in the name of the Father alone is sufficient.

LET NO ONE BE misled by the fact of the apostle's frequently omitting the name of the Father and of the Holy Spirit when making mention of baptism, or on this account imagine that the invocation of the names is not observed. "As many of you," he says, "as were baptized into Christ have put on Christ;"[240] and again, "As many of you as were baptized into Christ were baptized into his death."[241] For the naming of Christ is the confession of the whole,[242] showing forth as it does the God who gave, the Son who received, and the Spirit who is, the unction.[243] So we have learned from Peter, in the Acts, of "Jesus of Nazareth whom God anointed with the Holy Ghost;"[244] and in Isaiah, "The Spirit of the Lord is upon me, because the Lord hath anointed me;"[245] and the Psalmist, "Therefore God, even thy God, hath anointed thee with the oil of gladness above

---

[239] John 1:18. On the reading "only begotten God" Cf. note in Ch. 6. In this passage in St. Basil "God" is the reading of three MSS. at Paris, that at Moscow, that at the Bodleian, and that at Vienna. "Son" is read by Regius III., Regius I., Regius IV., and Regius V. in Paris, the three last being all of the 14th century, the one in the British Museum, and another in the Imperial Library at Vienna, which generally agrees with our own in the Museum.

[240] Gal. 3:27, R.V.

[241] Rom. 6:3, with change to 2d person.

[242] Cf. note in Ch. 10.

[243] "ἡ τοῦ Χριστοῦ προσηγορία ...δηλοῖ τόν τε Χρίσαντα Θεὸν καὶ τὸν Χρισθέντα Υἱὸν καὶ τὸ Χρίσμα τὸ Πνεῦμα."

[244] Acts 10:38.

[245] Is. 60:1.

thy fellows."[246] Scripture, however, in the case of baptism, sometimes plainly mentions the Spirit alone.[247]

"For into one Spirit,"[248] it says, "we were all baptized in[249] one body."[250] And in harmony with this are the passages: "You shall be baptized with the Holy Ghost,"[251] and "He shall baptize you with the Holy Ghost."[252] But no one on this account would be justified in calling that baptism a perfect baptism wherein only the name of the Spirit was invoked. For the tradition that has been given us by the quickening grace must remain forever inviolate. He who redeemed our life from destruction[253] gave us power of renewal, whereof the cause is ineffable and hidden in mystery, but bringing great salvation to our souls, so that to add or to take away anything[254] involves manifestly a falling away from the life everlasting. If then in baptism the separation of the Spirit from the Father and the Son is perilous to the baptizer, and of no advantage to the baptized, how can the rending asunder of the Spirit from Father and from Son be safe for us?[255] Faith and baptism are two kindred and inseparable ways of salvation: faith is perfected through baptism, baptism is established through faith, and both are completed by the same names. For as we believe in the Father and the Son and the Holy Ghost, so are we also baptized in the name of the Father and of the Son and of the Holy Ghost; first comes the confession, introducing us to salvation, and baptism follows, setting the seal upon our assent.

---

[246] Ps. 44:7 (LXX).

[247] No subject occurs in the original, but "Scripture" seems better than "the Apostle" of the Bened. Tr. "*Videtur fecisse mentionem*," moreover, is not the Latin for φαίνεται μνημονεύσας, but for φαίνεται μνημονεῦσαι.

[248] *Sic.*

[249] *Sic.*

[250] 1 Cor. 12:13, loosely quoted.

[251] Acts 1:5.

[252] Luke 3:16.

[253] Cf. Ps. 102:4 (LXX).

[254] Cf. Deut. 4:2, and Rev. 21:18, 19.

[255] Cf. note in Ch. 10.

CHAPTER THIRTEEN

Statement of the reason why in the writings of Paul the angels are associated with the Father and the Son.

IT IS, HOWEVER, OBJECTED that other beings which are enumerated with the Father and the Son are certainly not always glorified together with them. The apostle, for instance, in his charge to Timothy, associates the angels with them in the words, "I charge thee before God and the Lord Jesus Christ and the elect angels."[256] We are not for alienating the angels from the rest of creation, and yet, it is argued, we do not allow of their being reckoned with the Father and the Son. To this I reply, although the argument, so obviously absurd is it, does not really deserve a reply, that possibly before a mild and gentle judge, and especially before One who by His leniency to those arraigned before Him demonstrates the unimpeachable equity of His decisions, one might be willing to offer as witness even a fellow-slave; but for a slave to be made free and called a son of God and quickened from death can only be brought about by Him who has acquired natural kinship with us, and has been changed from the rank of a slave. For how can we be made kin with God by one who is an alien? How can we be freed by one who is himself under the yoke of slavery? It follows that the mention of the Spirit and that of angels are not made under like conditions. The Spirit is called on as Lord of life, and the angels as allies of their fellow-slaves and faithful witnesses of the truth. It is customary for the saints to deliver the commandments of God in the presence of witnesses, as also the apostle himself says to Timothy, "The things which thou hast heard of me among many witnesses, the same commit thou to faithful men;"[257] and now he calls the angels to witness, for he knows that angels shall be present with the Lord when He shall come in the glory of His Father to judge the world in righteousness. For He says, "Whoever shall confess me before men, him shall the Son of Man also confess before the

---
[256] 1 Tim. 5:21.
[257] 2 Tim. 2:2.

angels of God, but he that denieth Me before men shall be denied before the angels of God;"[258] and Paul in another place says, "When the Lord Jesus shall be revealed from heaven with his angels."[259] Thus he already testifies before the angels, preparing good proofs for himself at the great tribunal.

And not only Paul, but generally all those to whom is committed any ministry of the word, never cease from testifying, but call heaven and earth to witness on the ground that now every deed that is done is done within them, and that in the examination of all the actions of life they will be present with the judged. So it is said, "He shall call to the heavens above and to earth, that he may judge his people."[260] And so Moses when about to deliver his oracles to the people says, "I call heaven and earth to witness this day;"[261] and again in his song he says, "Give ear, O ye heavens, and I will speak, and hear, O earth, the words of my mouth;"[262] and Isaiah, "Hear, O heavens, and give ear, O earth;"[263] and Jeremiah describes astonishment in heaven at the tidings of the unholy deeds of the people: "The heaven was astonished at this, and was horribly afraid, because my people committed two evils."[264] And so the apostle, knowing the angels to be set over men as tutors and guardians, calls them to witness. Moreover, Joshua, the son of Nun, even set up a stone as witness of his words (already a heap somewhere had been called a witness by Jacob),[265] for he says, "Behold this stone shall be a witness unto you this day to the end of days, when ye lie to the Lord our God,"[266] perhaps believing that by God's power even the stones would speak to the conviction of the transgressors; or, if not, that at least each man's conscience would be wounded by the force of the reminder. In this manner, they who

---

[258] Luke 12:8, 9.
[259] 2 Thess. 1:7.
[260] Ps. 49:4 (LXX).
[261] Deut. 4:26.
[262] Deut. 32:1.
[263] Isa. 1:2.
[264] Jer. 2:12, 13 (LXX).
[265] Gen. 31:47.
[266] Josh. 24:27 (LXX).

have been entrusted with the stewardship of souls provide witnesses, whatever they may be, so as to produce them at some future day. But the Spirit is ranked together with God, not on account of the emergency of the moment, but on account of the natural fellowship; is not dragged in by us, but invited by the Lord.

CHAPTER FOURTEEN

Objection that some were baptized unto Moses and believed in him, and an answer to it; with remarks upon types.

BUT EVEN IF SOME are baptized unto the Spirit, it is not, it is urged, on this account right for the Spirit to be ranked with God. Some "were baptized unto Moses in the cloud and in the sea."[267] And it is admitted that faith even before now has been put in men; for "The people believed God and his servant Moses."[268] Why then, it is asked, do we, on account of faith and of baptism, exalt and magnify the Holy Spirit so far above creation, when there is evidence that the same things have before now been said of men? What, then, shall we reply? Our answer is that the faith in the Spirit is the same as the faith in the Father and the Son; and in like manner, too, the baptism. But the faith in Moses and in the cloud is, as it were, in a shadow and type. The nature of the divine is very frequently represented by the rough and shadowy outlines[269] of the types; but because divine things are prefigured by small and human things, it is obvious that we must not therefore conclude the divine nature to be small. The type is an exhibition of things expected, and gives an imitative anticipation of the future. So Adam was a type of "Him that was to come."[270] Typically, "That rock was Christ;"[271] and the water a type of

---

[267] 1 Cor. 10:2.

[268] Ex. 14:31 (LXX).

[269] σκιαγραφία, or shade-painting, is illusory scene-painting. Plato (*Crit.* 107 c.) calls it "indistinct and deceptive." Cf. Ar. *Eth. Nic.* i. 3, 4, "παχυλῶς καὶ ἐν τύπῳ." The τύπος gives the general design, not an exact anticipation.

[270] Rom. 5:14.

[271] 1 Cor. 10:4.

the living power of the word; as He says, "If any man thirst, let him come unto me and drink."[272] The manna is a type of the living bread that came down from heaven;[273] and the serpent on the standard,[274] of the passion of salvation accomplished by means of the cross, wherefore they who even looked thereon were preserved. So in like manner, the history of the exodus of Israel is recorded to show forth those who are being saved through baptism. For the firstborn of the Israelites were preserved, like the bodies of the baptized, by the giving of grace to them that were marked with blood. For the blood of the sheep is a type of the blood of Christ; and the firstborn, a type of the first-formed. And inasmuch as the first-formed of necessity exists in us, and, in sequence of succession, is transmitted till the end, it follows that "in Adam" we "all die,"[275] and that "death reigned"[276] until the fulfilling of the law and the coming of Christ. And the firstborn were preserved by God from being touched by the destroyer, to show that we who were made alive in Christ no longer die in Adam. The sea and the cloud for the time being led on through amazement to faith, but for the time to come they typically prefigured the grace to be. "Who is wise and he shall understand these things?"[277]—how the sea is typically a baptism bringing about the departure of Pharaoh, in like manner as this washing causes the departure of the tyranny of the devil. The sea slew the enemy in itself: and in baptism too dies our enmity towards God. From the sea the people came out unharmed: we too, as it were, alive from the dead, step up from the water "saved" by the "grace" of Him who called us.[278] And the cloud is a shadow of the gift of the Spirit, who cools the flame of our passions by the "mortification" of our "members."[279]

What then? Because they were typically baptized unto Moses, is

---

[272] John 7:37.
[273] John 6:49, 51.
[274] σημεῖον, as in the LXX. Cf. Numb. 21:9 and John 3:14.
[275] 1 Cor. 15:22.
[276] Rom. 5:17.
[277] Hos. 14:9.
[278] Eph. 2:5.
[279] Col. 3:5.

the grace of baptism therefore small? Were it so, and if we were in each case to prejudice the dignity of our privileges by comparing them with their types, not even one of these privileges could be reckoned great; then not the love of God, who gave His only begotten Son for our sins, would be great and extraordinary, because Abraham did not spare his own son;[280] then even the passion of the Lord would not be glorious, because a sheep typified the offering instead of Isaac; then the descent into hell was not fearful, because Jonah had previously typified the death in three days and three nights. The same prejudicial comparison is made also in the case of baptism by all who judge of the reality by the shadow, and, comparing the typified with the type, attempt by means of Moses and the sea to disparage at once the whole dispensation of the Gospel. What remission of sins, what renewal of life, is there in the sea? What spiritual gift is there through Moses? What dying[281] of sins is there? Those men did not die with Christ; wherefore they were not raised with Him.[282] They did not "bear the image of the heavenly;"[283] they did "bear about in the body the dying of Jesus;"[284] they did not "put off the old man;" they did not "put on the new man which is renewed in knowledge after the image of Him which created him."[285] Why then do you compare baptisms which have only the name in common, while the distinction between the things themselves is as great as might be that of dream and reality, that of shadow and figures with substantial existence?

But belief in Moses not only does not show our belief in the Spirit to be worthless, but, if we adopt our opponents' line of argument, it rather weakens our confession in the God of the universe. "The people," it is written, "believed the Lord and his servant Moses."[286] Moses then is joined with God, not with the Spirit; and he was a type not of the Spirit, but of Christ. For at that time in the ministry of the law, he

---

[280] Cf. Rom. 8:32.
[281] νέκρωσις. A.V. in 2 Cor. 4:10, "dying," Rom. 4:19, "deadness."
[282] Cf. Rom. 6:8.
[283] 1 Cor. 15:49.
[284] 2 Cor. 4:10.
[285] Col. 3:9, 10.
[286] Ex. 14:31.

by means of himself typified "the Mediator between God and men."[287] Moses, when mediating for the people in things pertaining to God, was not a minister of the Spirit; for the law was given, "ordained by angels in the hand of a mediator,"[288] namely Moses, in accordance with the summons of the people, "Speak thou with us,...but let not God speak with us."[289] Thus faith in Moses is referred to the Lord, the Mediator between God and men, who said, "Had ye believed Moses, ye would have believed me."[290] Is then our faith in the Lord a trifle, because it was signified beforehand through Moses? So then, even if men were baptized unto Moses, it does not follow that the grace given of the Spirit in baptism is small. I may point out, too, that it is usual in Scripture to say Moses and the law,[291] as in the passage, "They have Moses and the prophets."[292] When therefore it is meant to speak of the baptism of the law, the words are, "They were baptized unto Moses."[293] Why then do these calumniators of the truth, by means of the shadow and the types, endeavor to bring contempt and ridicule on the "rejoicing" of our "hope,"[294] and the rich gift of our God and Savior, who through regeneration renews our youth like the eagle's?[295] Surely it is altogether childish, and like a babe who must needs be fed on milk,[296] to be ignorant of the great mystery of our salvation; inasmuch as, in accordance with the gradual progress of our education, while being brought to perfection in our training for godliness,[297] we were first taught elementary and easier lessons, suited to our intelligence, while the Dispenser of our lots was ever leading us up, by gradually accustoming us, like eyes brought up in the dark, to

---

[287] 1 Tim. 2:5.
[288] Gal. 3:19.
[289] Ex. 20:19.
[290] John 5:46.
[291] *i.e.*, to mean by "Moses," the law.
[292] Luke 16:29.
[293] 1 Cor. 10:2.
[294] Heb. 3:6.
[295] Cf. Ps. 102:5 (LXX).
[296] Cf. Heb. 5:12.
[297] Cf. 1 Tim. 4:7.

the great light of truth. For He spares our weakness, and in the depth of the riches[298] of His wisdom, and the inscrutable judgments of His intelligence, used this gentle treatment, fitted for our needs, gradually accustoming us to see first the shadows of objects, and to look at the sun in water, to save us from dashing against the spectacle of pure unadulterated light, and being blinded. Just so the Law, having a shadow of things to come, and the typical teaching of the prophets, which is a dark utterance of the truth, have been devised means to train the eyes of the heart, in that hence the transition to the wisdom hidden in mystery[299] will be made easy. Enough so far concerning types; nor indeed would it be possible to linger longer on this topic, or the incidental discussion would become many times bulkier than the main argument.

CHAPTER FIFTEEN

Reply to the suggested objection that we are baptized "into water." Also concerning baptism.

WHAT MORE? VERILY, OUR opponents are well equipped with arguments. We are baptized, they urge, into water, and of course we shall not honor the water above all creation, or give it a share of the honor of the Father and of the Son. The arguments of these men are such as might be expected from angry disputants, leaving no means untried in their attack on him who has offended them, because their reason is clouded over by their feelings. We will not, however, shrink from the discussion even of these points. If we do not teach the ignorant, at least we shall not turn away before evil doers. But let us for a moment retrace our steps.

The dispensation of our God and Savior concerning man is a recall from the fall and a return from the alienation caused by disobedience to close communion with God. This is the reason for the sojourn of Christ in the flesh, the pattern life described in the Gospels, the suf-

---

[298] Rom. 11:33.
[299] 1 Cor. 2:7.

ferings, the cross, the tomb, the resurrection; so that the man who is being saved through imitation of Christ receives that old adoption. For perfection of life the imitation of Christ is necessary, not only in the example of gentleness,[300] lowliness, and long suffering set us in His life, but also of His actual death. So Paul, the imitator of Christ,[301] says, "being made conformable unto his death; if by any means I might attain unto the resurrection of the dead."[302] How then are we made in the likeness of His death?[303] In that we were buried[304] with Him by baptism. What then is the manner of the burial? And what is the advantage resulting from the imitation? First of all, it is necessary that the continuity of the old life be cut. And this is impossible unless a man be born again, according to the Lord's word;[305] for the regeneration, as indeed the name shows, is a beginning of a second life. So before beginning the second, it is necessary to put an end to the first. For just as in the case of runners who turn and take the second course,[306] a kind of halt and pause intervenes between the movements in the opposite direction, so also in making a change in lives it seemed necessary for death to come as mediator between the two, ending all that goes before, and beginning all that comes after. How then do we achieve the descent into hell? By imitating, through baptism, the burial of Christ. For the bodies of the baptized are, as it were, buried in the water. Baptism then symbolically signifies the putting off of the works of the flesh; as the apostle says, ye were "circumcised with the circumcision made without hands, in putting off the body of the sins of the flesh by the circumcision of Christ; buried

---

[300] ἀοργησία in Arist. *Eth.* iv. 5, 5, is the defect where meekness (πραότης) is the mean. In Plutarch, who wrote a short treatise on it, is a virtue. In Mark 3:5, Jesus looked round on them "with anger," μετ' ὀργῆς, but in Matt. 11:29, He calls Himself πρᾷος.

[301] Cf. 1 Cor. 11:1.

[302] Phil. 3:10, 11.

[303] Rom. 6:4, 5.

[304] A.V., "are buried." Grk. and R.V., "were buried."

[305] John 3:3.

[306] In the double course (δίαυλος) the runner turned (κάμπτω) the post at the end of the stadium. So "κάμψαι δίαυλον θάτερον κῶλον πάλιν" in Æsch. *Ag.* 335, for retracing one's steps another way.

with him in baptism."[307] And there is, as it were, a cleansing of the soul from the filth[308] that has grown on it from the carnal mind,[309] as it is written, "Thou shalt wash me, and I shall be whiter than snow."[310] On this account we do not, as is the fashion of the Jews, wash ourselves at each defilement, but own the baptism of salvation[311] to be one.[312] For there the death on behalf of the world is one, and one the resurrection of the dead, whereof baptism is a type. For this cause the Lord, who is the Dispenser of our life, gave us the covenant of baptism, containing a type of life and death, for the water fulfils the image of death, and the Spirit gives us the earnest of life. Hence it follows that the answer to our question why the water was associated with the Spirit[313] is clear: the reason is because in baptism two ends were proposed; on the one hand, the destroying of the body of sin,[314] that it may never bear fruit unto death;[315] on the other hand, our living unto the Spirit,[316] and having our fruit in holiness;[317] the water receiving the body as in a tomb figures death, while the Spirit pours in the quickening power, renewing our souls from the deadness of sin unto their original life. This then is what it is to be born again of water and of the Spirit, the being made dead being effected in the water, while our life is wrought in us through the Spirit. In three immersions,[318] then, and

---

[307] Col. 2:11, 12.

[308] Cf. 1 Pet. 3:21.

[309] τὸ σαρκικὸν φρόνημα. Cf. the φρόνημα τῆς σαρκός of Rom. 8:6. Cf. *Article ix.*

[310] Ps. 50:9 (LXX).

[311] Cf. 1 Pet. 3:21.

[312] Cf. Eph. 4:5.

[313] Cf. John 3:5.

[314] Cf. Rom. 6:6.

[315] Cf. Rom. 7:5.

[316] Cf. Gal. 5:25.

[317] Cf. Rom. 6:22.

[318] Trine immersion was the universal rule of the Catholic Church. Cf. Greg. Nyss. *The Great Catechism*, p. 502 of this edition. So Tertull. *de Cor. Mil.* c iii., *Aquam adituri, ibidem, sed et aliquanto prius in ecclesia, sub antistitis manu contestamur, nos renuntiare diabolo et pompæ et angelis ejus. Dehinc ter mergitamur.* Sozomen (vi. 26) says that Eunomius was alleged to be the first to maintain that baptism ought to be performed in one immersion and to corrupt in this man-

with three invocations, the great mystery of baptism is performed, to the end that the type of death may be fully figured, and that by the tradition of the divine knowledge the baptized may have their souls enlightened. It follows that if there is any grace in the water, it is not of the nature of the water, but of the presence of the Spirit. For baptism is "not the putting away of the filth of the flesh, but the answer of a good conscience towards God."[319] So in training us for the life that follows on the resurrection the Lord sets out all the manner of life required by the Gospel, laying down for us the law of gentleness, of endurance of wrong, of freedom from the defilement that comes of the love of pleasure, and from covetousness, to the end that we may of set purpose win beforehand and achieve all that the life to come of its inherent nature possesses. If therefore any one in attempting a definition were to describe the gospel as a forecast of the life that follows on the resurrection, he would not seem to me to go beyond what is meet and right. Let us now return to our main topic.

Through the Holy Spirit comes our restoration to paradise, our ascension into the kingdom of heaven, our return to the adoption of sons, our liberty to call God our Father, our being made partakers of the grace of Christ, our being called children of light, our sharing in eternal glory, and, in a word, our being brought into a state of all "fullness of blessing,"[320] both in this world and in the world to come, of all the good gifts that are in store for us, by promise hereof, through faith, beholding the reflection of their grace as though they were already present, we await the full enjoyment. If such is the

---

ner the tradition of the apostles, and Theodoret (Hæret. fab. iv. 3) describes Eunomius as abandoning the trine immersion, and also the invocation of the Trinity as baptizing into the death of Christ. Jeremy Taylor (*Ductor dubitantium*, iii. 4, Sect. 13) says, "In England we have a custom of sprinkling, and that but once....As to the number, though the Church of England hath made no law, and therefore the custom of doing it once is the more indifferent and at liberty, yet if the trine immersion be agreeable to the analogy of the mystery, and the other be not, the custom ought not to prevail, and is not to be complied with, if the case be evident or declared."

[319] 1 Pet. 3:21.
[320] Rom. 15:29.

earnest, what the perfection? If such the first fruits, what the complete fulfilment? Furthermore, from this too may be apprehended the difference between the grace that comes from the Spirit and the baptism by water: in that John indeed baptized with water, but our Lord Jesus Christ by the Holy Ghost. "I indeed," he says, "baptize you with water unto repentance; but he that cometh after me is mightier than I, whose shoes I am not worthy to bear: he shall baptize you with the Holy Ghost and with fire."[321] Here He calls the trial at the judgment the baptism of fire, as the apostle says, "The fire shall try every man's work, of what sort it is."[322] And again, "The day shall declare it, because it shall be revealed by fire."[323] And ere now there have been some who in their championship of true religion have undergone the death for Christ's sake, not in mere similitude, but in actual fact, and so have needed none of the outward signs of water for their salvation, because they were baptized in their own blood.[324] Thus I write not to disparage the baptism by water, but to overthrow the arguments[325] of those who exalt themselves against the Spirit; who confound things that are distinct from one another, and compare those which admit of no comparison.

---

[321] Matt. 3:11.

[322] 1 Cor. 3:13.

[323] Ibid.

[324] On the martyrs' baptism of blood, cf. Eus. vi. 4, on the martyrdom of the Catechumen Herais. So St. Cyril, of Jerusalem (*Cat. Lect.* iii. 10), "If a man receive not baptism, he has not salvation; excepting only the martyrs, even who without the water receive the kingdom. For when the Savior was ransoming the world through the cross, and was pierced in the side, He gave forth blood and water, that some in times of peace should be baptized in water; others in time of persecution, in their own blood." So Tertullian (*In Valentin*. ii.) of the Holy Innocents, "baptized in blood for Jesus' sake" (Keble), "*testimonium Christi sanguine litavere*."

[325] Τοὺς λογισμοὺς καθαιρῶν. Cf. 2 Cor. 10:4.

CHAPTER SIXTEEN

That the Holy Spirit is in every conception inseparable from the Father and the Son, alike in the creation of perceptible objects, in the dispensation of human affairs, and in the judgment to come.

LET US THEN REVERT to the point raised from the outset, that in all things the Holy Spirit is inseparable and wholly incapable of being parted from the Father and the Son. St. Paul, in the passage about the gift of tongues, writes to the Corinthians, "If ye all prophesy and there come in one that believeth not, or one unlearned, he is convinced of all, he is judged of all; and thus are the secrets of the heart made manifest; and so falling down on his face he will worship God and report that God is in you of a truth."[326] If then God is known to be in the prophets by the prophesying that is acting according to the distribution of the gifts of the Spirit, let our adversaries consider what kind of place they will attribute to the Holy Spirit. Let them say whether it is more proper to rank Him with God or to thrust Him forth to the place of the creature. Peter's words to Sapphira, "How is it that ye have agreed together to tempt the Spirit of the Lord? Ye have not lied unto men, but unto God,"[327] show that sins against the Holy Spirit and against God are the same; and thus you might learn that in every operation the Spirit is closely conjoined with, and inseparable from, the Father and the Son. God works the differences of operations, and the Lord the diversities of administrations, but all the while the Holy Spirit is present too of His own will, dispensing distribution of the gifts according to each recipient's worth. For, it is said, "there are diversities of gifts, but the same Spirit; and differences of administrations, but the same Lord; and there are diversities of operations, but it is the same God which worketh all in all."[328] "But all these," it is said, "worketh that one and the self-same Spirit, dividing

---

[326] 1 Cor. 14:24, 25.
[327] Acts 5:9 and 4. "Thou hast not lied," said to Ananias, interpolated into the rebuke of Sapphira.
[328] 1 Cor. 12:4, 5, 6.

to every man severally as He will."³²⁹ It must not however be supposed because in this passage the apostle names in the first place the Spirit, in the second the Son, and in the third God the Father, that therefore their rank is reversed. The apostle has only started in accordance with our habits of thought; for when we receive gifts, the first that occurs to us is the distributer, next we think of the sender, and then we lift our thoughts to the fountain and cause of the boons.

Moreover, from the things created at the beginning may be learnt the fellowship of the Spirit with the Father and the Son. The pure, intelligent, and supermundane powers are and are styled holy, because they have their holiness of the grace given by the Holy Spirit. Accordingly, the mode of the creation of the heavenly powers is passed over in Silence, for the historian of the cosmogony has revealed to us only the creation of things perceptible by sense. But do thou, who hast power from the things that are seen to form an analogy of the unseen, glorify the Maker by whom all things were made, visible and invisible, principalities and powers, authorities, thrones, and dominions, and all other reasonable natures whom we cannot name.³³⁰ And in the creation bethink thee first, I pray thee, of the original cause of all things that are made, the Father; of the creative cause, the Son; of the perfecting cause, the Spirit; so that the ministering spirits subsist by the will of the Father, are brought into being by the operation of the Son, and perfected by the presence of the Spirit. Moreover, the perfection of angels is sanctification and continuance in it. And let no one imagine me either to affirm that there are three original hypostases³³¹ or to allege the operation of the Son to be imperfect. For the first principle of existing things is One, creating through the Son and perfecting through the Spirit.³³² The operation of the Father who worketh all in all is not imperfect, neither is the creating work

---

³²⁹ 1 Cor. 12:11.

³³⁰ Cf. Col. 1:16.

³³¹ ὑποστάσεις, apparently used here as the equivalent of οὐσίαι, unless the negation only extends to ἀρχικάς. Cf. note in Ch. 5.

³³² Contrast the neuter τὸ ὄν of Pagan philosophy with the ὁ ὤν or ἐγώ εἰμι of Christian revelation.

of the Son incomplete if not perfected by the Spirit. The Father, who creates by His sole will, could not stand in any need of the Son, but nevertheless He wills through the Son; nor could the Son, who works according to the likeness of the Father, need co-operation, but the Son too wills to make perfect through the Spirit. "For by the word of the Lord were the heavens made, and all the host of them by the breath [the Spirit] of His mouth."[333] The Word then is not a mere significant impression on the air, borne by the organs of speech; nor is the Spirit of His mouth a vapor, emitted by the organs of respiration; but the Word is He who "was with God in the beginning" and "was God,"[334] and the Spirit of the mouth of God is "the Spirit of truth which proceedeth from the Father."[335] You are therefore to perceive three, the Lord who gives the order, the Word who creates, and the Spirit who confirms.[336] And what other thing could confirmation be than the perfecting according to holiness? This perfecting expresses the confirmation's firmness, unchangeableness, and fixity in good. But there is no sanctification without the Spirit. The powers of the heavens are not holy by nature; were it so there would in this respect be no difference between them and the Holy Spirit. It is in proportion to their relative excellence that they have their meed of holiness from the Spirit. The branding-iron is conceived of together with the fire; and yet the material and the fire are distinct. Thus too in the case of the heavenly powers; their substance is, peradventure, an aerial spirit, or an immaterial fire, as it is written, "Who maketh his angels spirits and his ministers a flame of fire;"[337] wherefore they exist in space and become visible, and appear in their proper bodily form to

---

[333] Ps. 32:6 (LXX).

[334] John 1:1.

[335] John 15:26.

[336] τὸν στερεοῦντα τὸ πνεῦμα. It is to be noticed here that St. Basil uses the masculine and more personal form in apposition with the neuter πνεῦμα, and not the neuter as in the creed of Constantinople, τὸ κύριον καὶ τὸ Ζωοποιὸν τὸ ἐκ τοῦ πατρὸς ἐκπορευόμενον, etc. There is scriptural authority for the masculine in the "ὅταν δὲ ἔλθῃ ἐκεῖνος, τὸ πνεῦμα τῆς ἀληθείας" of John 16:13. Cf. p. 15–17.

[337] Ps. 103:4 (LXX).

them that are worthy. But their sanctification, being external to their substance, superinduces their perfection through the communion of the Spirit. They keep their rank by their abiding in the good and true, and while they retain their freedom of will, never fall away from their patient attendance on Him who is truly good. It results that, if by your argument you do away with the Spirit, the hosts of the angels are disbanded, the dominions of archangels are destroyed, all is thrown into confusion, and their life loses law, order, and distinctness. For how are angels to cry "Glory to God in the highest"[338] without being empowered by the Spirit? For "No man can say that Jesus is the Lord but by the Holy Ghost, and no man speaking by the Spirit of God calleth Jesus accursed;"[339] as might be said by wicked and hostile spirits, whose fall establishes our statement of the freedom of the will of the invisible powers; being, as they are, in a condition of equipoise between virtue and vice, and on this account needing the succor of the Spirit. I indeed maintain that even Gabriel[340] in no other way foretells events to come than by the foreknowledge of the Spirit, by reason of the fact that one of the boons distributed by the Spirit is prophecy. And whence did he who was ordained to announce the mysteries of the vision to the Man of Desires[341] derive the wisdom whereby he was enabled to teach hidden things, if not from the Holy Spirit? The revelation of mysteries is indeed the peculiar function of the Spirit, as it is written, "God hath revealed them unto us by His Spirit."[342] And how could "thrones, dominions, principalities and powers"[343] live their blessed life, did they not "behold the face of the Father which is in heaven"?[344] But to behold it is impossible without the Spirit! Just as at night, if you withdraw the light from the house, the eyes fall blind and their faculties become inactive, and the worth of objects cannot be discerned, and gold is trodden on in ignorance as though it were

---

[338] Luke 2:14.
[339] 1 Cor. 12:3.
[340] Luke 1:11.
[341] "Man greatly beloved." A.V. and R.V. Dan. 10:11.
[342] 1 Cor. 2:10.
[343] Col. 1:16.
[344] Matt. 18:10.

iron, so in the order of the intellectual world it is impossible for the high life of Law to abide without the Spirit. For it so to abide were as likely as that an army should maintain its discipline in the absence of its commander, or a chorus its harmony without the guidance of the Coryphæus. How could the Seraphim cry "Holy, Holy, Holy,"[345] were they not taught by the Spirit how often true religion requires them to lift their voice in this ascription of glory? Do "all His angels" and "all His hosts"[346] praise God? It is through the co-operation of the Spirit. Do "thousand thousand" of angels stand before Him, and "ten thousand times ten thousand" ministering spirits?[347] They are blamelessly doing their proper work by the power of the Spirit. All the glorious and unspeakable harmony[348] of the highest heavens both in the service of God, and in the mutual concord of the celestial powers, can therefore only be preserved by the direction of the Spirit. Thus with those beings who are not gradually perfected by increase and advance,[349] but are perfect from the moment of the creation, there is in creation the presence of the Holy Spirit, who confers on them the grace that flows from Him for the completion and perfection of their essence.[350]

But when we speak of the dispensations made for man by our great God and Savior Jesus Christ,[351] who will gainsay their having been accomplished through the grace of the Spirit? Whether you wish to examine ancient evidence—the blessings of the patriarchs, the succor given through the legislation, the types, the prophecies, the valorous feats in war, the signs wrought through just men—or on the other hand the things done in the dispensation of the coming of our Lord

---

[345] Is. 6:3.

[346] Ps. 148:2 (LXX).

[347] Dan. 7:10.

[348] Cf. Job 38:7, though for first clause the lxx. reads ὅτε ἐγενήθη ἄστρα. On the Pythagorean theory of the harmony of the spheres *vide* Arist. *De Cœl*. ii. 9, 1.

[349] προκοπή. Cf. προέκοπτε of the boy Jesus in Luke 2:52.

[350] ὑπόστασις, apparently again used in its earlier identification with οὐσία.

[351] Titus 2:13, R.V. The A.V. favours the view, opposed to that of the Greek Fathers, that "the great God" means the Father. Cf. Theodoret in this edition, pp. 319 and 321 and notes.

in the flesh—all is through the Spirit. In the first place He was made an unction, and being inseparably present was with the very flesh of the Lord, according to that which is written, "Upon whom thou shalt see the Spirit descending and remaining on Him, the same is"[352] "my beloved Son;"[353] and "Jesus of Nazareth" whom "God anointed with the Holy Ghost."[354] After this every operation was wrought with the co-operation of the Spirit. He was present when the Lord was being tempted by the devil; for, it is said, "Jesus was led up of the Spirit into the wilderness to be tempted."[355] He was inseparably with Him while working His wonderful works;[356] for, it is said, "If I by the Spirit of God cast out devils."[357] And He did not leave Him when He had risen from the dead; for when renewing man, and, by breathing on the face of the disciples,[358] restoring the grace, that came of the inbreathing of God, which man had lost, what did the Lord say? "Receive ye the Holy Ghost: whose soever sins ye remit, they are remitted unto them; and whose soever ye retain, they are retained."[359] And is it not plain and incontestable that the ordering of the Church is effected through the Spirit? For He gave, it is said, "in the church, first Apostles, secondarily prophets, thirdly teachers, after that miracles, then gifts of

---

[352] John 1:33.
[353] Matt. 3:17.
[354] Acts 10:38.
[355] Matt. 4:1.
[356] δυνάμεις, rendered "wonderful works" in Matt. 7:22; "mighty works" in Matt. 11:20, Mark 6:14, and Luke 10:13; and "miracles" in Acts 2:22, 19:11, and Gal. 3:5.
[357] Matt. 12:28.
[358] Gen. 2:7 (LXX) is ἐνεφύσησεν εἰς τὸ πρόσωπον αὐτοῦ. "εἰς τὸ πρόσωπον" is thence imported into John 20:22. Mr. C.F.H. Johnston notes, "This addition… is found in the Prayer at the Little Entrance in the Liturgy of St. Mark. Didymus, in his treatise on the Holy Spirit, which we have only in St. Jerome's Latin Version, twice used 'insufflans in faciem corum,' §§6, 33. The text is quoted in this form by Epiphanius Adv. Hær. lxxiv. 13, and by St. Aug. De Trin. iv. 20." To these instances may be added Athan. Ep. i. § 8, and the versions of Upper and Lower Egypt, the Thebaic, known as the Sahidic, and the Memphitic, or Coptic, both ascribed to the 3rd century.
[359] John 20:22, 23.

ON THE HOLY SPIRIT

healing, helps, governments, diversities of tongues,"[360] for this order is ordained in accordance with the division of the gifts that are of the Spirit.[361]

Moreover, by anyone who carefully uses his reason it will be found that even at the moment of the expected appearance of the Lord from heaven the Holy Spirit will not, as some suppose, have no functions to discharge: on the contrary, even in the day of His revelation, in which the blessed and only potentate[362] will judge the world in righteousness,[363] the Holy Spirit will be present with Him. For who is so ignorant of the good things prepared by God for them that are worthy, as not to know that the crown of the righteous is the grace of the Spirit, bestowed in more abundant and perfect measure in that day, when spiritual glory shall be distributed to each in proportion as he shall have nobly played the man? For among the glories of the saints are "many mansions" in the Father's house,[364] that is differences of dignities: for as "star differeth from star in glory, so also is the resurrection of the dead."[365] They, then, that were sealed by the Spirit unto the day of redemption,[366] and preserve pure and undiminished the first fruits which they received of the Spirit, are they that shall hear the words "well done thou good and faithful servant; thou hast been faithful over a few things, I will make thee ruler over many things."[367] In like manner they which have grieved the Holy Spirit by the wickedness of their ways, or have not wrought for Him that gave to them, shall be deprived of what they have received, their grace being transferred to others; or, according to one of the evangelists, they shall even be wholly cut asunder[368]—the cutting asunder meaning

---

[360] 1 Cor. 12:28.
[361] Cf. 1 Cor. 12:11.
[362] 1 Tim. 6:15.
[363] Acts 17:31.
[364] παρὰ τῷ πατρί, (=*chez le Père*,) with little or no change of meaning, for ἐν τῇ οἰκίᾳ τοῦ πατρός μου. John 14:2.
[365] 1 Cor. 15:41, 42.
[366] Cf. Eph. 4:30.
[367] Matt. 25:21.
[368] Matt. 24:51.

complete separation from the Spirit. The body is not divided, part being delivered to chastisement, and part let off; for when a whole has sinned it were like the old fables, and unworthy of a righteous judge, for only the half to suffer chastisement. Nor is the soul cut in two—that soul the whole of which possesses the sinful affection throughout, and works the wickedness in co-operation with the body. The cutting asunder, as I have observed, is the separation for aye of the soul from the Spirit. For now, although the Spirit does not suffer admixture with the unworthy, He nevertheless does seem in a manner to be present with them that have once been sealed, awaiting the salvation which follows on their conversion; but then He will be wholly cut off from the soul that has defiled His grace. For this reason "In Hell there is none that maketh confession; in death none that remembereth God,"[369] because the succor of the Spirit is no longer present. How then is it possible to conceive that the judgment is accomplished without the Holy Spirit, wherein the word points out that He is Himself the prize[370] of the righteous, when instead of the earnest[371] is given that which is perfect, and the first condemnation of sinners, when they are deprived of that which they seem to have? But the greatest proof of the conjunction of the Spirit with the Father and the Son is that He is said to have the same relation to God which the spirit in us has to each of us. "For what man" it is said, "knoweth the things of a man, save the spirit of man which is in him? even so the things of God knoweth no man but the Spirit of God."[372]

On this point I have said enough.

---

[369] Ps. 6:5 (LXX) ὅτι οὐκ ἔστιν ἐν τῷ θανάτῳ ὁ μνημονεύων σου, ἐν δὲ τῷ ᾅδῃ τίς ἐξομολογήσεταί σοι; Vulg. "*In inferno autem quis confitebitur tibi?*"

[370] Phil. 3:14.

[371] 2 Cor. 1:22, v. 5.

[372] 1 Cor. 2:11.

CHAPTER SEVENTEEN

Against those who say that the Holy Ghost is not to be numbered with, but numbered under, the Father and the Son. Wherein moreover there is a summary notice of the faith concerning right sub-numeration.

WHAT, HOWEVER, THEY call sub-numeration,[373] and in what sense they use this word, cannot even be imagined without difficulty. It is well known that it was imported into our language from the "wisdom of the world;"[374] but a point for our present consideration will be whether it has any immediate relation to the subject under discussion. Those who are adepts in vain investigations tell us that, while some nouns are common and of widely extended denotation, others are more specific, and that the force of some is more limited than that of others. Essence, for instance, is a common noun, predicable of all things both animate and inanimate; while animal is more specific, being predicated of fewer subjects than the former, though of more than those which are considered under it, as it embraces both rational and irrational nature. Again, human is more specific than animal, and man than human, and than man the individual Peter, Paul, or John.[375] Do they then mean by sub-nu-

---

[373] "The word was used as a quasi-philosophical term to express the doctrine quoted by St. Basil, in § 13: it does not occur in the confession of Eunomius, which was prepared after this book, A.D. 382; but it was used by him in his *Liber Apologeticus* (before A.D. 365) against which St. Basil wrote." Rev. C.F.H. Johnston. For "ὑπαρίθμησις" the only authorities given by the lexicons are "ecclesiastical." But the importation from the "wisdom of the world" implies use in heathen philosophy.

[374] Cf. 1 Cor. 1:20.

[375] "This portion of the theory of general language is the subject of what is termed the doctrine of the Predicables; a set of distinctions handed down from Aristotle, and his follower Porphyry, many of which have taken a firm root in scientific, and some of them even in popular, phraseology. The predicables are a five-fold division of General Names, not grounded as usual on a difference in their meaning, that is, in the attribute which they connote, but on a difference in the kind of class which they denote. We may predicate of a thing five differ-

meration the division of the common into its subordinate parts? But I should hesitate to believe they have reached such a pitch of infatuation as to assert that the God of the universe, like some common quality conceivable only by reason and without actual existence in any hypostasis, is divided into subordinate divisions, and that then this subdivision is called sub-numeration. This would hardly be said even by men melancholy mad, for, besides its impiety, they are establishing the very opposite argument to their own contention. For the subdivisions are of the same essence as that from which they have been divided. The very obviousness of the absurdity makes it difficult for us to find arguments to confute their unreasonableness; so that really their folly looks like an advantage to them; just as soft and yielding bodies offer no resistance, and therefore cannot be struck a stout blow. It is impossible to bring a vigorous confutation to bear on a palpable absurdity. The only course open to us is to pass by their abominable impiety in silence. Yet our love for the brethren and the importunity of our opponents makes silence impossible.

What is it that they maintain? Look at the terms of their imposture. "We assert that connumeration is appropriate to subjects of equal dignity, and sub-numeration to those which vary in the direction of inferiority." "Why," I rejoined, "do you say this? I fail to understand your extraordinary wisdom. Do you mean that gold is numbered with gold, and that lead is unworthy of the connumeration, but, because of the cheapness of the material, is subnumerated to gold? And do you attribute so much importance to number as that it can either exalt the value of what is cheap, or destroy the dignity of what is valuable?

---

ent varieties of class-name:
  A *genus* of the thing (γένος).
  A *species* (εἶδος).
  A *differentia* (διαφορα).
  A *proprium* (ἰδιόν).
  An *accidens* (συμβεβηκός).
It is to be remarked of these distinctions, that they express, not what the predicate is in its own meaning, but what relation it bears to the subject of which it happens on the particular occasion to be predicated." *J. S. Mill, System of Logic,* i. 133.

Therefore, again, you will number gold under precious stones, and such precious stones as are smaller and without luster under those which are larger and brighter in color. But what will not be said by men who spend their time in nothing else but either 'to tell or to hear some new thing'?[376] Let these supporters of impiety be classed for the future with Stoics and Epicureans. What sub-numeration is even possible of things less valuable in relation to things very valuable? How is a brass obol to be numbered under a golden stater? "Because," they reply, "we do not speak of possessing two coins, but one and one." But which of these is subnumerated to the other? Each is similarly mentioned. If then you number each by itself, you cause an equality of value by numbering them in the same way but, if you join them, you make their value one by numbering them one with the other. But if the sub-numeration belongs to the one which is numbered second, then it is in the power of the counter to begin by counting the brass coin. Let us, however, pass over the confutation of their ignorance, and turn our argument to the main topic.

Do you maintain that the Son is numbered under the Father, and the Spirit under the Son, or do you confine your sub-numeration to the Spirit alone? If, on the other hand, you apply this sub-numeration also to the Son, you revive what is the same impious doctrine, the unlikeness of the substance, the lowliness of rank, the coming into being in later time, and once for all, by this one term, you will plainly again set circling all the blasphemies against the Only-begotten. To controvert these blasphemies would be a longer task than my present purpose admits of; and I am the less bound to undertake it because the impiety has been refuted elsewhere to the best of my ability.[377] If on the other hand they suppose the sub-numeration to benefit the Spirit alone, they must be taught that the Spirit is spoken of together with the Lord in precisely the same manner in which the Son is spoken of with the Father. "The name of the Father and of the Son and of the Holy Ghost"[378] is delivered in like manner, and,

---

[376] Acts 17:21.
[377] *i.e.* in the second book of his work against Eunomius.
[378] Matt. 28:19.

according to the co-ordination of words delivered in baptism, the relation of the Spirit to the Son is the same as that of the Son to the Father. And if the Spirit is co-ordinate with the Son, and the Son with the Father, it is obvious that the Spirit is also co-ordinate with the Father. When then the names are ranked in one and the same co-ordinate series,[379] what room is there for speaking on the one hand of connumeration, and on the other of sub-numeration? Nay, without exception, what thing ever lost its own nature by being numbered? Is it not the fact that things when numbered remain what they naturally and originally were, while number is adopted among us as a sign indicative of the plurality of subjects? For some bodies we count, some we measure, and some we weigh;[380] those which are by nature continuous we apprehend by measure; to those which are divided we apply number (with the exception of those which on account of their fineness are measured); while heavy objects are distinguished by the inclination of the balance. It does not however follow that, because we have invented for our convenience symbols to help us to arrive at the knowledge of quantity, we have therefore changed the nature of the things signified. We do not speak of "weighing under" one another things which are weighed, even though one be gold and the other tin; nor yet do we "measure under" things that are measured; and so in the same way we will not "number under" things which are numbered. And if none of the rest of things admits of sub-numeration how can they allege that the Spirit ought to be subnumerated? Laboring as they do under heathen unsoundness, they imagine that things which are inferior, either by grade of rank or subjection of substance, ought to be subnumerated.

---

[379] ουστοιχία, a series of similar things, as in Arist. *An. Pr.* ii. 21, 2. In the Pythagorean philosophy, a co-ordinate or parallel series. Arist. *Met.* i. 5, 6, and *Eth. Nic.* i. 6, 7.

[380] Cf. Wis. xi. 20. "Thou hast ordered all things in measure and number and weight."

CHAPTER EIGHTEEN

In what manner in the confession of the three hypostases we preserve the pious dogma of the Monarchia. Wherein also is the refutation of them that allege that the Spirit is subnumerated.[381]

IN DELIVERING THE FORMULA of the Father, the Son, and the Holy Ghost,[382] our Lord did not connect the gift with number. He did not say "into First, Second, and Third,"[383] nor yet "into one,

---

[381] The term Μοναρχία first acquired importance in patristic literature in Justin's work *De monarchia*, against Polytheism. Of the lost letter of Irenæus to the Roman Presbyter Florinus, who was deposed for heresy, presumably gnostic, the title, according to Eusebius (*H.E.* v. 20), was περὶ Μοναρχίας, ἢ περὶ τοῦ μὴ εἶναι τὸν θεὸν ποιητὴν κακῶν. Later it came to be used to express not the Divine unity as opposed to Polytheism or Oriental Dualism, but the Divine unity as opposed to Tritheism. *Vide* the words of Dionysius of Rome, as quoted by Athan. *De Decretis*, § 26, "Next let me turn to those who cut in pieces, divide, and destroy that most sacred doctrine of the church of God, the divine Monarchy, making it, as it were, three powers and divided subsistences and three godheads." So St. Basil *Cont. Eunom.* ii. Ἀρχὴ μὲν οὖν πατρὸς οὐδεμία, ἀρχὴ δὲ τοῦ υἱοῦ ὁ πατήρ. And in *Ep.* xxxviii. Ἀλλά τίς ἐστι δύναμις ἀγεννήτως καὶ ἀνάρχως ὑφεστῶσα ἥτις ἐςτὶν αἰτία τῆς ἀπάντων τῶν ὄντων αἰτίας, ἐκ γὰρ τοῦ πατρὸς ὁ υἱὸς δι' οὗ τὰ πάντα. And in *Ep.* cxxv. Ενα γὰρ οἴδαμεν ἀγέννητον καὶ μίαν τῶν πάντων ἀρχήν, τὸν πατέρα τοῦ κυρίου ἡμῶν Ἰησοῦ Χριστοῦ. On the doctrine and its exponents compare § 72 of the *De Sp. S.*
On the other hand "Monarchians" was a name connoting heresy when applied to those who pushed the doctrine of the Unity to an extreme, involving denial of a Trinity. Of these, among the more noteworthy were Paul of Samosata, bp. of Antioch, who was deposed in 269, a representative of thinkers who have been called dynamical monarchians, and Praxeas (supposed by some to be a nickname), who taught at Rome in the reign of Marcus Aurelius, and of whom Tertullian, the originator of the term patripassians, as applied to Monarchians, wrote "*Paracletum fugavit et patrem crucifixit.*" This heretical Monarchianism culminated in Sabellius, the "most original, ingenious, and profound of the Monarchians." Schaff. *Hist. Chr. Church*, i. 293. Cf. Gisseler, i. p. 127, Harnack's *Monarchianismus* in Herzog's *Real Encyclopædie*, Vol. x. Thomasius *Dog. Gesch.* i. p. 179, and Fialon *Et. Hist.* p. 241

[382] Matt. 28:19.

[383] Mr. C.F.H. Johnston quotes as instances of the application of the word "third" to the Holy Ghost; Justin Martyr (*Apol.* i. 13) "We honor the Spirit of prophecy in the third rank." Tertullian (*In Prax.* 8) "As the fruit from the tree

two, and three, but He gave us the boon of the knowledge of the faith which leads to salvation, by means of holy names. So that what saves us is our faith. Number has been devised as a symbol indicative of the quantity of objects. But these men, who bring ruin on themselves from every possible source, have turned even the capacity for counting against the faith. Nothing else undergoes any change in consequence of the addition of number, and yet these men in the case of the divine nature pay reverence to number, lest they should exceed the limits of the honor due to the Paraclete. But, O wisest sirs, let the unapproachable be altogether above and beyond number, as the ancient reverence of the Hebrews wrote the unutterable name of God in peculiar characters, thus endeavoring to set forth its infinite excellence. Count, if you must; but you must not by counting do damage to the faith. Either let the ineffable be honored by silence; or let holy things be counted consistently with true religion. There is one God and Father, one Only-begotten, and one Holy Ghost. We proclaim each of the hypostases singly; and, when count we must, we do not let an ignorant arithmetic carry us away to the idea of a plurality of Gods.

For we do not count by way of addition, gradually making increase from unity to multitude, and saying one, two, and three—nor yet first, second, and third. For "I," God, "am the first, and I am the last."[384] And hitherto we have never, even at the present time, heard of a second God. Worshipping as we do God of God, we both confess the distinction of the Persons, and at the same time abide by the Monarchy. We do not fritter away the theology[385] in a divided plurality, be-

---

is third from the root, and the rivulet from the river third from the source, and the flame from the ray third from the sun." Eunomius (*Lib. Apol.* § 25) "observing the teaching of Saints, we have learned from them that the Holy Spirit is third in dignity and order, and so have believed him to be third in nature also." On the last St. Basil (*Adv. Eunom.* ii.) rejoins "Perhaps the word of piety allows Him to come in rank second to the Son...although He is inferior to the Son in rank and dignity (that we may make the utmost possible concession) it does not reasonably follow thence that he is of a different nature." On the word "perhaps" a dispute arose at the Council of Florence, the Latins denying its genuineness.

[384] Is. 44:6.

[385] According to patristic usage θεολογία proper is concerned with all that

cause one Form, so to say, united[386] in the invariableness of the Godhead, is beheld in God the Father, and in God the Only begotten. For the Son is in the Father and the Father in the Son; since such as is the latter, such is the former, and such as is the former, such is the latter; and herein is the Unity. So that according to the distinction of Persons, both are one and one, and according to the community of Nature, one. How, then, if one and one, are there not two Gods? Because we speak of a king, and of the king's image, and not of two kings. The majesty is not cloven in two, nor the glory divided. The sovereignty and authority over us is one, and so the doxology ascribed by us is not plural but one;[387] because the honor paid to the image passes on to the prototype. Now what in the one case the image is by reason of imitation, that in the other case the Son is by nature; and as in works of art the likeness is dependent on the form, so in the case of the divine and uncompounded nature the union consists in the communion of the Godhead.[388] One, moreover, is the Holy Spirit, and we speak of Him singly, conjoined as He is to the one Father through the one Son, and through Himself completing the adorable and blessed Trinity. Of Him the intimate relationship to the Father and the Son is sufficiently declared by the fact of His not being ranked in the plurality of the creation, but being spoken of singly; for he is not one of many, but One. For as there is one Father and one Son, so is there one Holy Ghost. He is consequently as far removed from created Nature as reason requires the singular to be removed from compound and plural bodies; and He is in such wise united to the Father and to the Son as unit has affinity with unit.

And it is not from this source alone that our proofs of the natural

---

relates to the Divine and Eternal nature of our Lord. Cf. Bp. Lightfoot. *Ap Fathers*, Part II. vol. ii. p. 75.

[386] ἐνιζομένην. Var. lectiones are ἐνιζομένην, "seated in," and ἐνεικονιζομένην, "imaged in."

[387] Cf. the embolismus, or intercalated prayer in the *Liturgy of St. James*, as cited by Mr. C.F.H. Johnston. "For of thee is the kingdom and the power and the glory, of Father, of Son, and of Holy Ghost, now and ever."

[388] On the right use of the illustration of εἰκών, cf. Basil *Ep.* xxxviii., and Bp. Lightfoot's note on Col. 1:15. Cf. also John 1:18 and 14:9, 10.

communion are derived, but from the fact that He is moreover said to be "of God;"[389] not indeed in the sense in which "all things are of God,"[390] but in the sense of proceeding out of God, not by generation, like the Son, but as Breath of His mouth. But in no way is the "mouth" a member, nor the Spirit breath that is dissolved; but the word "mouth" is used so far as it can be appropriate to God, and the Spirit is a Substance having life, gifted with supreme power of sanctification. Thus, the close relation is made plain, while the mode of the ineffable existence is safeguarded. He is moreover styled 'Spirit of Christ,' as being by nature closely related to Him. Wherefore "If any man have not the Spirit of Christ, he is none of His."[391] Hence He alone worthily glorifies the Lord, for, it is said, "He shall glorify me,"[392] not as the creature, but as "Spirit of truth,"[393] clearly showing forth the truth in Himself, and, as Spirit of wisdom, in His own greatness revealing "Christ the Power of God and the wisdom of God."[394] And as Paraclete[395] He expresses in Himself the goodness of the Paraclete who

---

[389] 2 Cor. 1:12.

[390] 1 Cor. 11:12. George of Laodicea applied this passage to the Son, and wrote to the Arians: "Why complain of Pope Alexander (*i.e.* of Alexandria) for saying that the Son is from the Father....For if the apostle wrote All things are from God...He may be said to be from God in that sense in which all things are from God." Athan., *De Syn.* 17.

[391] Rom. 8:9.

[392] John 16:14.

[393] John 14:17.

[394] 1 Cor. 1:24.

[395] παράκλητος occurs five times in the N.T., and is rendered in A.V. in John 14:16 and 26, 15:26 and 16:7, *Comforter;* in 1 John 2:1 *Advocate*, as applied to the Son. In the text the Son, the Paraclete, is described as sending the Spirit, the Paraclete; in the second clause of the sentence it can hardly be positively determined whether the words τοῦ ὅθεν προῆλθεν refer to the Father or to the Son. The former view is adopted by Mr. C.F.H. Johnson, the latter by the editor of Keble's *Studia Sacra*, p. 176. The sequence of the sentence in John 15:26 might lead one to regard ὅθεν προῆλθεν as equivalent to παρὰ τοῦ Πατρὸς ἐκπορεύεται. On the other hand. St. Basil's avoidance of direct citation of the verb ἐκπορεύεται, his close connexion of τοῦ ἀποστείλαντος with ὅθεν προῆλθεν, and the close of the verse in St. John's gospel ἐκεῖνος μαρτυρήσει περὶ ἐμοῦ, suggest that the μεγαλωσύνη in St. Basil's mind may be the μεγαλωσύνη of the Son. At the same time, while the Western Church was in the main unanimous as to the

sent Him, and in His own dignity manifests the majesty of Him from whom He proceeded. There is then on the one hand a natural glory, as light is the glory of the sun; and on the other a glory bestowed judicially and of free will '*ab extra*' on them that are worthy. The latter is twofold. "A son," it is said, "honoreth his father, and a servant his master."[396] Of these two the one, the servile, is given by the creature; the other, which may be called the intimate, is fulfilled by the Spirit. For, as our Lord said of Himself, "I have glorified Thee on the earth: I have finished the work which thou gavest me to do;"[397] so of the Paraclete He says "He shall glorify me: for He shall receive of mine, and shall show it unto you."[398] And as the Son is glorified of the Father when He says "I have both glorified *it* and will glorify *it*[399] again,"[400] so is the Spirit glorified through His communion with both Father and Son, and through the testimony of the Only-begotten when He says "All manner of sin and blasphemy shall be forgiven unto men: but the blasphemy against the Holy Ghost shall not be forgiven unto men."

And when, by means of the power that enlightens us, we fix our eyes on the beauty of the image of the invisible God, and through the image are led up to the supreme beauty of the spectacle of the arche-

---

double procession, this passage from St. Basil is not quoted as an exception to the general current of the teaching of the Greek Fathers, who, as Bp. Pearson expresses it, "stuck more closely to the phrase and language of the Scriptures, saying that the spirit proceedeth from the Father." (Pearson *On the Creed*, Art. viii. where *vide* quotations) *Vide* also Thomasius, *Christ. Dogm.*, i. 270, *Namentlich auf letzere Bestimmung legten die griechischen Väter groszes Gewicht. Im Gegensatz gegen den macedonischen Irrtum, der den Geist für ein Geschüpf des Sohnes ansah, führte man die Subsistenz desselben ebenso auf den Vater zuruck wie die des Sohnes. Man lehrte, also, der heilige Geist geht vom Vater aus, der Vater ist die ἀρχή wie des Sohnes so auch des Geistes; aber mit der dem herkömmlichen Zuge des Dogma entsprechenden Näherbestimmung: nicht ἀμέσως, sondern ἐμμέσως, interventu filii geht der Geist vom Vater aus, also "durch den Sohn vom Vater." So die bedeutendsten Kirchenlehrer, während andere einfach bei der Formel stehen blieben; er gehe vom Vater aus.*

[396] Mal. 1:6.
[397] John 17:4.
[398] John 16:14.
[399] Four MSS. of the De S.S. read ἐδόξασά σε, a variation not appearing in MSS. of the Gospel.
[400] John 12:28.

type, then, I ween, is with us inseparably the Spirit of knowledge, in Himself bestowing on them that love the vision of the truth the power of beholding the Image, not making the exhibition from without, but in Himself leading on to the full knowledge. "No man knoweth the Father save the Son."[401] And so "no man can say that Jesus is the Lord but by the Holy Ghost."[402] For it is not said through the Spirit, but by the Spirit, and "God is a spirit, and they that worship Him must worship Him in spirit and in truth,"[403] as it is written "in thy light shall we see light,"[404] namely by the illumination of the Spirit, "the true light which lighteth every man that cometh into the world."[405] It results that in Himself He shows the glory of the Only begotten, and on true worshippers He in Himself bestows the knowledge of God. Thus, the way of the knowledge of God lies from One Spirit through the One Son to the One Father, and conversely the natural Goodness and the inherent Holiness and the royal Dignity extend from the Father through the Only-begotten to the Spirit. Thus, there is both acknowledgment of the hypostases and the true dogma of the Monarchy is not lost.[406] They on the other hand who support their sub-numeration by talking of first and second and third ought to be informed that into the undefiled theology of Christians they are importing the polytheism of heathen error. No other result can be achieved by the

---

[401] Matt. 11:27, "οὐδεὶς οἶδε τὸν πατέρα εἰ μὴ ὁ Υἱός" substituted for "οὐ δὲ τὸν πατέρα τὶς ἐπιγνώσκει εἰ μὴ ὁ Υἱός."

[402] 1 Cor. 12:3.

[403] John 4:24.

[404] Ps. 35:9 (LXX).

[405] John 1:9.

[406] Cf. note at beginning of the chapter, and the distinction between δόγμα and κήουγμα in § 66. "The great objection which the Eastern Church makes to the *Filioque* is, that it implies the existence of two ἀρχαὶ in the godhead; and if we believe in δύο ἄναρχοι; we, in effect, believe in two Gods. The unity of the Godhead can only be maintained by acknowledging the Father to be the sole Ἀρχὴ or πηγὴ θεοτήτος, who from all eternity has communicated His own Godhead to His co-eternal and consubstantial Son and Spirit. This reasoning is generally true. But, as the doctrine of the Procession of the Spirit from the Father and the Son presupposes the eternal generation of the Son from the Father; it does not follow, that that doctrine impugns the Catholic belief in the Μία Ἀρχή." Bp. Harold Browne, *Exp. xxxix Art.*, Note on Art v.

fell device of sub-numeration than the confession of a first, a second, and a third God. For us is sufficient the order prescribed by the Lord. He who confuses this order will be no less guilty of transgressing the law than are the impious heathen.

Enough has been now said to prove, in contravention of their error, that the communion of Nature is in no wise dissolved by the manner of sub-numeration. Let us, however, make a concession to our contentious and feeble-minded adversary, and grant that what is second to anything is spoken of in sub-numeration to it. Now let us see what follows. "The first man" it is said "is of the earth earthy, the second man is the Lord from heaven."[407] Again "that was not first which is spiritual but that which is natural and afterward that which is spiritual."[408] If then the second is subnumerated to the first, and the subnumerated is inferior in dignity to that to which it was subnumerated, according to you the spiritual is inferior in honor to the natural, and the heavenly man to the earthy.

CHAPTER NINETEEN

Against those who assert that the Spirit ought not to be glorified.

"BE IT SO," IT is rejoined, "but glory is by no means so absolutely due to the Spirit as to require His exaltation by us in doxologies." Whence then could we get demonstrations of the dignity of the Spirit, "passing all understanding,"[409] if His communion with the Father and the Son were not reckoned by our opponents as good for testimony of His rank? It is, at all events, possible for us to arrive to a certain extent at intelligent apprehension of the sublimity of His nature and of His unapproachable power, by looking at the meaning of His title, and at the magnitude of His operations, and by His good gifts bestowed on us or rather on all cre-

---
[407] 1 Cor. 15:47.
[408] 1 Cor. 15:46.
[409] Phil. 4:7.

ation. He is called Spirit, as "God is a Spirit,"[410] and "the breath of our nostrils, the anointed of the Lord."[411] He is called holy,[412] as the Father is holy, and the Son is holy, for to the creature holiness was brought in from without, but to the Spirit holiness is the fulfilment of nature, and it is for this reason that He is described not as being sanctified, but as sanctifying. He is called good,[413] as the Father is good, and He who was begotten of the Good is good, and to the Spirit His goodness is essence. He is called upright,[414] as "the Lord is upright,"[415] in that He is Himself truth,[416] and is Himself Righteousness,[417] having no divergence nor leaning to one side or to the other, on account of the immutability of His substance. He is called Paraclete, like the Only begotten, as He Himself says, "I will ask the Father, and He will give you another comforter."[418] Thus names are borne by the Spirit in common with the Father and the Son, and He gets these titles from His natural and close relationship. From what other source could they be derived? Again He is called royal,[419] Spirit of truth,[420] and Spirit of wisdom.[421] "The Spirit of God," it is said "hath made me,"[422] and God filled Bezaleel with "the divine Spirit of wisdom and understanding and knowledge."[423] Such names as these are super-eminent and mighty, but they do not transcend His glory.

And His operations, what are they? For majesty ineffable, and for numbers innumerable. How shall we form a conception of what ex-

---

[410] John 4:24.
[411] Lam. 4:20. Sic in A.V. and R.V., the reference being to Zedekiah. Cf. Jer. 39:5. The Vulgate reads, "*Spiritus oris nostri Christus Dominus*," from the Greek of the LXX quoted by St. Basil, "Πνεῦμα προσώπου ἡμῶν χριστὸς κύριος."
[412] 1 John 1:20.
[413] Ps. 142:10 (LXX).
[414] Ps. 50:10 (LXX).
[415] Ps. 91:15 (LXX).
[416] John 14:17; 15:26; 16:13; 1 John 5:6.
[417] 2 Cor. 3:8, 9.
[418] John 14:16, παράκλητον. Cf. Note on p. 29.
[419] Ps. 50:12 (LXX) πνεῦμα ἡγεμονικόν. Vulg. *spiritus principalis*.
[420] John 15:26, etc.
[421] Is. 11:2.
[422] Job 33:4.
[423] Ex. 31:3 (LXX).

tends beyond the ages? What were His operations before that creation whereof we can conceive? How great the grace which He conferred on creation? What the power exercised by Him over the ages to come? He existed; He pre-existed; He co-existed with the Father and the Son before the ages. It follows that, even if you can conceive of anything beyond the ages, you will find the Spirit yet further above and beyond. And if you think of the creation, the powers of the heavens were established by the Spirit,[424] the establishment being understood to refer to disability to fall away from good. For it is from the Spirit that the powers derive their close relationship to God, their inability to change to evil, and their continuance in blessedness. Is it Christ's advent? The Spirit is forerunner. Is there the incarnate presence? The Spirit is inseparable. Working of miracles, and gifts of healing are through the Holy Spirit. Demons were driven out by the Spirit of God. The devil was brought to naught by the presence of the Spirit. Remission of sins was by the gift of the Spirit, for "ye were washed, ye were sanctified...in the name of the Lord Jesus Christ, and in the holy Spirit of our God."[425] There is close relationship with God through the Spirit, for "God hath sent forth the Spirit of His Son into your hearts, crying Abba, Father."[426] The resurrection from the dead is effected by the operation of the Spirit, for "Thou sendest forth thy spirit, they are created; and Thou renewest the face of the earth."[427] If here creation may be taken to mean the bringing of the departed to life again, how mighty is not the operation of the Spirit, Who is to us the dispenser of the life that follows on the resurrection, and attunes our souls to the spiritual life beyond? Or if here by creation is meant the change to a better condition of those who in this life have fallen into sin, (for it is so understood according to the usage of Scripture, as in the words of Paul "if any man be in Christ he is a new creature"),[428] the renewal which takes place in this life, and the transmutation from our earthly

---

[424] Cf. Ps. 32:6 (LXX).
[425] 1 Cor. 6:11, R.V.
[426] Gal. 4:6.
[427] Ps. 103:30 (LXX).
[428] 2 Cor. 5:17.

and sensuous life to the heavenly conversation which takes place in us through the Spirit, then our souls are exalted to the highest pitch of admiration. With these thoughts before us are we to be afraid of going beyond due bounds in the extravagance of the honor we pay? Shall we not rather fear lest, even though we seem to give Him the highest names which the thoughts of man can conceive or man's tongue utter, we let our thoughts about Him fall too low?

It is the Spirit which says, as the Lord says, "Get thee down, and go with them, doubting nothing: for I have sent them."[429] Are these the words of an inferior, or of one in dread? "Separate me Barnabas and Saul for the work whereunto I have called them."[430] Does a slave speak thus? And Isaiah, "The Lord God and His Spirit hath sent me,"[431] and "the Spirit came down from the Lord and guided them."[432] And pray do not again understand by this guidance some humble service, for the Word witnesses that it was the work of God—"Thou leddest thy people," it is said "like a flock,"[433] and "Thou that leadest Joseph like a

---

[429] Acts 10:20.

[430] Acts 13:2.

[431] Isa. 48:16. Mr. C. F. Johnston remarks: "In Isaiah 48:16 St. Didymus, as translated by St. Jerome, gives *Spiritum suum*. The Targum has the same. St. Ambrose writes: '*Quis est qui dicit; misit me Dominus Deus et Spiritus Ejus; nisi Qui venit a Patre, ut salvos faceret peccatores? Quem ut audis, et Spiritus misit; ne cum legis quia Filius Spiritum mittit, inferioris esse Spiritum crederes potestatis*,' (*De Sp. S.* iii. 1, § 7.) The passage is quoted by St. Athanasius, St. Basil, St. Cyril Hieros., and, as far as the editor is aware, without any comment which would help to determine their way of understanding the case of τὸ πνεῦμα; but Origen, on the words 'Whosoever shall humble himself as this little child' (*Comm. in Evang.*, Matt. 13:18) says—quoting the original, which may be rendered, "'humbling himself as this little child is imitating the Holy Spirit, who humbled Himself for men's salvation. That the Savior and the Holy Ghost were sent by the Father for the salvation of men is made plain by Isaiah saying, in the person of the Savior, 'the Lord sent me, and His Spirit.' It must be observed, however, that the phrase is ambiguous, for either God sent and the Holy Ghost also sent, the Savior; or, as I understand, the Father sent both, the Savior and the Holy Ghost.'" The Vulgate and Beza both render "*Spiritus*." The order of the Hebrew is in favour of the nominative, as in the Vulgate and LXX cf. Note A on Chap. 48 of Isaiah in the *Speaker's Commentary*.

[432] Is. 62:14 (LXX).

[433] Ps. 76:20 (LXX).

flock,"[434] and "He led them on safely, so that they feared not."[435] Thus when you hear that when the Comforter is come, He will put you in remembrance, and "guide you into all truth,"[436] do not misrepresent the meaning.

But, it is said that "He maketh intercession for us."[437] It follows then that, as the suppliant is inferior to the benefactor, so far is the Spirit inferior in dignity to God. But have you never heard concerning the Only-begotten that He "is at the right hand of God, who also maketh intercession for us"?[438] Do not, then, because the Spirit is in you—if indeed He is at all in you—nor yet because He teaches us who were blinded, and guides us to the choice of what profits us—do not for this reason allow yourself to be deprived of the right and holy opinion concerning Him. For to make the loving kindness of your benefactor a ground of ingratitude were indeed a very extravagance of unfairness. "Grieve not the Holy Spirit;"[439] hear the words of Stephen, the first fruits of the martyrs, when he reproaches the people for their rebellion and disobedience; "you do always," he says, "resist the Holy Ghost;"[440] and again Isaiah—"They vexed His Holy Spirit, therefore He was turned to be their enemy;"[441] and in another passage, "the house of Jacob angered the Spirit of the Lord."[442] Are not these passages indicative of authoritative power? I leave it to the judgment of my readers to determine what opinions we ought to hold when we hear these passages; whether we are to regard the Spirit as an instrument, a subject, of equal rank with the creature, and a fellow servant of ourselves, or whether, on the contrary, to the ears of the pious the mere whisper of this blasphemy is not most grievous. Do you call the Spirit a servant? But, it is said, "the servant knoweth not what his

---
[434] Ps. 79:1 (LXX).
[435] Ps. 77:53 (LXX).
[436] John 16:13. Cf. 14:26.
[437] Rom. 8:26, 27.
[438] Rom. 8:34.
[439] Eph. 4:30.
[440] Acts 7:51.
[441] Is. 63:10.
[442] Ps. 105:32 (LXX); Micah 2:7.

Lord doeth,"[443] and yet the Spirit knoweth the things of God, as "the spirit of man that is in him."[444]

CHAPTER TWENTY

Against those who maintain that the Spirit is in the rank neither of a servant nor of a master, but in that of the free.

HE IS NOT A slave, it is said; not a master, but free. Oh, the terrible insensibility, the pitiable audacity, of them that maintain this! Shall I rather lament in them their ignorance or their blasphemy? They try to insult the doctrines that concern the divine nature[445] by comparing them with the human, and endeavor to apply to the ineffable nature of God that common custom of human life whereby the difference of degrees is variable, not perceiving that among men no one is a slave by nature. For men are either brought under a yoke of slavery by conquest, as when prisoners are taken in war; or they are enslaved on account of poverty, as the Egyptians were oppressed by Pharaoh; or, by a wise and mysterious dispensation, the worst children are by their fathers' order condemned to serve the wiser and the better;[446] and this any righteous enquirer into the circumstances would declare to be not a sentence of condemnation but a benefit. For it is more profitable that the man who, through lack of intelligence, has no natural principle of rule within himself, should become the chattel of another, to the end that, being guided by the reason of his master, he may be like a chariot with a charioteer, or a boat with a steersman seated at the tiller. For this reason Jacob by his father's blessing became lord of Esau,[447] in order that the foolish son, who had not intelligence, his proper guardian, might, even though he wished it not, be benefited by his prudent brother. So Canaan shall

---

[443] John 15:15.
[444] 1 Cor. 2:11.
[445] τὰ τῆς θεολογίας δόγματα. Cf. note on § 66.
[446] Cf. Gen. 9:25.
[447] Gen. 27:29.

be "a servant unto his brethren"[448] because, since his father Ham was unwise, he was uninstructed in virtue. In this world, then, it is thus that men are made slaves, but they who have escaped poverty or war, or do not require the tutelage of others, are free. It follows that even though one man be called master and another servant, nevertheless, both in view of our mutual equality of rank and as chattels of our Creator, we are all fellow slaves. But in that other world what can you bring out of bondage? For no sooner were they created than bondage was commenced. The heavenly bodies exercise no rule over one another, for they are unmoved by ambition, but all bow down to God, and render to Him alike the awe which is due to Him as Master and the glory which falls to Him as Creator. For "a son honoreth his father and a servant his master,"[449] and from all God asks one of these two things; for "if I then be a Father where is my honor? and if I be a Master where is my fear?"[450] Otherwise the life of all men, if it were not under the oversight of a master, would be most pitiable; as is the condition of the apostate powers who, because they stiffen their neck against God Almighty, fling off the reins of their bondage—not that their natural constitution is different; but the cause is in their disobedient disposition to their Creator. Whom then do you call free? Him who has no King? Him who has neither power to rule another nor willingness to be ruled? Among all existent beings no such nature is to be found. To entertain such a conception of the Spirit is obvious blasphemy. If He is a creature of course He serves with all the rest, for "all things," it is said "are thy servants,"[451] but if He is above Creation, then He shares in royalty.[452]

---

[448] Gen. 9:25.
[449] Mal. 1:6.
[450] Ibid.
[451] Ps. 118:91 (LXX).
[452] St. Basil's view of slavery is that (a) as regards our relation to God, all created beings are naturally in a condition of subservience to the Creator; (b) as regards our relationship to one another, slavery is not of nature, but of convention and circumstance. How far he is here at variance with the well known account of slavery given by Aristotle in the first book of the *Politics* will depend upon the interpretation we put upon the word "nature." "Is there," asks Aristo-

tle, "any one intended by nature to be a slave, and for whom such a condition is expedient and right, or rather is not all slavery a violation of nature? There is no difficulty in answering this question, on grounds both of reason and fact. For that some should rule, and others be ruled, is a thing not only necessary, but expedient; from the hour of their birth some are marked out for subjection, others for rule....Where, then, there is such a difference as that between soul and body, or between men and animals (as in the case of those whose business it is to use their body, and who can do nothing better), the lower sort are by nature slaves, and it is better for them, as for all inferiors, that they should be under the rule of a master....It is clear, then, that some men are by nature free and others slaves, and that for these latter slavery is both expedient and right." *Politics*, Bk. 1, Sec. 5. Here by *Nature* seems to be meant something like Basil's "lack of intelligence," and of the τὸ κατὰ φύσιν ἄρχον, which makes it "profitable" for one man to be the chattel of another (κτῆμα is livestock, especially *mancipium*. Cf. Shakespeare's K. and Pet., "She is my goods, my chattels." "Chattel" is a doublet of "cattle"). St. Basil and Aristotle are at one as to the advantage to the weak slave of his having a powerful protector; and this, no doubt, is the point of view from which slavery can be best apologized for.

Christianity did indeed do much to better the condition of the slave by asserting his spiritual freedom, but at first it did little more than emphasize the latter philosophy of heathendom, εἰ σῶμα δοῦλον, ἀλλ' ὁ νοῦς ἐλεύθερος (Soph., *frag. incert.* xxii.), and gave the highest meaning to such thoughts as those expressed in the late *Epigram* of Damascius (c. 530) on a dead slave:

Ζωσίμη ἡ πρὶν ἐοῦσα μόνῳ τῷ σώματι δούλη,
Καὶ τῷ σώματι νῦν εὗρεν ἐλευθερίην.

It is thought less of a slave's servitude to fellow man than of the slavery of bond and free alike to evil. Cf. Aug., *De Civit. Dei.* iv. cap. iii. "*Bonus etiamsi serviat liber est: malus autem si regnat servus est: nec est unius hominis, sed quod gravius est tot dominorum quot vitiorum.*" Chrysostom even explains St. Paul's non-condemnation of slavery on the ground that its existence, with that of Christian liberty, was a greater moral triumph than its abolition. (*In Genes. Serm.* v. 1.) Even so late as the sixth century the legislation of Justinian, though protective, supposed no natural liberty. "*Expedit enim respublicæ ne quis re suâ utatur male.*" *Instit.* i. viii. quoted by Milman, *Lat. Christ.* ii. 14. We must not therefore be surprised at not finding in a Father of the fourth century an anticipation of a later development of Christian sentiment. At the same time it was in the age of St. Basil that "the language of the Fathers assumes a bolder tone" (cf. *Dict. Christ. Ant.* ii. 1905), and "in the correspondence of Gregory Nazianzen we find him referring to a case where a slave had been made bishop over a small community in the desert. The Christian lady to whom he belonged endeavoured to assert her right of ownership, for which she was severely rebuked by St. Basil (cf. *Letter* CXV.) After St. Basil's death she again claimed the slave, whereupon Gregory addressed her a letter of grave remonstrance at her unchristian desire

CHAPTER TWENTY-ONE

Proof from Scripture that the Spirit is called Lord.

BUT WHY GET AN unfair victory for our argument by fighting over these undignified questions, when it is within our power to prove that the excellence of the glory is beyond dispute by adducing more lofty considerations? If, indeed, we repeat what we have been taught by Scripture, every one of the Pneumatomachi will peradventure raise a loud and vehement outcry, stop their ears, pick up stones or anything else that comes to hand for a weapon, and charge against us. But our own security must not be regarded by us before the truth. We have learnt from the Apostle, "the Lord direct your hearts into the love of God and into the patient waiting for Christ"[453] *for our tribulations*. Who is the Lord that directs into the love of God and into the patient waiting for Christ for tribulations? Let those men answer us who are for making a slave of the Holy Spirit. For if the argument had been about God the Father, it would certainly have said, 'the Lord direct you into His own love,' or if about the Son, it would have added 'into His own patience.' Let them then seek what other Person there is who is worthy to be honored with the title of Lord. And parallel with this is that other passage, "and the Lord make you to increase and abound in love one toward another, and toward all men, even as we do towards you; to the end He may establish your hearts unblamable in holiness before God, even our Father, at the coming of our Lord Jesus Christ with all His saints."[454]

---

to recall his brother bishop from his sphere of duty. Ep. 79," *id.*

[453] 2 Thess. 3:5. A note of the Benedictine Editors on this passage says: "It must be admitted that these words are not found in the sacred text and are wanting in three manuscripts of this work. Moreover, in the *Regius Quintus* they are only inserted by a second hand, but since they are shortly afterwards repeated by Basil, as though taken from the sacred context, I am unwilling to delete them, and it is more probable that they were withdrawn from the manuscripts from which they are wanting because they were not found in the apostle, then added, without any reason at all, to the manuscripts in which they occur."

[454] 1 Thess. 3:12, 13.

Now what Lord does he entreat to stablish the hearts of the faithful at Thessalonica, unblamable in holiness before God even our Father, at the coming of our Lord? Let those answer who place the Holy Ghost among the ministering spirits that are sent forth on service. They cannot. Wherefore let them hear yet another testimony which distinctly calls the Spirit Lord. "The Lord," it is said, "is that Spirit;" and again "even as from the Lord the Spirit."[455] But to leave no ground for objection, I will quote the actual words of the Apostle—"For even unto this day remaineth the same veil untaken away in the reading of the Old Testament, which veil is done away in Christ....Nevertheless, when it shall turn to the Lord, the veil shall be taken away. Now the Lord is that Spirit."[456] Why does he speak thus? Because he who abides in the bare sense of the letter, and in it busies himself with the observances of the Law, has, as it were, got his own heart enveloped in the Jewish acceptance of the letter, like a veil; and this befalls him because of his ignorance that the bodily observance of the Law is done away by the presence of Christ, in that for the future the types are transferred to the reality. Lamps are made needless by the advent of the sun; and, on the appearance of the truth, the occupation of the Law is gone, and prophecy is hushed into silence. He, on the contrary, who has been empowered to look down into the depth of the meaning of the Law, and, after passing through the obscurity of the letter, as through a veil, to arrive within things unspeakable, is like Moses taking off the veil when he spoke with God. He, too, turns from the letter to the Spirit. So with the veil on the face of Moses corresponds the obscurity of the teaching of the Law, and spiritual contemplation with the turning to the Lord. He, then, who in the reading of the Law takes away the letter and turns to the Lord—and the Lord is now called the Spirit—becomes moreover like Moses, who had his face glorified by the manifestation of God. For just as objects which lie near brilliant colors are themselves tinted by the brightness which

---

[455] 2 Cor. 3:17, 18, R.V. In *Adv. Eunom.* iii. 3 St. Basil had quoted v. 17 of the Son, making πνεῦμα descriptive of our Lord. "This was written," adds Mr. C.F.H. Johnston, "during St. Basil's presbyterate, at least ten years earlier."

[456] 2 Cor. 3:14, 16, 17.

is shed around, so is he who fixes his gaze firmly on the Spirit by the Spirit's glory somehow transfigured into greater splendor, having his heart lighted up, as it were, by some light streaming from the truth of the Spirit.[457] And, this is "being changed from[458] the glory" of the Spirit "into" His own "glory," not in miserl degree, nor dimly and indistinctly, but as we might expect any one to be who is enlightened by[459] the Spirit. Do you not, O man, fear the Apostle when he says "Ye are the temple of God, and the Spirit of God dwelleth in you"?[460] Could he ever have brooked to honor with the title of "temple" the quarters of a slave? How can he who calls Scripture "God-inspired,"[461] because it was written through the inspiration of the Spirit, use the language of one who insults and belittles Him?

CHAPTER TWENTY-TWO

Establishment of the natural communion of the Spirit from His being, equally with the Father and the Son, unapproachable in thought.[462]

MOREOVER, THE SURPASSING EXCELLENCE of the nature of the Spirit is to be learned not only from His having the same title as the Father and the Son, and sharing in their operations, but also from His being, like the Father and the Son, unapproachable in thought. For what our Lord says of the Father as being above and beyond human conception, and what He says of the Son, this same language He uses also of the Holy Ghost. "O righteous

---

[457] Cf. 2 Cor. 3:18.

[458] St. Basil gives ἀπό the sense of "*by.*" So Theodoret, Œcum., Theophylact, Bengel. Cf. Alford *in loc.* The German is able to repeat the prep., as in Greek and Latin, "*von einer Klarheit zu der andern, als vom Herrn.*"

[459] ἀπό.

[460] 1 Cor. 3:16.

[461] 2 Tim. 3:16.

[462] πρὸς θεωρίαν δυσέφικτον. The Benedictine Latin is "*incomprehensibilis,*" but this is rather ἀκατάληπτος. The "incomprehensible" of the Ath. Creed is "*immensus.*"

Father," He says, "the world hath not known Thee,"[463] meaning here by the world not the complex whole compounded of heaven and earth, but this life of ours subject to death,[464] and exposed to innumerable vicissitudes. And when discoursing of Himself He says, "Yet a little while and the world seeth me no more, but ye see me;"[465] again in this passage, applying the word *world* to those who being bound down by this material and carnal life, and beholding[466] the truth by material sight alone,[467] were ordained, through their unbelief in the resurrection, to see our Lord no more with the eyes of the heart. And He said the same concerning the Spirit. "The Spirit of truth," He says, "whom the world cannot receive, because it seeth Him not, neither knoweth Him: but ye know Him, for He dwelleth with you."[468] For the carnal man, who has never trained his mind to contemplation,[469] but rather keeps it buried deep in lust of the flesh,[470] as in mud, is powerless to look up to the spiritual light of the truth. And so the world, that is life enslaved by the affections of the flesh, can no more receive the grace of the Spirit than a weak eye the light of a sunbeam. But the Lord, who by His teaching bore witness to purity of life, gives to His disciples the power of now both beholding and contemplating the Spirit. For "now," He says, "Ye are clean through the word which I have spoken unto you,"[471] wherefore "the world cannot receive Him, because it seeth Him not,...but ye know Him; for he dwelleth with you."[472] And so

---

[463] John 17:25.

[464] ἐπίκηρος. The force of the word as applied to this life is illustrated by the 61st Epigram of Callimachus:
Τίς ξένος, ὦ ναυηγέ; Λεόντιχος ἐνθάδε νεκρὸν
εὗρεν ἐπ' αἰγιαλοῖς, χῶσε δὲ τῷδε τάφῳ
δακρύσας ἐπίκηρον ἑὸν βίον· οὐδὲ γὰρ αὐτὸς
ἥσυχος, αἰθυίης δ' ἴσα θαλασσοπορεῖ.

[465] John 14:19.

[466] ἐπιβλέποντας, the reading of the Viennese MS. vulgo ἐπιτρέποντας.

[467] μόνοις ὀφθαλμοῖς.

[468] John 14:17.

[469] ἀγύμναστον ἔχων τὸν νοῦν. Cf. Heb. 5:14.

[470] τῷ φρονήματι τῆς σαρκός. Cf. Rom. 8:6 τὸ γὰρ φρόνημα τῆς σαρκὸς θάνατος.

[471] John 15:3.

[472] John 14:17.

says Isaiah—"He that spread forth the earth and that which cometh out of it; he that giveth breath unto the people upon it, and Spirit to them that trample on it";[473] for they that trample down earthly things and rise above them are borne witness to as worthy of the gift of the Holy Ghost. What then ought to be thought of Him whom the world cannot receive, and Whom saints alone can contemplate through pureness of heart? What kind of honors can be deemed adequate to Him?

CHAPTER TWENTY-THREE

The glorifying of the enumeration of His attributes.[474]

NOW OF THE REST of the Powers each is believed to be in a circumscribed place. The angel who stood by Cornelius[475] was not at one and the same moment with Philip;[476] nor yet did the angel who spoke with Zacharias from the altar at the same time occupy his own post in heaven. But the Spirit is believed to have been operating at the same time in Habakkuk and in Daniel at Babylon,[477] and to have been at the prison with Jeremiah,[478] and with Eze-

---

[473] Is. 42:5 (LXX) πατοῦσιν αὐτήν. So St. Basil's argument requires us to translate the LXX. The "walk therein" of A.V. would not bear out his meaning. For this use of πατειν, cf. Soph., Ant. 745. οὐ γὰρ σέβεις τιμάς γε τὰς θεῶν πατῶν. So in the vulgate we read "*et spiritum calcantibus eam*,"—*calcare* bearing the sense of "trample on," as in Juvenal, *Sat.* x. 86, "*calcemus Cæsaris hostem.*" The Hebrew bears no such meaning.

[474] Here the Benedictine Editors begin Chapter xxiii., remarking that they do so "*cum plures* MSS. *codices. tum ipsam sermonis seriem et continuationem secuti. Liquet enim hic Basilium ad aliud argumentum transire.*" Another division of the text makes Chapter XXIII. begin with the words "But I do not mean by glory."

[475] Acts 10:3.

[476] Acts 8:26.

[477] Bel and the Dragon 34.

[478] Jer. 20:2 (LXX). εἰς τὸν καταρράκτην ὅς ἦν ἐν πύλῃ. Καταρράκτης τῶν πυλῶν occurs in Dion. Halic. viii. 67, in the same sense as the Latin *cataracta* (Livy xxvii. 27) *a portcullis*. The Vulgate has *in nervum*, which may either be *gyve* or *gaol*. The Hebrew="stocks", as in A.V. and R.V. καταρράκτης in the text of Basil and the LXX may be assumed to mean *prison*, from the notion of

kiel at the Chebar.[479] For the Spirit of the Lord filleth the world,[480] and "whither shall I go from thy spirit? or whither shall I flee from thy presence?"[481] And, in the words of the Prophet, "For I am with you, saith the Lord...and my spirit remaineth among you."[482] But what nature is it becoming to assign to Him who is omnipresent, and exists together with God? The nature which is all-embracing, or one which is confined to particular places, like that which our argument shows the nature of angels to be? No one would so say. Shall we not then highly exalt Him who is in His nature divine, in His greatness infinite, in His operations powerful, in the blessings He confers, good? Shall we not give Him glory? And I understand glory to mean nothing else than the enumeration of the wonders which are His own. It follows then that either we are forbidden by our antagonists even to mention the good things which flow to us from Him. or on the other hand that the mere recapitulation of His attributes is the fullest possible attribution of glory. For not even in the case of the God and Father of our Lord Jesus Christ and of the Only-begotten Son, are we capable of giving Them glory otherwise than by recounting, to the extent of our powers, all the wonders that belong to Them.

CHAPTER TWENTY-FOUR

Proof of the absurdity of the refusal to glorify the Spirit, from the comparison of things glorified in creation.

FURTHERMORE MAN IS "CROWNED with glory and honor,"[483] and "glory, honor and peace" are laid up by promise "to every man that worketh good."[484] There is moreover a special and peculiar glory for Israelites "to whom," it is said "pertaineth the adoption and

---

the barred grating over the door. Cf. Ducange s.v. *cataracta*.
[479] Ez. 1:1.
[480] Wis. 1:7.
[481] Ps. 138:7 (LXX).
[482] Hag. 2:4, 5.
[483] Ps. 8:5 (LXX).
[484] Rom. 2:10.

the glory...and the service,"[485] and the Psalmist speaks of a certain glory of his own, "that my glory may sing praise to Thee;"[486] and again "Awake up my glory"[487] and according to the Apostle there is a certain glory of sun and moon and stars,[488] and "the ministration of condemnation is glorious."[489] While then so many things are glorified, do you wish the Spirit alone of all things to be unglorified? Yet the Apostle says, "the ministration of the Spirit is glorious."[490] How then can He Himself be unworthy of glory? How according to the Psalmist can the glory of the just man be great[491] and according to you the glory of the Spirit none? How is there not a plain peril from such arguments of our bringing on ourselves the sin from which there is no escape? If the man who is being saved by works of righteousness glorifies even them that fear the Lord[492] much less would he deprive the Spirit of the glory which is His due.

Grant, they say, that He is to be glorified, but not with the Father and the Son. But what reason is there in giving up the place appointed by the Lord for the Spirit, and inventing some other? What reason is there for robbing of His share of glory Him Who is everywhere associated with the Godhead; in the confession of the Faith, in the baptism of redemption, in the working of miracles, in the indwelling of the saints, in the graces bestowed on obedience? For there is not even one single gift which reaches creation without the Holy Ghost;[493] when not even a single word can be spoken in defense of Christ except by them that are aided by the Spirit, as we have learnt in the Gospels from our Lord and Savior.[494] And I know not whether anyone who has been partaker of the Holy Spirit will consent that we

---

[485] Rom. 9:4.
[486] Ps. 29:12 (LXX).
[487] Ps. 56:8 (LXX).
[488] Cf. 1 Cor. 15:41.
[489] 2 Cor. 3:9.
[490] 2 Cor. 3:8.
[491] Cf. Ps. 20:5 (LXX).
[492] Cf. Ps. 14 (LXX).
[493] Cf. Matt. 28:19; 1 Cor. 12:11; Rom. 8:11; 1 Pet. 1:2.
[494] Matt. 10:19, 20.

should overlook all this, forget His fellowship in all things, and tear the Spirit asunder from the Father and the Son. Where then are we to take Him and rank Him? With the creature? Yet all the creature is in bondage, but the Spirit maketh free. "And where the Spirit of the Lord is, there is liberty."[495] Many arguments might be adduced to them that it is unseemly to coordinate the Holy Spirit with created nature, but for the present I will pass them by. Were I indeed to bring forward, in a manner befitting the dignity of the discussion, all the proofs always available on our side, and so overthrow the objections of our opponents, a lengthy dissertation would be required, and my readers might be worn out by my prolixity. I therefore propose to reserve this matter for a special treatise,[496] and to apply myself to the points now more immediately before us.

Let us then examine the points one by one. He is good by nature, in the same way as the Father is good, and the Son is good; the creature on the other hand shares in goodness by choosing the good. He knows "The deep things of God;"[497] the creature receives the manifestation of ineffable things through the Spirit. He quickens together with God, who produces and preserves all things alive,[498] and together with the Son, who gives life. "He that raised up Christ from the dead," it is said, "shall also quicken your mortal bodies by the spirit that dwelleth in you;"[499] and again "my sheep hear my voice,...and I give unto them eternal life;"[500] but "the Spirit" also, it is said, "giveth

---

[495] 2 Cor. 3:17.

[496] Mr. C.F.H. Johnston conjectures the allusion to be to Hom. xxiv. "*Contra Sabellianos et Arium et Anomœos.*"

[497] 1 Cor. 2:10, 11.

[498] In 1 Tim. 6:13, St. Paul writes τοῦ θεοῦ τοῦ ζωοποιοῦντος πάντα. In the text St. Basil writes τὰ πάντα ζωογονοῦντος. The latter word is properly distinguished from the former as meaning not to make alive after death, but to engender alive. In Luke 17:33, it is rendered in A.V. "preserve." In Acts 7:19, it is "to the end they might not *live.*" On the meaning of ζωογονεῖν in the LXX, and the Socinian arguments based on its use in Luke 17:33, cf. Pearson, *On the Creed*, Art. V. note to p. 257 Ed. 1676.

[499] Rom. 8:11.

[500] John 10:27–28.

life,"[501] and again "the Spirit," it is said, "is life, because of righteousness."[502] And the Lord bears witness that "it is the Spirit that quickeneth; the flesh profiteth nothing."[503] How then shall we alienate the Spirit from His quickening power, and make Him belong to lifeless nature? Who is so contentious, who is so utterly without the heavenly gift,[504] and unfed by God's good words, who is so devoid of part and lot in eternal hopes, as to sever the Spirit from the Godhead and rank Him with the creature?

Now it is urged that the Spirit is in us as a gift from God, and that the gift is not reverenced with the same honor as that which is attributed to the giver. The Spirit is a gift of God, but a gift of life, for the law of "the Spirit of life," it is said, "hath made" us "free;"[505] and a gift of power, for "ye shall receive power after that the Holy Ghost is come upon you."[506] Is He on this account to be lightly esteemed? Did not God also bestow His Son as a free gift to mankind? "He that spared not His own Son," it is said, "but delivered Him up for us all, how shall He not with Him also freely give us all things?"[507] And in another place, "that we might truly know the things that are freely given us of God,"[508] in reference to the mystery of the Incarnation. It follows then that the maintainers of such arguments, in making the greatness of God's loving kindness an occasion of blasphemy, have really surpassed the ingratitude of the Jews. They find fault with the Spirit because He gives us freedom to call God our Father. "For God hath sent forth the Spirit of His Son into" our "hearts crying Abba, Father,"[509] that the voice of the Spirit may become the very voice of them that have received him.

---

[501] 2 Cor. 3:6.
[502] Rom. 8:10.
[503] John 6:63.
[504] Cf. Heb. 6:4.
[505] Rom. 8:2.
[506] Acts 1:8.
[507] Rom. 8:32.
[508] 1 Cor. 2:12.
[509] Gal. 4:6.

CHAPTER TWENTY-FIVE

That Scripture uses the words "in" or "by," ἐν, in place of "with." Wherein also it is proved that the word "and" has the same force as "with."

IT IS, HOWEVER, ASKED by our opponents, how it is that Scripture nowhere describes the Spirit as glorified together with the Father and the Son, but carefully avoids the use of the expression "with the Spirit," while it everywhere prefers to ascribe glory "in Him" as being the fitter phrase. I should, for my own part, deny that the word in [or by] implies lower dignity than the word "with;" I should maintain on the contrary that, rightly understood, it leads us up to the highest possible meaning. This is the case where, as we have observed, it often stands instead of *with*; as for instance, "I will go into thy house in burnt offerings,"[510] instead of *with* burnt offerings and "he brought them forth also by silver and gold,"[511] that is to say *with* silver and gold and "thou goest not forth *in* our armies"[512] instead of *with* our armies, and innumerable similar passages. In short I should very much like to learn from this newfangled philosophy what kind of glory the Apostle ascribed by the word *in*, according to the interpretation which our opponents proffer as derived from Scripture, for I have nowhere found the formula "To Thee, O Father, be honor and glory, through Thy only begotten Son, *by* [or *in*] the Holy Ghost,"—a form which to our opponents comes, so to say, as naturally as the air they breathe. You may indeed find each of these clauses separately,[513] but they will nowhere be able to show them to us arranged in this conjunction. If, then, they want exact conformity to what is written, let them give us exact references. If, on the other hand, they make concession to custom, they must not make us an

---

[510] Ps. 65:13 (LXX).
[511] Ps. 104:37 (LXX).
[512] Ps. 43:9 (LXX).
[513] In Eph. 2:18 they are combined, but no Scriptural doxology uses ἐν of the Spirit.

exception to such a privilege.

As we find both expressions in use among the faithful, we use both; in the belief that full glory is equally given to the Spirit by both. The mouths, however, of revilers of the truth may best be stopped by the preposition which, while it has the same meaning as that of the Scriptures, is not so wieldy a weapon for our opponents, (indeed it is now an object of their attack) and is used instead of the conjunction *and*. For to say "Paul and Silvanus and Timothy"[514] is precisely the same thing as to say Paul *with* Timothy and Silvanus; for the connection of the names is preserved by either mode of expression. The Lord says "The Father, the Son and the Holy Ghost."[515] If I say the Father and the Son *with* the Holy Ghost shall I make, any difference in the sense? Of the connection of names by means of the conjunction *and* the instances are many. We read "The grace of our Lord Jesus Christ and the love of God and the fellowship of the Holy Ghost,"[516] and again "I beseech you for the Lord Jesus Christ's sake, and for the love of the Spirit."[517] Now if we wish to use *with* instead of *and*, what difference shall we have made? I do not see; unless any one according to hard and fast grammatical rules might prefer the conjunction as copulative and making the union stronger, and reject the preposition as of inferior force. But if we had to defend ourselves on these points I do not suppose we should require a defense of many words. As it is, their argument is not about syllables nor yet about this or that sound of a word, but about things differing most widely in power and in truth. It is for this reason that, while the use of the syllables is really a matter of no importance whatever, our opponents are making the endeavor to authorize some syllables, and hunt out others from the Church. For my own part, although the usefulness of the word is obvious as soon as it is heard, I will nevertheless set forth the arguments which led our fathers to adopt the reasonable

---

[514] 1 Thess. 1:1.
[515] Matt. 28:19.
[516] 2 Cor. 13:13.
[517] Rom. 15:30.

course of employing the preposition *"with."*[518] It does indeed equally well with the preposition "and," confute the mischief of Sabellius;[519] and it sets forth quite as well as *"and"* the distinction of the hypostases, as in the words "I and my Father will come,"[520] and "I and my Father are one."[521] In addition to this the proof it contains of the eternal fellowship and uninterrupted conjunction is excellent. For to say that the Son is *with* the Father is to exhibit at once the distinction of the hypostases, and the inseparability of the fellowship. The same thing is observable even in mere human matters, for the conjunction *"and"* intimates that there is a common element in an action, while the preposition "with" declares in some sense as well the communion in action. As, for instance—Paul and Timothy sailed to Macedonia, but both Tychicus and Onesimus were sent to the Colossians. Hence we learn that they did the same thing. But suppose we are told that they sailed *with*, and were sent *with*? Then we are informed in addition that they carried out the action in company with one another. Thus while the word *"with"* upsets the error of Sabellius as no other

---

[518] "St. Basil's statement of the reason of the use of μετά, σύν, in the Doxology, is not confirmed by any earlier or contemporary writer, as far as the editor is aware, nor is it contradicted." Rev. C.F.H. Johnston.

[519] "Sabellius has been usually assigned to the middle of third century, Mr. Clinton giving A.D. 256–270 as his active period. The discovery of the *Philosophumena* of Hippolytus has proved this to be a mistake, and thrown his period back to the close of the second and beginning of the third century.... He was in full activity in Rome during the Episcopate of Zephyrinus, A.D. 198–217." Professor Stokes in *D. C. Biog.* iv. 569. For Basil's views of Sabellianism *vide* Epp. CCX., CCXIV., CCXXXV. In his *Hær. Fab. Conf.* ii. 9 Theodoret writes: "Sabellius said that Father, Son, and Holy Ghost were one Hypostasis; one Person under three names; and he describes the same now as Father, now as Son, now as Holy Ghost. He says that in the old Testament He gave laws as Father, was incarnate in the new as Son, and visited the Apostles as Holy Ghost." So in the Ἔκθεσις τῆς κατὰ μέρος πίστεως, a work falsely attributed to Gregory Thaumaturgus, and possibly due to Apollinaris, (cf. Theod., *Dial.* iii.) "We shun Sabellius, who says that Father and Son are the same, calling Him who speaks Father, and the Word, remaining in the Father and at the time of creation manifested, and, on the completion of things returning to the Father, Son. He says the same of the Holy Ghost."

[520] Apparently an inexact reference to John 14:23.

[521] John 10:30.

word can, it routs also sinners who err in the very opposite direction; those, I mean, who separate the Son from the Father and the Spirit from the Son, by intervals of time.[522]

As compared with *"in,"* there is this difference, that while *"with"* sets forth the mutual conjunction of the parties associated—as, for example, of those who sail with, or dwell with, or do anything else in common, *"in"* shows their relation to that matter in which they happen to be acting. For we no sooner hear the words "sail in" or "dwell in" than we form the idea of the boat or the house. Such is the distinction between these words in ordinary usage; and laborious investigation might discover further illustrations. I have no time to examine into the nature of the syllables. Since then it has been shown that *"with"* most clearly gives the sense of conjunction, let it be declared, if you will, to be under safe-conduct, and cease to wage your savage and truceless war against it. Nevertheless, though the word is naturally thus auspicious, yet if any one likes, in the ascription of praise, to couple the names by the syllable "and," and to give glory, as we have taught in the Gospel, in the formula of baptism, Father and Son and Holy Ghost,[523] be it so: no one will make any objection. On these conditions, if you will, let us come to terms. But our foes would rather surrender their tongues than accept this word. It is this that rouses against us their implacable and truceless war. We must offer the ascription of glory to God, it is contended, *in* the Holy Ghost, and not *and* to the Holy Ghost, and they passionately cling to this word *in*, as though it lowered the Spirit. It will therefore be not unprofitable to speak at greater length about it; and I shall be astonished if they do not, when they have heard what we have to urge, reject the *in* as itself a traitor to their cause, and a deserter to the side of the glory of the Spirit.

---

[522] *i.e.*, The Arians, who said of the Son, "There was when he was not;" and the Pneumatomachi, who made the Spirit a created being.

[523] Matt. 28:19.

CHAPTER TWENTY-SIX

That the word "in," in as many senses as it bears, is understood of the Spirit.

NOW, SHORT AND simple as this utterance is, it appears to me, as I consider it, that its meanings are many and various. For of the senses in which "*in*" is used, we find that all help our conceptions of the Spirit. *Form* is said to be *in Matter*; *Power* to be *in* what is capable of it; *Habit* to be *in* him who is affected by it; and so on.[524] Therefore, inasmuch as the Holy Spirit perfects rational beings, completing their excellence, He is analogous to Form. For he, who no longer "lives after the flesh,"[525] but, being "led by the Spirit of God,"[526] is called a Son of God, being "conformed to the image of the Son of God,"[527] is described as spiritual. And as is the power of seeing in the healthy eye, so is the operation of the Spirit in the purified soul. Wherefore also Paul prays for the Ephesians that they may have their "eyes enlightened" by "the Spirit of wisdom."[528] And as the art in him who has acquired it, so is the grace of the Spirit in the recipient ever present, though not continuously in operation. For as the art is potentially in the artist, but only in operation when he is working in accordance with it, so also the Spirit is ever present with those that are worthy, but works, as need requires, in prophecies, or in healings, or in some other actual carrying into effect of His potential action.[529] Furthermore as in our bodies is health, or heat, or,

---

[524] Cf. Note on Chapter iii. p. 4. In the Aristotelian philosophy, εἶδος, or Forma, is the τὸ τί ἦν εἶναι, the essence or formal cause. Cf. Ar., *Met*. vi. 7, 4. εἶδος δὲ λέγω τὸ τί ἦν εἶναι ἑκάστον καὶ τὴν πρώτην οὐσίαν. Δύναμις, or Potentia, is potential action or existence, as opposed to ἐνέργεια, *actus*, actual action or existence, or ἐντελέχεια. Cf. Ar., *Met*., viii. 3, 9, and viii. 8, 11. Sir W. Hamilton, *Metaph*. i. 178–180.

[525] Rom. 8:12.
[526] Rom. 8:14.
[527] Rom. 8:29.
[528] Eph. 1:17, 18.
[529] ἐν ἄλλοις τισι δυνάμεων ἐνεργήμασι. The Benedictine translation is *in aliis miraculorum operationibus.*" It is of course quite true that δύναμιςis one of the

generally, their variable conditions, so, very frequently is the Spirit in the soul; since He does not abide with those who, on account of the instability of their will, easily reject the grace which they have received. An instance of this is seen in Saul,[530] and the seventy elders of the children of Israel, except Eldad and Medad, with whom alone the Spirit appears to have remained,[531] and, generally, any one similar to these in character. And like reason in the soul, which is at one time the thought in the heart, and at another speech uttered by the tongue,[532] so is the Holy Spirit, as when He "beareth witness with our spirit,"[533] and when He "cries in our hearts, Abba, Father,"[534] or when He speaks on our behalf, as it is said, "It is not ye that speak, but the Spirit of our Father which speaketh in you."[535] Again, the Spirit is conceived of, in relation to the distribution of gifts, as a whole in parts. For we all are "members one of another, having gifts differing according to the grace that is given us."[536] Wherefore "the eye cannot say to the hand, I have no need of thee; nor again the head to the feet, I have no need of you,"[537] but all together complete the Body of Christ in the Unity of the Spirit, and render to one another the needful aid that comes of the gifts. "But God hath set the members in the body, every one of them, as it hath pleased Him."[538] But "the members have the

---

four words used in the New Testament for miracle, and often has that sense, but here the context suggest the antithesis between potential and actual operation, and moreover non-miraculous (in the ordinary sense) operations of the Spirit need not be excluded; in a deep sense all His operations are miraculous. ἐνέργημα is an uncommon word, meaning the work wrought by ἐνέργεια or operation.

[530] 1 Sam. 16:14.

[531] Numb. 11:25, 26, LXX. and R.V. "did so no more" for "did not cease" of A.V.

[532] The distinction between the λόγος ἐνδιάθετος, thought, and the λογος πορφορικός, speech, appears first in Philo. II. 154. On the use of the term in Catholic Theology cf. Dr. Robertson's note on Ath., De Syn. § xxvi. p. 463 of the Ed. in this series. Also, Dorner, Div. I. i. p. 338, note.

[533] Rom. 8:16.

[534] Gal. 6:4.

[535] Matt. 10:20.

[536] Rom. 12:5, 6.

[537] 1 Cor. 12:21.

[538] 1 Cor. 12:18, slightly varied in order.

same care for one another,"[539] according to the inborn spiritual communion of their sympathy. Wherefore, "whether one member suffer, all the members suffer with it; or one member be honored, all the members rejoice with it."[540] And as parts in the whole so are we individually in the Spirit, because we all "were baptized in one body into one spirit."[541]

It is an extraordinary statement, but it is none the less true, that the Spirit is frequently spoken of as the *place* of them that are being sanctified, and it will become evident that even by this figure the Spirit, so far from being degraded, is rather glorified. For words applicable to the body are, for the sake of clearness, frequently transferred in scripture to spiritual conceptions. Accordingly, we find the Psalmist, even in reference to God, saying "Be Thou to me a champion God and a strong place to save me"[542] and concerning the Spirit "behold there is place by me, and stand upon a rock."[543] Plainly meaning the place or contemplation in the Spirit wherein, after Moses had entered thither, he was able to see God intelligibly manifested to him. This is the special and peculiar place of true worship; for it is said "Take heed to thyself that thou offer not thy burnt offerings in every place...but in the place the Lord thy God shall choose."[544] Now what is a spiritual burnt offering? "The sacrifice of praise."[545] And in what place do we offer it? In the Holy Spirit. Where have we learnt this? From the Lord himself in the words "The true worshippers shall worship the Father in spirit and in truth."[546] This place Jacob saw and said "The Lord is in

---

[539] 1 Cor. 12:25.
[540] 1 Cor. 12:26.
[541] An inversion of 1 Cor. 12:3.
[542] Ps. 70:3 (LXX).
[543] Ex. 33:21 (LXX).
[544] Deut. 12:13, 14.
[545] Ps. 49:14 (LXX).
[546] John 4:23. With this interpretation, cf. Athan., *Epist.* i. *Ad Serap.* § 33, "Hence it is shown that the Truth is the Son Himself...for they worship the Father, but in Spirit and in Truth, confessing the Son and the Spirit in him; for the Spirit is inseparable from the Son as the Son is inseparable from the Father."

this place."⁵⁴⁷ It follows that the Spirit is verily the place of the saints and the saint is the proper place for the Spirit, offering himself as he does for the indwelling of God, and called God's Temple.⁵⁴⁸ So Paul speaks in Christ, saying "In the sight of God we speak in Christ,"⁵⁴⁹ and Christ in Paul, as he himself says "Since ye seek a proof of Christ speaking in me."⁵⁵⁰ So also in the Spirit he speaketh mysteries,⁵⁵¹ and again the Spirit speaks in him.⁵⁵²

In relation to the originate,⁵⁵³ then, the Spirit is said to *be in* them

---

⁵⁴⁷ Gen. 28:16.
⁵⁴⁸ 1 Cor. 6:19.
⁵⁴⁹ 2 Cor. 2:17.
⁵⁵⁰ 2 Cor. 13:3.
⁵⁵¹ 1 Cor. 14:2.
⁵⁵² 1 Peter 1:11.
⁵⁵³ ἐν τοῦς γενητοῖς, as in the Bodleian MS. The Benedictine text adopts the common reading γεννητοις, with the note, "*Sed discrimen illud parvi momenti.*" If St. Basil wrote γεννητοῖς, he used it in the looser sense of mortal: in its strict sense of "begotten" it would be singularly out of place here, as the antithesis of the reference to the Son, who isγεννητός, would be spoilt. In the terminology of theology, so far from being "*parvi momenti*," the distinction is vital. In the earlier Greek philosophy ἀγένητος and ἀγέννητος are both used as nearly synonymous to express unoriginate eternal. Cf. Plat., *Phæd.* 245 D., ἀρχὴ δὲ ἀγένητόν, with Plat., *Tim.* 52 A., Τουτων δὲ οὕτως ἐχόντων ὁμολογητέον ἓν μὲν εἶναι τὸ κατὰ ταὐτὰ εἶδος ἔχον ἀγέννητον καὶ ἀνώλεθρον. And the earliest patristic use similarly meant by γεννητός and ἀγέννητος created and uncreated, as in Ign., *Ad Eph.* vii., where our Lord is called γεννητὸς καὶ ἀγέννητος, ἐν ἀνθρώπω Θεὸς, ἐν θανάτω ζωὴ ἀληθινή. Cf. Bp. Lightfoot's note. But "such language is not in accordance with later theological definitions, which carefully distinguished between γενητός and γεννητός, between ἀγένητοςand ἀγέννητος; so that γενητός, ἀγένητος, respectively denied and affirmed the eternal existence, being equivalent to κτιστός, ἄκτιστος, while γεννητός, ἀγέννητος described certain ontological relations, whether in time or in eternity. In the later theological language, therefore, the Son was γεννητός even in His Godhead. See esp. Joann. Damasc., *De Fid. Orth.* i. 8 (I. p. 135, Lequin), χρὴ γὰρ εἰδέναι ὅτι τὸ ἀγένητον, διὰ τοῦ ἑνὸς ν γραφόμενον, τὸ ἄκτιστον ἢ τὸ μὴ γενόμενον σημαίνει, τὸ δὲ ἀγέννητον, διὰ τῶν δύο νν γραφόμενον, δηλοῖ τὸ μὴ γεννηθέν; whence he draws the conclusion that μόνος ὁ πατὴρ ἀγέννητος and μόνος ὁ υἱός γεννητός." Bp. Lightfoot, *Ap. Fathers*, Pt. II. Vol. II. p. 90, where the history of the worlds is exhaustively discussed. At the time of the Arian controversy the Catholic disputants were chary of employing these terms, because of the base uses to which their opponents put them; so St. Basil, *Contra Eunom.* iv. protests against the

"in divers portions and in divers manners,"[554] while in relation to the Father and the Son it is more consistent with true religion to assert Him not to *be in* but to *be with*. For the grace flowing from Him when He dwells in those that are worthy, and carries out His own operations, is well described as existing in those that are able to receive Him. On the other hand His essential existence before the ages, and His ceaseless abiding with Son and Father, cannot be contemplated without requiring titles expressive of eternal conjunction. For absolute and real co-existence is predicated in the case of things which are mutually inseparable. We say, for instance, that heat exists in the hot iron, but in the case of the actual fire it co-exists; and, similarly, that health exists in the body, but that life co-exists with the soul. It follows that wherever the fellowship is intimate, congenital,[555] and inseparable, the word *with* is more expressive, suggesting, as it does, the idea of inseparable fellowship. Where on the other hand the grace flowing from the Spirit naturally comes and goes, it is properly and truly said to exist *in*, even if on account of the firmness of the recipients' disposition to good the grace abides with them continually. Thus whenever we have in mind the Spirit's proper rank, we contemplate Him as being *with* the Father and the Son, but when we think of the grace that flows from Him operating on those who participate in it, we say that the Spirit is *in* us. And the doxology which we offer "in the Spirit" is not an acknowledgment of His rank; it is rather a confession of our own weakness, while we show that we are not sufficient to glorify Him of ourselves, but our sufficiency[556] is in the Holy Spirit. Enabled in, [or by,] Him we render thanks to our God for the benefits we have received, according to the measure of our purification from evil, as we receive one a larger and another a smaller share of the aid of the Spirit, that we may offer "the sacrifice of praise to God."[557] According

---

Arian argument εἰ ἀγέννητος ὁ πατὴρ γεννητὸς δὲ ὁ υἱός, οὐ τῆς αὐτῆς οὐσιας. Cf. Ath., *De Syn.* in this series, p. 475, and *De Decretis*, on Newman's confusion of the terms, p. 149 and 169.

[554] Heb. 1:1.
[555] συμφυής.
[556] Cf. 2 Cor. 3:5.
[557] Heb. 13:15.

to one use, then, it is thus that we offer our thanksgiving, as the true religion requires, in the Spirit; although it is not quite unobjectionable that any one should testify of himself "the Spirit of God is in me, and I offer glory after being made wise through the grace that flows from Him." For to a Paul it is becoming to say "I think also that I have the Spirit of God,"[558] and again, "that good thing which was committed to thee keep by the Holy Ghost which dwelleth in us."[559] And of Daniel it is fitting to say that "the Holy Spirit of God is in him,"[560] and similarly of men who are like these in virtue.

Another sense may however be given to the phrase, that just as the Father is seen in the Son, so is the Son in the Spirit. The "worship in the Spirit" suggests the idea of the operation of our intelligence being carried on in the light, as may be learned from the words spoken to the woman of Samaria. Deceived as she was by the customs of her country into the belief that worship was local, our Lord, with the object of giving her better instruction, said that worship ought to be offered "in Spirit and in Truth,"[561] plainly meaning by the Truth, Himself. As then we speak of the worship offered in the Image of God the Father as worship in the Son, so too do we speak of worship in the Spirit as showing in Himself the Godhead of the Lord. Wherefore even in our worship the Holy Spirit is inseparable from the Father and the Son. If you remain outside the Spirit you will not be able even to worship at all; and on your becoming in Him you will in no wise be able to dissever Him from God—any more than you will divorce light from visible objects. For it is impossible to behold the Image of the invisible God except by the enlightenment of the Spirit, and impracticable for him to fix his gaze on the Image to dissever the light from the Image, because the cause of vision is of necessity seen at the same time as the visible objects. Thus fitly and consistently do we behold the "Brightness of the glory" of God by means of the illumination of the Spirit, and by means of the "Express Image" we are led up to Him

---

[558] 1 Cor. 7:40.
[559] 2 Tim. 1:14.
[560] Dan. 4:8 (LXX).
[561] John 4:24.

of whom He is the Express Image and Seal, graven to the like.[562]

CHAPTER TWENTY-SEVEN

Of the origin of the word "with," and what force it has. Also concerning the unwritten laws of the church.

THE WORD "*IN*," SAY our opponents, "is exactly appropriate to the Spirit, and sufficient for every thought concerning Him. Why then, they ask, have we introduced this new phrase, saying, "*with* the Spirit" instead of "*in* the Holy Spirit," thus employing an expression which is quite unnecessary, and sanctioned by no usage in the churches? Now it has been asserted in the previous portion of this treatise that the word "*in*" has not been specially allotted to the Holy Spirit, but is common to the Father and the Son. It has also been, in my opinion, sufficiently demonstrated that, so far from detracting anything from the dignity of the Spirit, it leads all, but those whose thoughts are wholly perverted, to the most sublime height. It remains for me to trace the origin of the word "*with*;" to explain what force it has, and to show that it is in harmony with Scripture.

[563]Of the beliefs and practices whether generally accepted or pub-

---

[562] Cf. note on § 15. So Athan. *in Matt.* xi. 22. Σφραγὶς γάρ ἐστιν ἰσότυπος ἐν ἑαυτῷ δεικνὺς τὸν πατέρα. Cf. Athan., *De Dec.* § 20, and note 9 in this series, p. 163. Cf. also Greg. Nyss., *In Eunom.* ii. 12.

[563] The genuineness of this latter portion of the Treatise was objected to by Erasmus on the ground that the style is unlike that of Basil's soberer writings. Bp. Jeremy Taylor follows Erasmus (Vol. vi. ed. 1852, p. 427). It was vindicated by Casaubon, who recalls St. John Damascene's quotation of the *Thirty Chapters to Amphilochius*. Mr. C.F.H. Johnston remarks, "The later discovery of the Syriac Paraphrases of the whole book pushes back this argument to about one hundred years from the date of St. Basil's writing. The peculiar care taken by St. Basil for the writing out of the treatise, and for its safe arrival in Amphilochius' hands, and the value set upon it by the friends of both, make the forgery of half the present book, and the substitution of it for the original within that period, almost incredible." Section 66 is quoted as an authoritative statement on the right use of Tradition "as a guide to the right understanding of Holy Scripture, for the right ministration of the Sacraments, and the preservation of sacred rights and ceremonies in the purity of their original institution," in

licly enjoined which are preserved in the Church[564] some we possess

---

Philaret's *Longer Catechism of the Eastern Church*.

St. Basil is, however, strong on the supremacy of Holy Scripture, as in the passages quoted in Bp. H. Browne, *On the xxxix Articles*: "Believe those things which are written; the things which are not written seek not." (*Hom. xxix. adv. Calum. S. Trin.*) "It is a manifest defection from the faith, and a proof of arrogance, either to reject anything of what is written, or to introduce anything that is not." (*De Fide.* i.) cf. also Letters CV. and CLIX. On the right use of Tradition cf. Hooker, *Ecc. Pol.* lxv. 2, "Lest, therefore, the name of tradition should be offensive to any, considering how far by some it hath been and is abused, we mean by traditions ordinances made in the prime of Christian Religion, established with that authority which Christ hath left to His Church for matters indifferent, and in that consideration requisite to be observed, till like authority see just and reasonable causes to alter them. So that traditions ecclesiastical are not rudely and in gross to be shaken off, because the inventors of them were men."
Cf. Tert., *De Præsc.* 36, 20, 21, "*Constat omnem doctrinam quæ cum illis ecclesiis apostolicis matricibus et originalibus fidei conspiret veritati deputandam, id sine dubio tenentem quod ecclesiæ ab apostolis, apostoli a Christo, Christus a Deo accepit.*" Vide Thomasius, *Christ. Dogm.* i. 105.

[564] "τῶς ἐν τῇ Ἐκκλησίᾳ· πεφυλαγμένων δογμάτων καὶ κηρυγμάτων." To give the apparent meaning of the original seems impossible except by some such paraphrase as the above. In Scripture δόγμα, which occurs five times (Luke 2:1, Acts 16:4, 17:7, Eph. 2:15, and Col. 2:14), always has its proper sense of decree or ordinances. Cf. Bp. Lightfoot, on Col. 2:14, and his contention that the Greek Fathers generally have mistaken the force of the passage in understanding δόγματα in both Col. and Eph. to mean the doctrines and precepts of the Gospel. Κήρυγμα occurs eight times (Matt. 12:41, Luke 11:32, Rom. 16:25, 1 Cor. 1:21, 2:4, 15:14, 2 Tim 4:17, and Tit. 1:3), always in the sense of preaching or proclamation.

"The later Christian sense of δόγμα, meaning *doctrine*, came from its secondary classical use, where it was applied to the authoritative and categorical 'sentences' of the philosophers: cf. Just. Mart., *Apol.* i. 7. οἱ ἐν Ἕλλησι τὰ αὐτοῖς ἀρεστὰ δογματίσαντες ἐκ παντὸς τῷ ἑνὶ ὀνόματι φιλοσοφίας προσαγορεύοντα, καίπερ τῶν δογμάτων ἐναντίων ὄντων." [All the sects in general among the Greeks are known by the common name of philosophy, though their doctrines are different.] Cic., *Acad.* ii. 19. '*De suis decretis quæ philosophi vocant* δόγματα.'...There is an approach towards the ecclesiastical meaning in Ignat., *Mag.* 13, βεβαιωθῆσαι ἐν τοῖς δόγμασι τοῦ κυρίου καὶ τῶν ἀποστόλων." Bp. Lightfoot in Col. 2:14. The "doctrines" of heretics are also called δόγματα, as in Basil, *Ep.* CCLXI. and Socr., *E. H.* iii. 10. Cf. Bp. Bull, *in Serm.* 2, "The dogmata or tenets of the Sadducees." In Orig., *c. Cels.* iii. p. 135, Ed. Spencer, 1658, δόγμα is used of the gospel or teaching of our Lord.

The special point about St. Basil's use of δόγματα is that he uses the word of doctrines and practices privately and tacitly sanctioned in the Church

derived from written teaching; others we have received delivered to us "in a mystery"[565] by the tradition of the apostles; and both of these in relation to true religion have the same force. And these no one will gainsay—no one, at all events, who is even moderately versed in the institutions of the Church. For were we to attempt to reject such customs as have no written authority, on the ground that the importance they possess is small, we should unintentionally injure the Gospel in

---

(like ἀπόρρητα, which is used of the esoteric doctrine of the Pythagoreans, Plat., Phæd. 62. B.), while he reserves κηρύγματα for what is now often understood by δόγματα, i.e. "legitima synodo decreta." Cf. Ep. LII., where he speaks of the great κήρυγμα of the Fathers at Nicæa. In this he is supported by Eulogius, Patriarch of Alexandria, 579–607, of whom Photius (Cod. ccxxx. Migne Pat. Gr. ciii. p. 1027) writes, "In this work," i.e. Or. II. "he says that of the doctrines (διδαγμάτων) handed down in the church by the ministers of the word, some areδόγματα, and others κηρύγματα. The distinction is that δόγματα are announced with concealment and prudence, and are often designedly compassed with obscurity, in order that holy things may not be exposed to profane persons nor pearls cast before swine. Κηρύγματα, on the other hand, are announced without any concealment." So the Benedictine Editors speak of Origen (c. Cels. i. 7) as replying to Celsus, "prædicationem Christianorum toti orbi notiorem esse quam placita philosophorum: sed tamen fatetur, ut apud philosophos, ita etiam apud Christianos nonulla esse veluti interiora, quæ post exteriorem et propositam omnibus doctrinam tradantur." Of κηρύματα they note, "Videntur hoc nomine designari leges ecclesiasticæ et canonum decreta quæ promulgari in ecclesia mos erat, ut neminem laterent." Mr. C.F.H. Johnston remarks: "The ὁμοούσιον, which many now-a-days would call the Nicene dogma (τὰ τοῦ ὁμοουσίου δόγματα, Soc., E.H. iii. 10) because it was put forth in the Council of Nicæa, was for that reason called not δόγμα, but κήρυγμα, by St. Basil, who would have said that it became the κήρυγμα (definition) of that Council, because it had always been the δόγμα of the Church."

In extra theological philosophy, a dogma has all along meant a certainly expressed opinion whether formally decreed or not. So Shaftesbury, Misc. Ref. ii. 2, "He who is certain, or presumes to say he knows, is in that particular whether he be mistaken or in the right a dogmatist." Cf. Littré S.V. for a similar use in French. In theology, the modern Roman limitation of dogma to decreed doctrine is illustrated by the statement of Abbé Bérgier (Dict. de Théol. Ed. 1844) of the Immaculate Conception of the Blessed Virgin. "Or, *nous convenons que ce n'est pas un dogme de foi*," because, though a common opinion among Romanists, it had not been so asserted at the Council of Trent. Since the publication of Pius IX's Edict of 1854 it has become, to ultramontanists, a "dogma of faith."

[565] 1 Cor. 2:7. Whether there is or is not here a conscious reference to St. Paul's words, there seems to be both in the text and in the passage cited an employment of μυστήριον in its proper sense of a secret revealed to the initiated.

its very vitals; or, rather, should make our public definition a mere phrase and nothing more.[566] For instance, to take the first and most general example, who is thence who has taught us in writing to sign with the sign of the cross those who have trusted in the name of our Lord Jesus Christ? What writing has taught us to turn to the East at the prayer? Which of the saints has left us in writing the words of the invocation at the displaying[567] of the bread of the Eucharist and the

---

[566] *i.e.* if nothing were of weight but what was written, what need of any authorization at all? There is no need of κήρυγμα for a δόγμα expressly written in Scripture.

[567] ἐπὶ τῇ ἀναδείξει. The Benedictine note is: "*Non respicit Basilius ad ritum ostensionis Eucharistiæ, ut multi existimarunt, sed potius ad verba Liturgiæ ipsi ascriptæ, cum petit sacerdos, ut veniat Spiritus sanctus* ἁγιάσαι καὶ ἀναδεῖξαι τὸν μὲν ἄρτον τοῦτον αὐτὸ τὸ τίμιον σῶμα τοῦ κυρίου. *Haec autem verba* ἐπὶ τῇ ἀναδείξει, *sic reddit Erasmus,* cum ostenditur. *Vituperat eum Ducæus; sicque ipse vertit,* cum conficitur, *atque hanc interpretationem multis exemplis confirmat. Videtur tamen nihil prorsus vitii habitura haec interpretatio,* Invocationis verba cum ostenditur panis Eucharistiæ, *id est,* cum panis non jam panis est, sed panis Eucharistiæ, sive corpus Christi ostenditur; et in liturgia, *ut sanctificet et ostendat hunc quidem panem, ipsum pretiosum corpus Domini. Nam 1°Cur eam vocem reformidemus, qua Latini uti non dubitant, ubi de Eucharistia loquuntur? Quale est illud Cypriani in epistola 63 ad Cæcilium:* Vino Christi sanguis ostenditur. *Sic etiam Tertullianus I. Marc. c. 14:* Panem quo ipsum corpus suum repræsentat *2° Ut Græce,* ἀναδεῖξαι, ἀποφαίνειν, *ita etiam Latine,* ostendere, *corpus Christi præsens in Eucharistia significatione quodam modo exprimit. Hoc enim verbum non solum panem fieri corpus Domini significat, sed etiam fidem nostram excitat, ut illud corpus sub specie panis videndum, tegendum, adorandum ostendi credamus. Quemadmodum Irenæus, cum ait lib. iv. cap. 33:* Accipiens panem suum corpus esse confitebatur, et temperamentum calicis suum sanguinem conformavit, *non solum mutationem panis et vini in corpus et sanguinem Christi exprimit, sed ipsam etiam Christi asseverationem, quæ hanc nobis mutationem persuadet: sic qui corpus Christi in Eucharistia ostendi et repræsentari dicunt, non modo jejuno et exiliter loqui non videntur, sed etiam acriores Christi præsentis adorandi stimulos subjicere. Poterat ergo retineri interpretatio Erasmi; sed quia viris eruditis displicuit, satius visum est quid sentirem in hac nota exponere.*"

This view of the meaning of ἀναδείκνυσθαι and ἀνάδειξις as being equivalent to ποιεῖν and ποίησιςis borne out and illustrated by Suicer, S.V. "*Ex his jam satis liquere arbitror* ἀναδεῖξαι *apud Basilium id esse quod alii Græci patres dicunt* ποιεῖν velἀποφαίνειν σῶμα χριστοῦ."

It is somewhat curious to find Bellarmine (*De Sacr. Euch.* iv. § 14) interpreting the prayer to Godεὐλογῆσαι καὶ ἁγιάσαι καὶ ἀναδεῖξαι to mean "ostende *per effectum salutarem in mentibus nostris istum panem salutificatum non esse panem vulgarem sed cœlestem.*"

cup of blessing? For we are not, as is well known, content with what the apostle or the Gospel has recorded, but both in preface and conclusion we add other words as being of great importance to the validity of the ministry, and these we derive from unwritten teaching. Moreover, we bless the water of baptism and the oil of the chrism, and besides this the catechumen who is being baptized. On what written authority do we do this? Is not our authority silent and mystical tradition? Nay, by what written word is the anointing of oil[568] itself taught? And whence comes the custom of baptizing thrice?[569] And as to the other customs of baptism from what Scripture do we derive the renunciation of Satan and his angels? Does not this come from that unpublished and secret teaching which our fathers guarded in a silence out of the reach of curious meddling and inquisitive investigation? Well had they learnt the lesson that the awful dignity of the mysteries is best preserved by silence. What the uninitiated are not even allowed to look at was hardly likely to be publicly paraded about in written documents. What was the meaning of the mighty Moses in not making all the parts of the tabernacle open to everyone? The profane he stationed without the sacred barriers; the first courts he conceded to the purer; the Levites alone he judged worthy of being servants of the Deity; sacrifices and burnt offerings and the rest of the priestly functions he allotted to the priests; one chosen out of all he admitted to the shrine, and even this one not always but on only one day in the year, and of this one day a time was fixed for his entry so that he might gaze on the Holy of Holies amazed at the strangeness and novelty of the sight. Moses was wise enough to know that contempt stretches to the trite and to the obvious, while a keen interest is naturally associated with the unusual and the unfamiliar. In the same manner, the Apostles and Fathers who laid down laws for

---

[568] For the unction of catechumens cf. *Ap. Const.* vii. 22; of the baptized, Tertullian, *De Bapt.* vii.; of the confirmed, *id.* viii.; of the sick *vide* Plumptre on St. James 5:14, in *Cambridge Bible for Schools.* Cf. *Letter* clxxxviii.

[569] For trine immersion an early authority is Tertullian, *c. Praxeam* xxvi. Cf. Greg. Nyss., *De Bapt.* ὕδατι ἑαυτοὺς ἐγκρύπτομεν ...καὶ τρίτον τοῦτο ποιήσαντες. *Dict. Ch. Ant.* i. 161.

the Church from the beginning thus guarded the awful dignity of the mysteries in secrecy and silence, for what is bruited abroad random among the common folk is no mystery at all. This is the reason for our tradition of unwritten precepts and practices, that the knowledge of our dogmas may not become neglected and contemned by the multitude through familiarity. "Dogma" and "Kerugma" are two distinct things; the former is observed in silence; the latter is proclaimed to all the world. One form of this silence is the obscurity employed in Scripture, which makes the meaning of "dogmas" difficult to be understood for the very advantage of the reader: Thus we all look to the East[570] at our prayers, but few of us know that we are seeking our own old country,[571] Paradise, which God planted in Eden in the East.[572] We pray standing,[573] on the first day of the week, but we do not all know the reason. On the day of the resurrection (or "standing again" Grk. ἀνάστασις) we remind ourselves of the grace given to us by standing at prayer, not only because we rose with Christ,[574] and are bound to "seek those things which are above,"[575] but because the day seems to us to be in some sense an image of the age which we expect, wherefore, though it is the beginning of days, it is not called by Moses *first*, but *one*.[576] For he says, "There was evening, and there was morning, one day," as though the same day often recurred. Now "one" and "eighth" are the same, in itself distinctly indicating that really "one" and "eighth" of which the Psalmist makes mention in certain titles of the Psalms, the state which follows after this present time, the day which knows no waning or eventide, and no succes-

---

[570] Cf. my note on Theodoret in this series, p. 112.

[571] Heb. 11:14, R.V.

[572] Gen. 2:8.

[573] The earliest posture of prayer was standing, with the hands extended and raised towards heaven, and with the face turned to the East. Cf. early art, and specially the figures of "oranti." Their rich dress indicates less their actual station in this life than the expected felicity of Paradise. *Vide, Dict. Christ. Ant.* ii. 1684.

[574] "Stood again with"—συναναστάντες.

[575] Col. 3:1.

[576] Gen. 1:5. Heb. LXX. Vulg. R.V. Cf. p. 64.

sor, that age which endeth not or groweth old.[577] Of necessity, then, the church teaches her own foster children to offer their prayers on that day standing, to the end that through continual reminder of the endless life we may not neglect to make provision for our removal thither. Moreover, all Pentecost is a reminder of the resurrection expected in the age to come. For that one and first day, if seven times multiplied by seven, completes the seven weeks of the holy Pentecost; for, beginning at the first, Pentecost ends with the same, making fifty revolutions through the like intervening days. And so it is a likeness of eternity, beginning as it does and ending, as in a circling course, at the same point. On this day, the rules of the church have educated us to prefer the upright attitude of prayer, for by their plain reminder they, as it were, make our mind to dwell no longer in the present but in the future. Moreover, every time we fall upon our knees and rise from off them we show by the very deed that by our sin we fell down to earth, and by the loving kindness of our Creator were called back to heaven.

Time will fail me if I attempt to recount the unwritten mysteries of the Church. Of the rest I say nothing; but of the very confession of our faith in Father, Son, and Holy Ghost, what is the written source? If it be granted that, as we are baptized, so also under the obligation to believe, we make our confession in like terms as our baptism, in accordance with the tradition of our baptism and in conformity with the principles of true religion, let our opponents grant us too, the right to be as consistent in our ascription of glory as in our confession of faith. If they deprecate our doxology on the ground that it lacks written authority, let them give us the written evidence for the confession of our faith and the other matters which we have enumerated. While the unwritten traditions are so many, and their bearing on "the mystery of godliness"[578] is so important, can they refuse to

---

[577] *Vide* Titles to Pss. 6 and 12. in A.V. "upon Sheminith," marg. "the eighth." LXX ὑπὲρ τῆς ὀγδόης. Vulg. *pro octava*. On various explanations of the Hebrew word *vide* Dict Bib. S. V. where Dr. Aldis Wright inclines to the view that it is a tune or key, and that the Hebrews were not acquainted with the octave.

[578] 1 Tim. 3:16.

allow us a single word which has come down to us from the Fathers—which we found, derived from untutored custom, abiding in unperverted churches—a word for which the arguments are strong, and which contributes in no small degree to the completeness of the force of the mystery?

The force of both expressions has now been explained. I will proceed to state once more wherein they agree and wherein they differ from one another—not that they are opposed in mutual antagonism, but that each contributes its own meaning to true religion. The preposition "*in*" states the truth rather relatively to ourselves; while "*with*" proclaims the fellowship of the Spirit with God. Wherefore we use both words, by the one expressing the dignity of the Spirit; by the other announcing the grace that is with us. Thus we ascribe glory to God both "in" the Spirit, and "with" the Spirit; and herein it is not our word that we use, but we follow the teaching of the Lord as we might a fixed rule, and transfer His word to things connected and closely related, and of which the conjunction in the mysteries is necessary. We have deemed ourselves under a necessary obligation to combine in our confession of the faith Him who is numbered with Them at Baptism, and we have treated the confession of the faith as the origin and parent of the doxology. What, then, is to be done? They must now instruct us either not to baptize as we have received, or not to believe as we were baptized, or not to ascribe glory as we have believed. Let any man prove if he can that the relation of sequence in these acts is not necessary and unbroken; or let any man deny if he can that innovation here must mean ruin everywhere. Yet they never stop dinning in our ears that the ascription of glory "*with*" the Holy Spirit is unauthorized and unscriptural and the like. We have stated that so far as the sense goes it is the same to say, "glory be to the Father and to the Son *and* to the Holy Ghost," and "glory be to the Father and to the Son *with* the Holy Ghost." It is impossible for anyone to reject or cancel the syllable "and," which is derived from the very words of our Lord, and there is nothing to hinder the acceptance of its equivalent. What amount of difference and similarity there is between the two we have already shown. And our argument is confirmed by the fact that the Apostle uses either word indifferently—saying at one time "in the name of the Lord Jesus and by the Spirit of our God;"[579] at another "when ye are gathered together, and my Spirit, with the power of our Lord Jesus,"[580] with no idea that it makes any difference to the connection of the names whether he use the conjunction or the preposition.

Chapter Twenty-Eight

That our opponents refuse to concede in the case of the Spirit the terms which Scripture uses in the case of men, as reigning together with Christ.

BUT LET US SEE if we can bethink us of any defense of this usage of our fathers; for they who first originated the expression are more open to blame than we ourselves. Paul in his Letter to the Colossians says, "And you, being dead in your sins and the uncircumcision...hath He quickened together with"[581] Christ. Did then God give to a whole people and to the Church the boon of the life with Christ, and yet the life with Christ does not belong to the Holy Spirit? But if this is impious even to think of, is it not rightly reverent so to make our confession, as They are by nature in close conjunction? Furthermore, what boundless lack of sensibility does it not show in these men to confess that the Saints are with Christ, (if, as we know is the case, Paul, on becoming absent from the body, is present with the Lord,[582] and, after departing, is with Christ[583]) and, so far as lies in their power, to refuse to allow to the Spirit to be with Christ even to the same extent as men? And Paul calls himself a "laborer together with God"[584] in the dispensation of the Gospel; will they bring an indictment for impiety against us, if we apply the term "fellow-laborer"

---

[579] 1 Cor. 6:11.
[580] 1 Cor. 5:4.
[581] Col. 2:13.
[582] Cf. 2 Cor. 5:8.
[583] Cf. Phil. 1:23.
[584] 1 Cor. 3:9.

to the Holy Spirit, through whom in every creature under heaven the Gospel bringeth forth fruit?[585] The life of them that have trusted in the Lord "is hidden," it would seem, "with Christ in God, and when Christ, who is our life, shall appear, then shall" they themselves also "appear with Him in glory;"[586] and is the Spirit of life Himself, "Who made us free from the law of sin,"[587] not with Christ, both in the secret and hidden life with Him, and in the manifestation of the glory which we expect to be manifested in the saints? We are "heirs of God and joint heirs with Christ,"[588] and is the Spirit without part or lot in the fellowship of God and of His Christ? "The Spirit itself beareth witness with our spirit that we are the children of God;"[589] and are we not to allow to the Spirit even that testimony of His fellowship with God which we have learnt from the Lord? For the height of folly is reached if we through the faith in Christ which is in the Spirit[590] hope that we shall be raised together with Him and sit together in heavenly places,[591] whenever He shall change our vile body from the natural to the spiritual,[592] and yet refuse to assign to the Spirit any share in the sitting together, or in the glory, or anything else which we have received from Him. Of all the boons of which, in accordance with the indefeasible grant of Him who has promised them, we have believed ourselves worthy, are we to allow none to the Holy Spirit, as though they were all above His dignity? It is yours according to your merit to be "ever with the Lord," and you expect to be caught up "in the clouds to meet the Lord in the air and to be ever with the Lord."[593] You declare the man who numbers and ranks the Spirit with the Father and the Son to be guilty of intolerable impiety. Can you really now deny

---

[585] Cf. Col. 1:6.
[586] Col. 3:3, 4.
[587] Rom. 8:2.
[588] Rom. 8:17.
[589] Rom. 8:16, 17. In this passage A.V. follows the neuter of the Greek original. R.V. has substituted "himself."
[590] Cf. Gal. 5:5.
[591] Cf. Eph. 2:6.
[592] Cf. Phil. 3:21, and 1 Cor. 15:44.
[593] 1 Thess. 4:17.

that the Spirit is with Christ?

I am ashamed to add the rest. You expect to be glorified together with Christ; ("if so be that we suffer with him that we may be also glorified together;"[594]) but you do not glorify the "Spirit of holiness"[595] together with Christ, as though He were not worthy to receive equal honor even with you. You hope to "reign with"[596] Christ; but you "do despite unto the Spirit of grace"[597] by assigning Him the rank of a slave and a subordinate. And I say this not to demonstrate that so much is due to the Spirit in the ascription of glory, but to prove the unfairness of those who will not ever give so much as this, and shrink from the fellowship of the Spirit with Son and Father as from impiety. Who could touch on these things without a sigh?[598] Is it not so plain as to be within the perception even of a child that this present state of things preludes the threatened eclipse of the faith? The undeniable has become the uncertain. We profess belief in the Spirit, and then we quarrel with our own confessions. We are baptized, and begin to fight again. We call upon Him as the Prince of Life, and then despise Him as a slave like ourselves. We received Him with the Father and the Son, and we dishonor Him as a part of creation. Those who "know not what they ought to pray for,"[599] even though they be induced to utter a word of the Spirit with awe, as though coming near His dignity, yet prune down all that exceeds the exact proportion of their speech. They ought rather to bewail their weakness, in that we are powerless to express in words our gratitude for the benefits which we are actually receiving; for He "passes all understanding,"[600] and convicts speech of its natural inability even to approach His dignity in the least degree; as it is written in the Book of Wisdom,[601] "Exalt Him as much as you can, for even yet will He far exceed; and when you exalt

---

[594] Rom. 8:17.
[595] Rom. 1:4.
[596] 2 Tim. 2:12.
[597] Heb. 10:29.
[598] Cf. Verg., *Æn.* ii. *Quis talia fando...temperet a lacrymis?*
[599] Rom. 8:26.
[600] Phil. 4:7.
[601] *i.e.* of Jesus the Son of Sirach, or Ecclus. 43:30.

Him put forth all your strength, and be not weary, for you can never go far enough." Verily terrible is the account to be given for words of this kind by you who have heard from God who cannot lie that for blasphemy against the Holy Ghost there is no forgiveness.[602]

CHAPTER TWENTY-NINE

Enumeration of the illustrious men in the Church who in their writings have used the word "with."

IN ANSWER TO THE objection that the doxology in the form "with the Spirit" has no written authority, we maintain that if there is no other instance of that which is unwritten, then this must not be received. But if the greater number of our mysteries are admitted into our constitution without written authority, then, in company with the many others, let us receive this one. For I hold it apostolic to abide also by the unwritten traditions. "I praise you," it is said, "that ye remember me in all things, and keep the ordinances as I delivered them to you;"[603] and "Hold fast the traditions which ye have been taught whether by word, or our Epistle."[604] One of these traditions is the practice which is now before us, which they who ordained from the beginning, rooted firmly in the churches, delivering it to their successors, and its use through long custom advances pace by pace with time. If, as in a Court of Law, we were at a loss for documentary evidence, but were able to bring before you a large number of witnesses, would you not give your vote for our acquittal? I think so; for "at the mouth of two or three witnesses shall the matter be established."[605] And if we could prove clearly to you that a long period of time was in our favor, should we not have seemed to you to urge with reason that this suit ought not to be brought into court against us? For ancient dogmas inspire a certain sense of awe, venerable as they

---

[602] Luke 12:10.
[603] 1 Cor. 11:2.
[604] 2 Thess. 2:15.
[605] Deut. 19:15.

are with a hoary antiquity. I will therefore give you a list of the supporters of the word (and the time too must be taken into account in relation to what passes unquestioned). For it did not originate with us. How could it? We, in comparison with the time during which this word has been in vogue, are, to use the words of Job, "but of yesterday."[606] I myself, if I must speak of what concerns me individually, cherish this phrase as a legacy left me by my fathers. It was delivered to me by one[607] who spent a long life in the service of God, and by him I was both baptized, and admitted to the ministry of the church. While examining, so far as I could, if any of the blessed men of old used the words to which objection is now made, I found many worthy of credit both on account of their early date, and also a characteristic in which they are unlike the men of today—because of the exactness of their knowledge. Of these some coupled the word in the doxology by the preposition, others by the conjunction, but were in no case supposed to be acting divergently—at least so far as the right sense of true religion is concerned.

There is the famous Irenæus,[608] and Clement of Rome;[609] Dionysius of Rome,[610] and, strange to say, Dionysius of Alexandria, in his second Letter to his namesake, on "Conviction and Defense," so concludes. I will give you his very words. "Following all these, we, too, since we have received from the presbyters who were before us a form and rule, offering thanksgiving in the same terms with them, thus conclude our Letter to you. To God the Father and the Son our Lord Jesus Christ, with the Holy Ghost, glory and might for ever and ever; amen." And no one can say that this passage has been altered. He would not have so persistently stated that he had received a form and rule if he had said "*in* the Spirit." For of this phrase the use is

---

[606] Job 8:9.

[607] *i.e.* Dianius, bp. of the Cappadocian Cæsarea, who baptized St. Basil c. 357 on his return from Athens, and ordained him Reader. He was a waverer, and signed the creed of Ariminum in 359; Basil consequently left him, but speaks reverentially of him in Ep. 51.

[608] † c. 200.

[609] † 100.

[610] † 269.

abundant: it was the use of *"with"* which required defense. Dionysius moreover in the middle of his treatise thus writes in opposition to the Sabellians, "If by the hypostases being three they say that they are divided, there are three, though they like it not. Else let them destroy the divine Trinity altogether." And again: "most divine on this account after the Unity is the Trinity."[611] Clement, in more primitive fashion, writes, "God lives, and the Lord Jesus Christ, and the Holy Ghost."[612] And now let us hear how Irenæus, who lived near the times of the Apostles, mentions the Spirit in his work "Against the Heresies."[613] "The Apostle rightly calls *carnal* them that are unbridled and carried away to their own desires, having no desire for the Holy Spirit,"[614] and in another passage Irenæus says, "The Apostle exclaimed that flesh and blood cannot inherit the kingdom of the heavens lest we, being without share in the divine Spirit, fall short of the kingdom of the heavens." If anyone thinks Eusebius of Palestine[615] worthy of credit on account of his wide experience, I point further to the very words he uses in discussing questions concerning the polygamy of the ancients. Stirring up himself to his work, he writes "invoking the holy God of the Prophets, the Author of light, through our Savior Je-

---

[611] Dionysius was Patriarch of Alexandria A.D. 247–265. Basil's "strange to say" is of a piece with the view of Dionysius' heretical tendencies expressed in Letter ix. *q.v.* Athanasius, however, (*De Sent. Dionysii*) was satisfied as to the orthodoxy of his predecessor. Bp. Westcott (*Dict. C. Biog.* i. 851) quotes Lumper (*Hist. Pat.* xii. 86) as supposing that Basil's charge against Dionysius of sowing the seeds of the Anomœan heresy was due to imperfect acquaintance with his writings. In Letter clxxxviii. Basil calls him "the Great," which implies general approval.

[612] Clem. Rom., *Ep. ad Cor.* lviii. Bp. Lightfoot's *Ap. Fathers*, Pt. I. ii. 169.

[613] Irenæus is near the Apostles in close connexion, as well as in time, through his personal knowledge of Polycarp. *Vide*his *Ep. to Florinus*quoted in Euseb., *Ecc. Hist.* v. 20. In his work *On the Ogdoad*, quoted in the same chapter, Irenæus says of himself that he τὴν πρωτὴν τῶν Ἀποστολῶν κατειληφέναι την διαδοχήν "had himself had the nearest succession of the Apostles."

[614] The reference is presumably to 1 Cor. 2:11 and 3:1.

[615] *i.e.*Eusebius of Cæsarea, the historian, so called to distinguish him from his namesake of Nicomedia. Cf. Theodoret, *Ecc. Hist.* i. 1. The work is not extant. It may be that mentioned by Eusebius in his Præp. Evang. vii. 8, 20 under the title of περὶ τῆς τῶν παλαιῶν ἀνδρῶν πολυπαιδίας.

sus Christ, with the Holy Spirit."

Origen, too, in many of his expositions of the Psalms, we find using the form of doxology *"with* the Holy Ghost." The opinions which he held concerning the Spirit were not always and everywhere sound; nevertheless, in many passages even he himself reverently recognizes the force of established usage, and expresses himself concerning the Spirit in terms consistent with true religion. It is, if I am not mistaken, in the Sixth[616] Book of his *Commentary on the Gospel of St. John* that he distinctly makes the Spirit an object of worship. His words are— "The washing or water is a symbol of the cleaning of the soul which is washed clean of all filth that comes of wickedness;[617] but none the less is it also by itself, to him who yields himself to the God-head of the adorable Trinity, through the power of the invocations, the origin and source of blessings." And again, in his *Exposition of the Epistle to the Romans* "the holy powers," he says, "are able to receive the Only-begotten, and the Godhead of the Holy Spirit." Thus I apprehend, the powerful influence of tradition frequently impels men to express themselves in terms contradictory to their own opinions.[618] Moreover

---

[616] The quotation is from the *Eighth* Book.

[617] Cf. 1 Pet. 3:21.

[618] As to Origen's unorthodoxy concerning the Holy Spirit St. Basil may have had in his mind such a passage as the following from the First Book of the *De Principiis*, extant in the original in Justinian, *Ep. ad Mennam*. Migne, Pat. Gr. xi. p. 150. ὅτι ὁ μὲν θεὸς καὶ πατὴρ συνέχων τὰ πάντα φθάνει εἰς εκαστον τῶν ὄντων μεταδιδοὺς ἑκάστῳ ἀπὸ τοῦ ἰδίου τὸ εἶναι· ὧν γάρ ἐστιν· ἐλάττων δὲ παρὰ τὸν πατέρα ὁ Υἱός φθάνει ἐπὶ μόνα τὰ λογικά· δεύτερος γάρ ἐστι τοῦ πατρός· ἔτι δὲ ἧττον τὸ πνεῦμα τὸ ἅγιον ἐπὶ μόνους τοὺς ἁγίους διικνούμενον· ὥστε κατὰ τοῦτο μείζων ἡ δύναμις τοῦ Πατρὸς παρὰ τὸν Υἱόν καὶ τὸ πνεῦμα τὸ ἅγιον πλείων δὲ ἡ τοῦ Υἱοῦ παρὰ τὸ πνεῦμα τὸ ἅγιον The work does not even exist as a whole in the translation of Rufinus, who omitted portions, and St. Jerome thought that Rufinus had misrepresented it. Photius (*Biblioth. cod.* viii.) says that Origen, in asserting in this work that the Son was made by the Father and the Spirit by the Son, is most blasphemous. Bp. Harold Browne, however (*Exposition of the xxxix. Art.* p. 113, n. 1), is of opinion that if Rufinus fairly translated the following passage, Origen cannot have been fairly charged with heresy concerning the Holy Ghost: "*Ne quis sane existimet nos ex eo quod diximus Spiritum sanctum solis sanctis præstari. Patris vero et Filii beneficia vel inoperationes pervenire ad bonos et malos, justos et injustos, prætulisse per hoc Patri et Filio Spiritum Sanctum, vel majorem ejus per hoc asserere dignitatem; quod utique val-*

this form of the doxology was not unknown even to Africanus the historian. In the Fifth Book of his *Epitome of the Times* he says, "we who know the weight of those terms, and are not ignorant of the grace of faith, render thanks to the Father, who bestowed on us His own creatures, Jesus Christ, the Savior of the world and our Lord, to whom be glory and majesty with the Holy Ghost, forever."[619] The rest of the passages may peradventure be viewed with suspicion; or may really have been altered, and the fact of their having been tampered with will be difficult to detect because the difference consists in a single syllable. Those however which I have quoted at length are out of the reach of any dishonest manipulation, and can easily be verified from the actual works.

I will now adduce another piece of evidence which might perhaps seem insignificant, but because of its antiquity must in nowise be omitted by a defendant who is indicted on a charge of innovation. It seemed fitting to our fathers not to receive the gift of the light at eventide in silence, but, on its appearing, immediately to give thanks. Who was the author of these words of thanksgiving at the lighting of the lamps, we are not able to say. The people, however, utter the ancient form, and no one has ever reckoned guilty of impiety those who say, "We praise Father, Son, and God's Holy Spirit."[620] And if anyone

---

de inconsequens est. Proprietatem namque gratiæ ejus operisque descripsimus. Porro autem nihil in Trinitate majus minusve dicendum est, quum unius Divinitatis Fons verbo ac ratione sua teneat universa, spiritu vero oris sui quæ digna sunt, sanctificatione sanctificet, sicut in Psalmo scriptum est verbo domini cœli firmati sunt et spiritu oris ejus omnis virtus eorum." *De Princ.* I. iii. 7. On the obligations of both Basil and Gregory of Nazianzus to Origen, cf. Socrates iv. 26.

[619] Of the chief writings of Julius Africanus (called Sextus Africanus by Suidas), who wrote at Emmaus and Alexandria c. 220, only fragments remain. A *Letter to Origen* is complete. His principal work was a *Chronicon* from the Creation to A.D. 221, in Five Books. Of this Dr. Salmon (*D.C.B.* i. 56) thinks the doxology quoted by Basil was the conclusion.

[620] Ps. 140 (LXX) was called ὁ ἐπιλύχνιος ψαλμός (*Ap. Const.* viii. 35). In the Vespers of the Eastern Church an evening hymn is sung, translated in *D.C.A.* i. 634, "Joyful Light of the holy glory of the immortal Father, the heavenly, the holy, the blessed Jesus Christ, we having come to the setting of the sun and beholding the evening light, praise God, Father, Son, and Holy Ghost. It is meet

knows the Hymn of Athenogenes,[621] which, as he was hurrying on to his perfecting by fire, he left as a kind of farewell gift[622] to his friends, he knows the mind of the martyrs as to the Spirit. On this head I shall say no more.

But where shall I rank the great Gregory,[623] and the words uttered by him? Shall we not place among Apostles and Prophets a man who walked by the same Spirit as they;[624] who never through all his days diverged from the footprints of the saints; who maintained, as long as he lived, the exact principles of evangelical citizenship? I am sure that we shall do the truth a wrong if we refuse to number that soul with the people of God, shining as it did like a beacon in the Church of God; for by the fellow-working of the Spirit the power which he had over demons was tremendous, and so gifted was he with the grace of the word "for obedience to the faith among...the nations,"[625] that, although only seventeen Christians were handed over to him, he brought the whole people alike in town and country through knowledge to God. He too by Christ's mighty name commanded even rivers to change their course,[626] and caused a lake, which afforded a ground of quarrel to some covetous brethren, to dry up.[627] Moreover

---

at all times that thou shouldest be hymned with auspicious voices, Son of God, Giver of Life: wherefore the world glorifieth thee."

[621] Identified by some with two early hymns, Δόξα ἐν ὑψίστοις, and φῶς ἱλαρόν.

[622] The MSS. vary between ἐξιτήριον andἀλεξιτήριον, farewell gift and amulet or charm. In *Ep.* cciii. 299 Basil says that our Lord gave His disciples peace as an ἐξιτήριον δῶρον, using the word, but in conjunction with δῶρον. Greg. Naz.,*Orat.* xiv. 223 speaks of our Lord leaving peace "ὥσπερ ἄλλο τι ἐξιτήριον."

[623] *i.e.* Gregory, bishop of Neocæsarea, known as Gregorius Thaumaturgus, or Gregory the Wonder-worker. To the modern reader "Gregory the Great" more naturally suggests Gregory of Nazianzus, but this he hardly was to his friend and contemporary, though the title had accrued to him by the time of the accepted Ephesine Council in 431 (*vide* Labbe, vol. iv. p. 1192) Gregory the Wonder-worker, † c. 270.

[624] 2 Cor. 12:18.

[625] Rom. 1:5.

[626] *e.g.* according to the legend, the Lycus. Cf. Newman, *Essays on Miracles*, p. 267.

[627] The story is told by Gregory of Nyssa, *Life of Greg. Thaum.* Migne xlvi.

his predictions of things to come were such as in no wise to fall short of those of the great prophets. To recount all his wonderful works in detail would be too long a task. By the superabundance of gifts, wrought in him by the Spirit in all power and in signs and in marvels, he was styled a second Moses by the very enemies of the Church. Thus, in all that he through grace accomplished, alike by word and deed, a light seemed ever to be shining, token of the heavenly power from the unseen which followed him. To this day he is a great object of admiration to the people of his own neighborhood, and his memory, established in the churches ever fresh and green, is not dulled by length of time. Thus not a practice, not a word, not a mystic rite has been added to the Church besides what he bequeathed to it. Hence truly on account of the antiquity of their institution many of their ceremonies appear to be defective.[628] For his successors in the administration of the Churches could not endure to accept any subsequent discovery in addition to what had had his sanction. Now one of the institutions of Gregory is the very form of the doxology to which objection is now made, preserved by the Church on the authority of his tradition; a statement which may be verified without much trouble by anyone who likes to make a short journey. That our Firmilian held this belief is testified by the writings which he has left.[629] The contemporaries also of the illustrious Meletius say that he was of this opinion. But why quote ancient authorities? Now in the East are not the maintainers of true religion known chiefly by this one term, and separated from their adversaries as by a watchword? I have heard from a certain Mesopotamian, a man at once well skilled in the language and of unperverted opinions, that by the usage of his country it is impossible for anyone, even though he may wish to do so, to express himself in any other way, and that they are compelled by the id-

---

926–930.

[628] The Neocæsareans appear to have entertained a Puritan objection to the antiphonal psalmody becoming general in the Church in the time of Basil. Cf. *Ep.* ccvii.

[629] Firmilian, like Gregory the Wonder-worker, a pupil of Origen, was bishop of Cæsarea from before A.D. 232 (Euseb. vi. 26) to 272 (Euseb. vii. 30). By some his death at Tarsus is placed in 264 or 5.

iom of their mother tongue to offer the doxology by the syllable "and," or, I should more accurately say, by their equivalent expressions. We Cappadocians, too, so speak in the dialect of our country, the Spirit having so early as the division of tongues foreseen the utility of the phrase. And what of the whole West, almost from Illyricum to the boundaries of our world? Does it not support this word?

How then can I be an innovator and creator of new terms, when I adduce as originators and champions of the word whole nations, cities, custom going back beyond the memory of man, men who were pillars of the church and conspicuous for all knowledge and spiritual power? For this cause this banded array of foes is set in motion against me, and town and village and remotest regions are full of my calumniators. Sad and painful are these things to them that seek for peace, but great is the reward of patience for sufferings endured for the Faith's sake. So besides these let sword flash, let axe be whetted, let fire burn fiercer than that of Babylon, let every instrument of torture be set in motion against me. To me nothing is more fearful than failure to fear the threats which the Lord has directed against them that blaspheme the Spirit.[630] Kindly readers will find a satisfactory defense in what I have said, that I accept a phrase so dear and so familiar to the saints, and confirmed by usage so long, inasmuch as, from the day when the Gospel was first preached up to our own time, it is shown to have been admitted to all full rights within the churches, and, what is of greatest moment, to have been accepted as bearing a sense in accordance with holiness and true religion. But before the great tribunal what have I prepared to say in my defense? This; that I was in the first place led to the glory of the Spirit by the honor conferred by the Lord in associating Him with Himself and with His Father at baptism;[631] and secondly by the introduction of each of us to the knowledge of God by such an initiation; and above all by the fear of the threatened punishment shutting out the thought of all indignity and unworthy conception. But our opponents, what will they say?

---

[630] Cf. Matt. 12:31.
[631] Matt. 28:19.

After showing neither reverence for the Lord's honor[632] nor fear of His threats, what kind of defense will they have for their blasphemy? It is for them to make up their mind about their own action or even now to change it. For my own part I would pray most earnestly that the good God will make His peace rule in the hearts of all,[633] so that these men who are swollen with pride and set in battle array against us may be calmed by the Spirit of meekness and of love; and that if they have become utterly savage, and are in an untamable state, He will grant to us at least to bear with long suffering all that we have to bear at their hands. In short "to them that have in themselves the sentence of death,"[634] it is not suffering for the sake of the Faith which is painful; what is hard to bear is to fail to fight its battle. The athlete does not so much complain of being wounded in the struggle as of not being able even to secure admission into the stadium. Or perhaps this was the time for silence spoken of by Solomon the wise.[635] For, when life is buffeted by so fierce a storm that all the intelligence of those who are instructed in the word is filled with the deceit of false reasoning and confounded, like an eye filled with dust, when men are stunned by strange and awful noises, when all the world is shaken and everything tottering to its fall, what profits it to cry, as I am really crying, to the wind?

CHAPTER THIRTY

Exposition of the present state of the Churches.

TO WHAT THEN SHALL I liken our present condition? It may be compared, I think, to some naval battle which has arisen out of time old quarrels, and is fought by men who cherish a

---

[632] The Benedictine version for τὰς τιμὰς τοῦ κυρίου is *honorem quem Dominus tribuit Spiritui*. The reading of one MS. is τὰς φωνάς. There is authority for either sense of the genitive with τιμή, i.e. the honors *due to the Lord* or *paid by the Lord*.
[633] Cf. Col. 3:15.
[634] 2 Cor. 1:9.
[635] Eccl. 3:7.

deadly hate against one another, of long experience in naval warfare, and eager for the fight. Look, I beg you, at the picture thus raised before your eyes. See the rival fleets rushing in dread array to the attack. With a burst of uncontrollable fury they engage and fight it out. Fancy, if you like, the ships driven to and fro by a raging tempest, while thick darkness falls from the clouds and blackens all the scenes so that watchwords are indistinguishable in the confusion, and all distinction between friend and foe is lost. To fill up the details of the imaginary picture, suppose the sea swollen with billows and whirled up from the deep, while a vehement torrent of rain pours down from the clouds and the terrible waves rise high. From every quarter of heaven the winds beat upon one point, where both the fleets are dashed one against the other. Of the combatants some are turning traitors; some are deserting in the very thick of the fight; some have at one and the same moment to urge on their boats, all beaten by the gale, and to advance against their assailants. Jealousy of authority and the lust of individual mastery splits the sailors into parties which deal mutual death to one another. Think, besides all this, of the confused and unmeaning roar sounding over all the sea, from howling winds, from crashing vessels, from boiling surf, from the yells of the combatants as they express their varying emotions in every kind of noise, so that not a word from admiral or pilot can be heard. The disorder and confusion is tremendous, for the extremity of misfortune, when life is despaired of, gives men license for every kind of wickedness. Suppose, too, that the men are all smitten with the incurable plague of mad love of glory, so that they do not cease from their struggle each to get the better of the other, while their ship is actually settling down into the deep.

Turn now I beg you from this figurative description to the unhappy reality. Did it not at one time[636] appear that the Arian schism, after its separation into a sect opposed to the Church of God, stood itself alone in hostile array? But when the attitude of our foes against us was changed from one of long standing and bitter strife to one of open

---

[636] *i.e.* after the condemnation of Arius at Nicæa.

warfare, then, as is well known, the war was split up in more ways than I can tell into many subdivisions, so that all men were stirred to a state of inveterate hatred alike by common party spirit and individual suspicion.[637] But what storm at sea was ever so fierce and wild as this tempest of the Churches? In it every landmark of the Fathers has been moved; every foundation, every bulwark of opinion has been shaken:

---

[637] In Ep. ccxlii. written in 376, St. Basil says: "This is the thirteenth year since the outbreak of the war of heretics against us." 363 is the date of the Acacian Council of Antioch; 364 of the accession of Valens and Valentian, of the Semi-Arian Synod of Lampsacus, and of St. Basil's ordination to the priesthood and book against Eunomius. On the propagation by scission and innumerable subdivisions of Arianism Cannon Bright writes:

The extraordinary versatility, the argumentative subtlety, and the too frequent profanity of Arianism are matters of which a few lines can give no idea. But it is necessary, in even the briefest notice of this long-lived heresy, to remark on the contrast between its changeable inventiveness and the simple steadfastness of Catholic doctrine. On the one side, some twenty different creeds (of which several, however, were rather negatively than positively heterodox) and three main sects, the Semi-Arians, with their formula of Homoiousion, *i.e.* the Son is like in essence to the Father; the Acacians, vaguely calling Him like (Homoion); the Aetians, boldly calling Him unlike, as much as to say He is in no sense Divine. On the other side, the Church with the Nicene Creed, confessing Him as Homoousion, 'of one essence with the Father,' meaning thereby, as her great champion repeatedly bore witness, to secure belief in the reality of the Divine Sonship, and therefore in the real Deity, as distinguished from the titular deity which was so freely conceded to Him by the Arians." Cannon Bright, *St. Leo on the Incarnation*, p. 140 Socrates (ii. 41), pausing at 360, enumerates, after Nicæa:

1. 1st of Antioch (omitted the ὁμοούσιον, a.d. 341).
2. 2nd of Antioch (omitted the ὁμοούσιον, a.d. 341).
3. The Creed brought to Constans in Gaul by Narcissus and other Arians in 342.
4. The Creed "sent by Eudoxius of Germanicia into Italy," *i.e.* the "Macrostich," or "Lengthy Creed," rejected at Milan in 346.
5. The 1st Creed of Sirmium; *i.e.* the Macrostich with 26 additional clauses, 351.
6. The 2nd Sirmian Creed. The "manifesto;" called by Athanasius (*De Synod.* 28) "the blasphemy," 357.
7. The 3rd Sirmian, or "dated Creed," in the consulship of Flavius Eusebius and Hypatius, May 22d, 359.
8. The Acacian Creed of Seleucia, 359.
9. The Creed of Ariminum adopted at Constantinople, as revised at Nike.

everything buoyed up on the unsound is dashed about and shaken down. We attack one another. We are overthrown by one another. If our enemy is not the first to strike us, we are wounded by the comrade at our side. If a foeman is stricken and falls, his fellow soldier tramples him down. There is at least this bond of union between us that we hate our common foes, but no sooner have the enemy gone by than we find enemies in one another. And who could make a complete list of all the wrecks? Some have gone to the bottom on the attack of the enemy, some through the unsuspected treachery of their allies, some from the blundering of their own officers. We see, as it were, whole churches, crews and all, dashed and shattered upon the sunken reefs of disingenuous heresy, while others of the enemies of the Spirit[638] of Salvation have seized the helm and made shipwreck of the faith.[639] And then the disturbances wrought by the princes of the world[640] have caused the downfall of the people with a violence unmatched by that of hurricane or whirlwind. The luminaries of the world, which God set to give light to the souls of the people, have been driven from their homes, and a darkness verily gloomy and disheartening has settled on the Churches.[641] The terror of universal ruin is already imminent, and yet their mutual rivalry is so unbounded as to blunt all sense of danger. Individual hatred is of more importance than the general and common warfare, for men by whom the immediate gratification of ambition is esteemed more highly than the rewards that await us in a time to come, prefer the glory of getting the better of their opponents to securing the common welfare of mankind. So all men alike, each

---

[638] On the authority of the MS. of the tenth century at Paris, called by the Ben. Editors *Regius Secundus*, they read for πνεύματος πάθους, denying πνευματος to be consistent with the style and practice of Basil, who they say, never uses the epithet σωτήριος of the Spirit. Mr. C.F.H. Johnston notes that St. Basil "always attributes the saving efficacy of Baptism to the presence of the Spirit, and here applies the word to Him." In § 35, we have τὸ σωτήριον βάπτισυα.

[639] 1 Tim. 1:19.

[640] 1 Cor. 2:6.

[641] Among the bishops exiled during the persecution of Valens were Meletius of Antioch, Eusebius of Samosata, Pelagius of Laodicea, and Barses of Edessa. Cf. Theodoret, *Hist. Ecc.* iv. 12 *sq*. Cf. Ep. 195.

as best he can, lift the hand of murder against one another. Harsh rises the cry of the combatants encountering one another in dispute; already all the Church is almost full of the inarticulate screams, the unintelligible noises, rising from the ceaseless agitations that divert the right rule of the doctrine of true religion, now in the direction of excess, now in that of defect. On the one hand are they who confound the Persons and are carried away into Judaism;[642] on the other hand are they that, through the opposition of the natures, pass into heathenism.[643] Between these opposite parties inspired Scripture is powerless to mediate; the traditions of the apostles cannot suggest terms of arbitration. Plain speaking is fatal to friendship, and disagreement in opinion all the ground that is wanted for a quarrel. No oaths of confederacy are so efficacious in keeping men true to sedition as their likeness in error. Everyone is a theologian though he has his soul branded with more spots than can be counted. The result is that innovators find a plentiful supply of men ripe for faction, while self-appointed scions of the house of place-hunters[644] reject the government[645] of the Holy Spirit and divide the chief dignities of the Churches. The institutions of the Gospel have now everywhere been thrown into confusion by want of discipline; there is an indescribable pushing for the chief places while every self-advertiser tries to force himself into high office. The result of this lust for ordering is that our

---

[642] The identification of an unsound Monarchianism with Judaism is illustrated in the *1st Apology of Justin Martyr*, e.g. in § lxxxiii. (Reeves' Trans.). "The Jews, therefore, for maintaining that it was the Father of the Universe who had the conference with Moses, when it was the very Son of God who had it, and who is styled both Angel and Apostle, are justly accused by the prophetic spirit and Christ Himself, for knowing neither the Father nor the Son; for they who affirm the Son to be the Father are guilty of not knowing the Father, and likewise of being ignorant that the Father of the Universe has a Son, who, being the Logos and First-begotten of God, is God."

[643] *i.e.* the Arians, whose various ramifications all originated in a probably well-meant attempt to reconcile the principles of Christianity with what was best in the old philosophy, and a failure to see that the ditheism of Arianism was of a piece with polytheism.

[644] The word σπουδαρχίδης is a comic patronymic of σπουδάρχης, a place-hunter, occurring in *the Acharnians* of Aristophanes, 595.

[645] οἰκονομία.

people are in a state of wild confusion for lack of being ordered;[646] the exhortations of those in authority are rendered wholly purposeless and void, because there is not a man but, out of his ignorant impudence, thinks that it is just as much his duty to give orders to other people, as it is to obey anyone else.

So, since no human voice is strong enough to be heard in such a disturbance, I reckon silence more profitable than speech, for if there is any truth in the words of the Preacher, "The words of wise men are heard in quiet,"[647] in the present condition of things any discussion of them must be anything but becoming. I am moreover restrained by the Prophet's saying, "Therefore the prudent shall keep silence in that time, for it is an evil time,"[648] a time when some trip up their neighbors' heels, some stamp on a man when he is down, and others clap their hands with joy, but there is not one to feel for the fallen and hold out a helping hand, although according to the ancient law he is not uncondemned, who passes by even his enemy's beast of burden fallen under his load.[649] This is not the state of things now. Why not? The love of many has waxed cold;[650] brotherly concord is destroyed, the very name of unity is ignored, brotherly admonitions are heard no more, nowhere is there Christian pity, nowhere falls the tear of sympathy. Now there is no one to receive "the weak in faith,"[651] but mutual hatred has blazed so high among fellow clansmen that they are more delighted at a neighbor's fall than at their own success. Just as in a plague, men of the most regular lives suffer from the same sickness as the rest, because they catch the disease by communication with the infected, so nowadays by the evil rivalry which possesses our souls we are carried away to an emulation in wickedness, and are all of us each as bad as the others. Hence merciless and sour sit the judges of the erring; unfeeling and hostile are the critics of the well-disposed.

---

[646] ἀναρχία ἀπὸ φιλαρχίας.
[647] Eccl. 9:17.
[648] Amos 5:13.
[649] Ezek. 23:5.
[650] Matt. 24:12.
[651] Rom. 14:1.

And to such a depth is this evil rooted among us that we have become more brutish than the brutes; they do at least herd with their fellows, but our most savage warfare is with our own people.

For all these reasons I ought to have kept silence, but I was drawn in the other direction by love, which "seeketh not her own,"[652] and desires to overcome every difficulty put in her way by time and circumstance. I was taught too by the children at Babylon,[653] that, when there is no one to support the cause of true religion, we ought alone and all unaided to do our duty. They from out of the midst of the flame lifted up their voices in hymns and praise to God, reeking not of the host that set the truth at naught, but sufficient, three only that they were, with one another. Wherefore we too are undismayed at the cloud of our enemies, and, resting our hope on the aid of the Spirit, have, with all boldness, proclaimed the truth. Had I not so done, it would truly have been terrible that the blasphemers of the Spirit should so easily be emboldened in their attack upon true religion, and that we, with so mighty an ally and supporter at our side, should shrink from the service of that doctrine, which by the tradition of the Fathers has been preserved by an unbroken sequence of memory to our own day. A further powerful incentive to my undertaking was the warm fervor of your "love unfeigned,"[654] and the seriousness and taciturnity of your disposition; a guarantee that you would not publish what I was about to say to all the world—not because it would not be worth making known, but to avoid casting pearls before swine.[655] My task is now done. If you find what I have said satisfactory, let this make an end to our discussion of these matters. If you think any point requires further elucidation, pray do not hesitate to pursue the investigation with all diligence, and to add to your information by putting any uncontroversial question. Either through me or through others the Lord will grant full explanation on matters which have yet to be made clear, according to the knowledge supplied to the worthy by the Holy Spirit. Amen.

---

[652] 1 Cor. 13:5.
[653] Dan. 3:12 *seqq*.
[654] Rom. 12:9 and 2 Cor. 6:6.
[655] Matt. 7:6.

SECTION TWO
Letters to Amphilochius
by Saint Basil of Caesarea

TRANSLATED WITH NOTES BY
The Rev. Blomfield Jackson, M.A.
Vicar of Saint Bartholomew's, Moor Lane, and Fellow of King's College, London

Letter 150[1]
TO AMPHILOCHIUS IN THE NAME OF HERACLIDAS[2]

I REMEMBER OUR OLD conversations with one another, and am forgetful neither of what I said, nor of what you said. And now public life has no hold upon me. For although I am the same in heart and have not yet put off the old man, nevertheless, outwardly and by withdrawing myself far from worldly life, I seem already to have begun to tread the way of Christian conversation. I sit apart, like men who are on the point of embarking on the deep, looking out at what is before me. Mariners, indeed, need winds to make their voyage prosperous; I on the other hand want a guide to take me by the hand and conduct me safely through life's bitter waves. I feel that I need first a curb for my young manhood, and then pricks to drive me to the course of piety. Both these seem to be provided by reason, which at one time disciplines my unruliness of soul, and at another time my sluggishness. Again, I want other remedies that I may wash off the impurity of habit. You know how, long accustomed as I was to the Forum, I am lavish of words, and do not guard myself against the thoughts put into my mind by the evil one. I am the servant too of honor, and cannot easily give up thinking great things of myself. Against all this I feel that I need a great instructor. Then, further, I conclude that it is of no small importance, nor of benefit only for a

---

[1] Placed in 373.
[2] Amphilochius, not yet consecrated to Iconium, had abandoned his profession as an advocate, and was living in retirement at Ozizala, a place not far from Nazianzus, the see of his uncle Gregory, devoted to the care of his aged father, whose name he bore. Heraclidas, it appears, had also renounced the bar, and devoted himself to religious life; but did not join Amphilochius on the ground that he was living in Basil's hospital at Cæsarea. Cf. the letters of Gregory, first cousin of Amphilochius. On the relationship, see Bp. Lightfoot in D.C.B. i. p. 104, and pedigree in prolegomena.

little while, that the soul's eye should be so purged that, after being freed from all the darkness of ignorance, as though from some blinding humor, one can gaze intently on the beauty of the glory of God. All this I know very well that your wisdom is aware of; I know that you would wish that I might have someone to give me such help, and if ever God grant me to meet you I am sure that I shall learn more about what I ought to heed. For now, in my great ignorance, I can hardly even form a judgment as to what I lack. Yet I do not repent of my first impulse; my soul does not hang back from the purpose of a godly life as you have feared for me, nobly and becomingly doing everything in your power, lest, like the woman of whom I have heard the story, I should turn back and become a pillar of salt.[3] I am still, however, under the restraint of external authority; for the magistrates are seeking me like a deserter. But I am chiefly influenced by my own heart, which testifies to itself of all that I have told you.

Since you have mentioned our bond, and have announced that you mean to prosecute, you have made me laugh in this my dejection, because you are still an advocate and do not give up your shrewdness. I hold, unless, indeed, like an ignorant man, I am quite missing the truth, that there is only one way to the Lord, and that all who are journeying to Him are travelling together and walking in accordance with one "bond" of life. If this be so, wherever I go how can I be separated from you? How can I cease to live with you, and with you serve God, to Whom we have both fled for refuge? Our bodies may be separated by distance, but God's eye still doubtless looks upon us both; if indeed a life like mine is fit to be beheld by the divine eyes; for I have read somewhere in the Psalms that the eyes of the Lord are upon the righteous.[4] I do indeed pray that with you and with all that are like minded with you, I may be associated, even in body, and that night and day with you and with any other true worshipper of God I may bow my knees to our Father which is in heaven; for I know that communion in prayer brings great gain. If, as often as it is my lot to lie and groan in a different corner, I am always to be accused of lying,

---

[3] Cf. Gen. 19:26.
[4] Ps. 33:15.

I cannot contend against your argument, and already condemn myself as a liar, if with my own carelessness I have said anything which brings me under such a charge.

I was lately at Cæsarea, in order to learn what was going on there. I was unwilling to remain in the city itself, and betook myself to the neighboring hospital, that I might get there what information I wanted. According to his custom the very godly bishop visited it, and I consulted him as to the points which you had urged upon me. It is not possible for me to remember all that he said in reply; it went far beyond the limits of a letter. In sum, however, what he said about poverty was this, that the rule ought to be that everyone should limit his possessions to one garment. For one proof of this he quoted the words of John the Baptist "he that hath two coats let him impart to him that hath none;"[5] and for another our Lord's prohibition to His disciples to have two coats.[6] He further added "If thou wilt be perfect go and sell that thou hast and give to the poor."[7] He said too that the parable of the pearl bore on this point, because the merchant, who had found the pearl of great price, went away and sold all that he had and bought it; and he added too that no one ought even to permit himself the distribution of his own property, but should leave it in the hands of the person entrusted with the duty of managing the affairs of the poor; and he proved the point from the acts of the apostles,[8] because they sold their property and brought and laid it at the feet of the apostles, and by them it was distributed to each as every man had need.[9] For he said that experience was needed in order to distinguish between cases of genuine need and of mere greedy begging. For whoever gives to the afflicted gives to the Lord, and from

---

[5] Luke 3:11.

[6] Matt. 10:10.

[7] Matt. 19:21.

[8] Acts 4:35.

[9] It will be observed that St. Basil's quotation here does not quite bear out his point. There is no "by them" in Acts 4:35. "Distribution was made unto every man according as he had need." In Acts 2:45 the primitive communists are said themselves to have "parted to all men as every man had need," the responsibility of distribution being apparently retained.

the Lord shall have his reward; but he who gives to every vagabond casts to a dog, a nuisance indeed from his importunity, but deserving no pity on the ground of want.

He was moreover the first to speak shortly, as befits the importance of the subject, about some of the daily duties of life. As to this I should wish you to hear from himself, for it would not be right for me to weaken the force of his lessons. I would pray that we might visit him together, that so you might both accurately preserve in your memory what he said, and supply any omissions by your own intelligence. One thing that I do remember, out of the many which I heard, is this; that instruction how to lead the Christian life depends less on words, than on daily example. I know that, if you had not been detained by the duty of succoring your aged father, there is nothing that you would have more greatly esteemed than a meeting with the bishop, and that you would not have advised me to leave him in order to wander in deserts. Caves and rocks are always ready for us, but the help we get from our fellow man is not always at hand. If, then, you will put up with my giving you advice, you will impress on your father the desirability of his allowing you to leave him for a little while in order to meet a man who, alike from his experience of others and from his own wisdom, knows much, and is able to impart it to all who approach him.

Letter 161[10]
TO AMPHILOCHIUS ON HIS CONSECRATION AS BISHOP

BLESSED BE GOD WHO from age to age chooses them that please Him, distinguishes vessels of election, and uses them for the ministry of the Saints. Though you were trying to flee, as you confess, not from me, but from the calling you expected through me, He has netted you in the sure meshes of grace, and has brought you into the midst of Pisidia to catch men for the Lord, and draw the devil's prey from the deep into the light. You, too, may

---
[10] Placed in 374.

say as the blessed David said, "Whither shall I go from thy Spirit? or whither shall I flee from thy presence."[11] Such is the wonderful work of our loving Master. "Asses are lost"[12] that there may be a king of Israel. David, however, being an Israelite was granted to Israel; but the land which has nursed you and brought you to such a height of virtue, possesses you no longer, and sees her neighbor beautified by her own adornment. But all believers in Christ are one people; all Christ's people, although He is hailed from many regions, are one Church; and so our country is glad and rejoices at the dispensation of the Lord, and instead of thinking that she is one man the poorer, considers that through one man she has become possessed of whole Churches. Only may the Lord grant me both to see you in person, and, so long as I am parted from you, to hear of your progress in the gospel, and of the good order of your Churches.

Play the man, then, and be strong, and walk before the people whom the Most High has entrusted to your hand. Like a skillful pilot, rise in mind above every wave lifted by heretical blasts; keep the boat from being whelmed by the salt and bitter billows of false doctrine; and wait for the calm to be made by the Lord so soon as there shall have been found a voice worthy of rousing Him to rebuke the winds and the sea. If you wish to visit me, now hurried by long sickness towards the inevitable end, do not wait for an opportunity, or for the word from me. You know that to a father's heart every time is suitable to embrace a well-loved son, and that affection is stronger than words. Do not lament over a responsibility transcending your strength. If you had been destined to bear the burden unaided, it would have been not merely heavy; it would have been intolerable. But if the Lord shares the load with you, "cast all your care upon the Lord"[13] and He will Himself act. Only be exhorted ever to give heed

---

[11] Psalm 138:7 (LXX).

[12] 1 Sam. 9:3. So six mss. Editors have substituted "enemies." The letter does not exist in the *Codex Harlæanus*. Ὄνοι is supposed to mean that Faustinus and John, the predecessors of Amphilochius in the see of Iconium, were not very wise bishops. ἐχθροί might mean that they were Arian. Cf. *Letter* cxxxviii.

[13] Cf. Ps. 54:22 (LXX) and 1 Pet. 5:7.

lest you be carried away by wicked customs. Rather change all previous evil ways into good by the help of the wisdom given you by God. For Christ has sent you not to follow others, but yourself to take the lead of all who are being saved. I charge you to pray for me, that, if I am still in this life, I may be permitted to see you with your Church. If, however, it is ordained that I now depart, may I see all of you hereafter with the Lord, your Church blooming like a vine with good works, and yourself like a wise husbandman and good servant giving meat in due season to his fellow-servants and receiving the reward of a wise and trusty steward. All who are with me salute your reverence. May you be strong and joyful in the Lord. May you be preserved glorious in the graces of the Spirit and of wisdom.

Letter 176[14]

TO AMPHILOCHIUS, BISHOP OF ICONIUM[15]

GOD GRANT THAT WHEN this letter is put into your hands, it may find you in good health, quite at leisure, and as you would wish to be. For then it will not be in vain that I send you this invitation to be present at our city, to add greater dignity to the annual festival which it is the custom of our Church to hold in honor of the martyrs.[16] For be sure my most honored and dear friend, that our people here, though they have had experience of many, desire no one's presence so eagerly as they do yours; so affectionate an impression has your short intercourse with them left behind. So, then, that the Lord may be glorified, the people delighted, the martyrs honored, and that I in my old age may receive the attention due to me from my true son, do not refuse to travel to me with all speed. I will beg you too to anticipate the day of assembly, that so we may converse at leisure and may comfort one another by the interchange of spiritual gifts.

---

[14] Placed in 374.

[15] An invitation to feast of St. Eupsychius, with a request to arrive three days before the actual day of the festival, which was observed on the 7th of September. (Cf. *Letter* c. and note, and the invitation to the Pontic bishops in cclii.)

[16] *i.e.* Damas and Eupsychius.

The day is the fifth of September.[17] Come then three days beforehand in order that you may also honor with your presence the Church[18] of the Hospital. May you by the grace of the Lord be kept in good health and spirits in the Lord, praying for me and for the Church of God.

Letter 188[19]
TO AMPHILOCHIUS, CONCERNING THE CANONS[20]

"EVEN A FOOL," IT is said, "when he asks questions," is counted wise.[21] But when a wise man asks questions, he makes even a fool wise. And this, thank God, is my case, as often as I receive a letter from your industrious self. For we become more learned and wiser than we were before, merely by asking questions, because we are taught many things which we did not know; and our anxiety to answer them acts as a teacher to us. Assuredly at the present time, though I have never before paid attention to the points you raise, I have been forced to make accurate enquiry, and to turn over in my mind both whatever I have heard from the elders, and all that I have been taught in conformity with their lessons.

I. As to your enquiry about the Cathari,[22] a statement has already been made, and you have properly reminded me that it is right to follow the custom obtaining in each region, because those, who at the

---

[17] So the date stands in eight MSS. However it arose, 5th is a mistake for 7th, the day of St. Eupsychius in the Greek Kalendar.

[18] Μνήμη. The Ben. Ed. understand by this word the church erected by Basil in his hospital (Cf. *Letter* xciv.) at Cæsarea. In illustration of the use of μνήμη in this sense Du Cange cites *Act. Conc. Chalced.* i. 144, and explains it as being equivalent to *"memoria,"* i.e. *"ædes sacra in qua extat sancti alicujus sepulcrum."* Cf. *Nomocan. Photii* v. § 1. For the similar use of *"memoria,"* in Latin, Cf. Aug., *De Civ. Dei.* xxii. 10: "*Nos autem martyribus nostris non templa sicut diis sed*memorias*sicut hominibus mortuis fabricamus.*"

[19] Placed in 347 (Publisher's correction: 374).

[20] In this letter Basil replies to several questions of Amphilochius concerning the Canons, and also concerning the interpretation of some passages of Holy Scripture. Maran dates it at the end of 374.

[21] Prov. 17:28 (LXX).

[22] *i.e.* the followers of Novatian. Cf. Eusebius vi. 43. Cf. *De. Sp. Scto.* ch. x. p. 17 and note.

time gave decision on these points, held different opinions concerning their baptism. But the baptism of the Pepuzeni[23] seems to me to have no authority; and I am astonished how this can have escaped Dionysius,[24] acquainted as he was with the canons. The old authorities decided to accept that baptism which in nowise errs from the faith. Thus, they used the names of heresies, of schisms, and of unlawful congregations.[25] By *heresies* they meant men who were altogether broken off and alienated in matters relating to the actual faith; by *schisms*[26] men who had separated for some ecclesiastical reasons and questions capable of mutual solution; by *unlawful congregations* gatherings held by disorderly presbyters or bishops or by uninstructed laymen. As, for instance, if a man be convicted of crime, and prohibited from discharging ministerial functions, and then refuses to submit to the canons, but arrogates to himself episcopal and ministerial rights, and persons leave the Catholic Church and join him, this is unlawful assembly. To disagree with members of the Church about repentance, is *schism*. Instances of *heresy* are those of the Manichæans, of the Val-

---

[23] Or Pepuziani, another name for the Montanists. "Epiphanius may safely be disregarded, who, treating of the Montanists, in the 48th section of his work on heresies, treats of the Pepuziani, in the 49th, as a kindred, but distinct, sect." Dr. Salmon in *D.C.B.* iv. 303. The name is derived from Pepuza in Western Phrygia, the Montanist, or Cataphrygian, "Jerusalem." (Eus. *H.E.* v. 18.)

[24] *i.e.* of Alexandria. Jerome (*Vir. illust.* lxix.) says that he agreed with Cyprian and the African Synod on the rebaptizing of heretics. The Ben. note says: "*Videtur hac in re major auctoritas Basilio attribuenda quam Hieronymo. Plus operæ insumpserat Basilius in ea re examinanda.*"

[25] παρασυναγωγή.

[26] Archbp. Trench (*N.T. Syn.* 330) quotes Augustine (*Con. Crescon. Don.* ii. 7): "Schisma *est recens congregationis ex aliquâ sententiarum diversitate dissensio;* hæresis *autem schisma inveteratum;*" and Jerome (*Ep. ad Tit.* iii. 10): "*Inter* hæresim *et* schisma *hoc esse arbitrantur, quod* hæresis *perversum dogma habeat;* schisma *propter episcopalem dissensionem ab ecclesiâ separetur; quod quidem in principio aliquâ ex parte intelligi queat. Cæterum nullum schisma non sibi aliquam confingit hæresim, ut recte ab ecclesia recessisse videatur.*"

To these may be added Aug. (*Quæst. in Matt.* xi. 2): "*Solet autem etiam quæri schismatici quid ab hæreticis distent, et hoc inveniri quod schismaticos non fides diversa faciat sed communionis disrupta societas. Sed utrum inter zizania numerandi sint dubitari potest, magis autem videntur spicis corruptis esse similiores, vel paleis aristarum fractis, vel scissis et de segete abruptis.*"

entinians, of the Marcionites, and of these Pepuzenes; for with them there comes in at once their disagreement concerning the actual faith in God. So it seemed good to the ancient authorities to reject the baptism of heretics altogether, but to admit that of schismatics,[27] on the ground that they still belonged to the Church.

As to those who assembled in unlawful congregations, their decision was to join them again to the Church, after they had been brought to a better state by proper repentance and rebuke, and so, in many cases, when men in orders[28] had rebelled with the disorderly, to receive them on their repentance, into the same rank. Now the Pepuzeni are plainly heretical, for, by unlawfully and shamefully applying to Montanus and Priscilla the title of the Paraclete, they have blasphemed against the Holy Ghost. They are, therefore, to be condemned for ascribing divinity to men; and for outraging the Holy Ghost by comparing Him to men. They are thus also liable to eternal

---

[27] τῶν ἀποσχισάντων, ὡς ἔτι ἐκ τῆς ἐκκλησίας ὄντων.

The Ben. note is "*Quod autem addit Basilius, ut adhuc ex Ecclesia exsistentium, non idcirco addit quod schismaticos in Ecclesiæ membris numeraret. Illius verba si quis in deteriorem partem rapiat, facilis et expedita responsio, Nam sub finem hujus, canonis de Encratitis ipsis, id est, de hæreticis incarnationem et Dei singularitatem negantibus, ait sibi non jam integrum esse eos qui huic sectæ conjuncti sunt* ab Ecclesia separare, *quia duos eorum episcopos sine baptismo ac sine nova ordinatione receperat. Nemo autem suspicabitur Basilium ejusmodi hæreticos ab Ecclesia alienissimos non judicasse. Quare quidquid schismaticis tribuit, in sola baptismi societate positum est. Nam cum Cyprianus et Firmilianus schismaticos et hæreticos ita ab Ecclesia distractos crederent, ut nihil prosus ad eos ex fontibus Ecclesiæ perflueret; Basilius huic sententiæ non assentitur, et in schismaticis quia fidem Ecclesiæ retinent, vestigium quoddam agnoscit necessitudinis et societatis cum Ecclesia, ita ut valida sacramentorum administratio ab Ecclesia ad illos permanare possit. Hinc sibi integrum negat detestandos hæreticos* ab Ecclesia separare, *quorum baptisma ratum habuerat. Idem docent duo præstantissimi unitatis defensores. Optatus et Augustinus.* Quod enim scissum est, *inquit Optatus lib. iii. n. 9,* ex parte divisum est, non ex toto: cum constet merito, quia nobis et vobis ecclesiastica una est conversatio, et si hominum litigant mentes, non litigant sacramenta. *Vid. lib. iv. n. 2. Sic etiam Augustinus lib. i.* De baptismo n. 3: Itaque isti (*hæretici et schismatici*) in quibusdam rebus nobiscum sunt: in quibus autem nobiscum non sunt, ut veniendo accipiant, vel redeundo recipiant, adhortamur. *Vid. lib. iii. n. 26. Sic ex Basilio hæretici nobiscum sunt quoad baptisma.*"

[28] τοὺς ἐν βαθμῷ.

damnation, inasmuch as blasphemy against the Holy Ghost admits of no forgiveness. What ground is there, then, for the acceptance of the baptism of men who baptize into the Father and the Son and Montanus or Priscilla? For those who have not been baptized into the names delivered to us have not been baptized at all. So that, although this escaped the vigilance of the great Dionysius, we must by no means imitate his error. The absurdity of the position is obvious in a moment, and evident to all who are gifted with even a small share of reasoning capacity.

The Cathari are schismatics; but it seemed good to the ancient authorities, I mean Cyprian and our own[29] Firmilianus, to reject all these, Cathari, Encratites,[30] and Hydroparastatæ,[31] by one common condemnation, because the origin of separation arose through schism, and those who had apostatized from the Church had no longer on them the grace of the Holy Spirit, for it ceased to be imparted when the continuity was broken. The first separatists had received their ordination from the Fathers, and possessed the spiritual gift by the laying on of their hands. But they who were broken off had become laymen, and, because they are no longer able to confer on others that grace of the Holy Spirit from which they themselves are fallen away, they had no authority either to baptize or to ordain. And therefore, those who were from time to time baptized by them, were ordered, as though baptized by laymen, to come to the church to be purified by the Church's true baptism. Nevertheless, since it has seemed to some of those of Asia that, for the sake of management of the majority, their baptism should be accepted, let it be accepted. We must, however, perceive the iniquitous action of the Encratites; who, in order to shut themselves out from being received back by the Church have endeavored for the future to anticipate readmission by a peculiar baptism of their own, violating, in this manner even their

---

[29] As being one of Basil's predecessors in the see of Cæsarea.

[30] "*Hoc Encratitarum facinore non corrupta essentialis baptismi forma. Sed novæ quædam adjectæ cærimoniæ.*" Ben. Ed.

[31] *i.e.* those who used water instead of wine in the Eucharist, as Tatian and his followers. Cf. Clem. Al., *Strom*. i. 19 and Cyprian. *Ep*. lxiii.

own special practice.[32] My opinion, therefore, is that nothing being distinctly laid down concerning them, it is our duty to reject their baptism, and that in the case of anyone who has received baptism from them, we should, on his coming to the church, baptize him. If, however, there is any likelihood of this being detrimental to general discipline, we must fall back upon custom, and follow the fathers who have ordered what course we are to pursue. For I am under some apprehension lest, in our wish to discourage them from baptizing, we may, through the severity of our decision, be a hindrance to those who are being saved. If they accept our baptism, do not allow this to distress us. We are by no means bound to return them the same favor, but only strictly to obey canons. On every ground let it be enjoined that those who come to us from their baptism be anointed[33] in

---

[32] The Ben. note points out that the improper proceeding of the Encratites consisted not in any corruption of the baptismal formula, but in the addition of certain novel ceremonies, and proceeds: "*Nam in canone 47 sic eos loquentes inducit.* In Patrem et Filium et Spiritum baptizati sumus. *Hinc eorum baptisma ratum habet, si qua inciderit magni momenti causa. Quod autem ait hoc facinus eos incipere,* ut reditum sibi in Ecclesiam intercludant, *videtur id prima specie in eam sententiam accipiendum, quasi Encratitæ baptisma suum ea mente immutassent, ut Catholicos ad illud rejiciendum incitarent, sicque plures in secta contineret odium et fuga novi baptismatis. Abhorrebat enim ab omnium animis iteratus baptismus, ut pluribus exemplis probat Augustinus, lib. v. De baptismo, n. 6. Videtur ergo prima specie Encratitis, ea, quam dixi, exstitisse causa, cur baptismum immutarent. Atque ita hunc locum interpretatur Tillemontius, tom. iv. p. 628. Sic etiam illius exemplo interpretatus sum in Præf. novæ Cypriani operum editioni præmissa cap. 4. p. 12. Sed huic interpretationi non convenit cum his quæ addit Basilius. Vereri enim se significat ne Catholici, dum Encratitas ab hac baptismi immutatione deterrere volunt, nimium restricti sint et severi in eorum baptismo rejiciendo. Sperabant ergo Catholici tardiores ad ejus modi baptisma Encratitas futuros, si illud Catholici ratum habere nollent; nedum ipsi Encratitæ baptismatis immutationem eo consilio induxerint, ut ejusmodi baptisma a Catholicis rejiceretur. Quamobrem hæc verba,* ut reditum sibi in Ecclesiam intercludant, *non consilium et propositum Encratitarum designant, sed incommodum quod ex eorum facinore consequebatur; velut si dicamus aliquem scelus admittere, ut æternam sibi damnationem accersat.*"

[33] St. Cyprian (*Ep.* lxx.) says that heretics who have no true altar cannot have oil sanctified by the altar. "Gregory of Nazianzus, *Orat.* (xlviii in Jul.) speaks of oil sanctified or consecrated on the spiritual or divine table; Optatus of Milevis (*c. Don.* vii. 102) says that this ointment is compounded (*conditur*) in the name of Christ; and the Pseudo-Dionysius (*De Hierarch. Eccles.* c. 4) mentions the use

the presence of the faithful, and only on these terms approach the mysteries. I am aware that I have received into episcopal rank Izois and Saturninus from the Encratite following.[34] I am precluded therefore from separating from the Church those who have been united to their company, inasmuch as, through my acceptance of the bishops, I have promulgated a kind of canon of communion with them.

II. The woman who purposely destroys her unborn child is guilty of murder. With us there is no nice enquiry as to its being formed or unformed. In this case it is not only the being about to be born who is vindicated, but the woman in her attack upon herself; because in most cases women who make such attempts die. The destruction of the embryo is an additional crime, a second murder, at all events if we regard it as done with intent. The punishment, however, of these women should not be for life, but for the term of ten years. And let their treatment depend not on mere lapse of time, but on the character of their repentance.

III. A deacon who commits fornication after his appointment to the diaconate is to be deposed. But, after he has been rejected and ranked among the laity, he is not to be excluded from communion. For there is an ancient canon that those who have fallen from their degree are to be subjected to this kind of punishment alone.[35]

Herein, as I suppose, the ancient authorities followed the old rule "Thou shalt not avenge twice for the same thing."[36] There is this further reason too, that laymen, when expelled from the place of the faithful, are from time to time restored to the rank whence they have fallen; but the deacon undergoes once for all the lasting penalty of deposition. His deacon's orders not being restored to him, they rested at this one punishment. So far is this as regards what depends on law laid down. But generally, a truer remedy is the departure from sin. Wherefore

---

of the sign of the cross in the consecration of it." D.C.A. i. 355.

[34] This is the only known reference to these two bishops.

[35] "*Respicit, ni falor, ad canonem 25 apostolorum, ad quem Balsamon et Zonaras observant nonnulla esse peccata, quibus excommunicatio, non solum depositio, infligitur; velut si quis pecunia, vel magistratus potentia, sacerdotium assequatur, ut sancitur Can. 29 et 30.*" Ben. note.

[36] Nahum 1:9 (LXX).

that man will give me full proof of his cure who, after rejecting grace for the sake of the indulgence of the flesh, has then, through bruising of the flesh[37] and the enslaving of it[38] by means of self-control, abandoned the pleasures whereby he was subdued. We ought therefore to know both what is of exact prescription and what is of custom; and, in cases which do not admit of the highest treatment, to follow the traditional direction.

IV. In the case of trigamy and polygamy they laid down the same rule, in proportion, as in the case of digamy; namely one year for digamy (some authorities say two years); for trigamy men are separated for three and often for four years; but this is no longer described as marriage at all, but as polygamy; nay rather as limited fornication. It is for this reason that the Lord said to the woman of Samaria, who had five husbands, "he whom thou now hast is not thy husband."[39] He does not reckon those who had exceeded the limits of a second marriage as worthy of the title of husband or wife. In cases of trigamy we have accepted a seclusion of five years, not by the canons, but following the precept of our predecessors. Such offenders ought not to be altogether prohibited from the privileges of the Church; they should be considered deserving of hearing after two or three years, and afterwards of being permitted to stand in their place; but they must be kept from the communion of the good gift, and only restored to the place of communion after showing some fruit of repentance.

V. Heretics repenting at death ought to be received; yet to be received, of course, not indiscriminately, but on trial of exhibition of true repentance and of producing fruit in evidence of their zeal for salvation.[40]

---

[37] "*Duo veteres libri* συντριμμοῦ τῆς καρδίας." Ben. note.

[38] Cf. 1 Cor. 9:27.

[39] John 4:18. For the more usual modern interpretation that the sixth union was an unlawful one, *cf. Bengel. Matrimonium hoc sextum non erat legitimum, vel non consummatum, aut desertio aliudve impedimentum intercesserat, ex altera utra parte.*

[40] τῶν κανονικῶν. The Greek is of either gender. The Ben. note is: *Clericos sive eos qui in canone recensentur hac voce designari hactenus existimarunt Basilii interpretes, ac ipsi etiam Zonares et Balsamon. Sed ut canonicas sive sacras virgines interpreter, plurimis rationum momentis adducor: 1. Basilius hoc nomine clericos appellare non so-*

VI. The fornication of canonical persons is not to be reckoned as wedlock, and their union is to be completely dissolved, for this is both profitable for the security of the Church and will prevent the heretics from having a ground of attack against us, as though we induced men to join us by the attraction of liberty to sin.

VII. Abusers of themselves with mankind, and with beasts, as also murderers, wizards, adulterers, and idolaters, are deserving of the same punishment. Whatever rule you have in the case of the rest, observe also in their case. There can, however, be no doubt that we ought to receive those who have repented of impurity committed in ignorance for thirty years.[41] In this case there is ground for forgiveness in ignorance, in the spontaneity of confession, and the long extent of time. Perhaps they have been delivered to Satan for a whole age of man that they may learn not to behave unseemly;[42] wherefore order them to be received without delay, especially if they shed tears to move your mercy, and show a manner of living worthy of compassion.[43]

---

let, sed sacras virgines, ut persici potest ex epistolis 52 et 175; 2. præscriptum Basilii non convenit in clericos, quorum nonnullis, nempe lectoribus et aliis ejus modi venia dabatur ineundi matrimonii, quamvis in canone recenserentur; 3. prohibet Basilius ejusmodi stupra quæ honesto matrimonii nomine prætexi solebant. At id non inconcessum erat matrimonium, alios vero matrimonium post ordinationem inire nulla prorsus Ecclesia patiebatur, aut certe matrimonii pretium erat depositio. Contra virginibus nubentibus non longior pœna pluribus in locis imponebatur, quam digamis, ut perspicitur ex canone 18, ubi Basilius hance consuetudinem abrogat, ac virginum matrimonia instar adulterii existimat.

[41] So the MSS. But the Ben. note points out that there must be some error, if a sin knowingly committed was punished by excommunication for fifteen years (Canons lviii., lxii., lxiii.), and one unwittingly committed by a punishment of twice the duration.

[42] Cf. 1 Tim. 1:20.

[43] The Ben. note continues: *"Deinde vero testatur Basilius eos fere hominis ætatem satanæ traditos fuisse. At ætas hominis (γενεά) sæpe annorum viginti spatio existimatur; velut cum ait Dionysius Alexandrinus Alexandrinus apud Eusebium, lib. vii. cap. 21. Israelitas in deserto fuisse duabus ætatibus. Ipse Basilius in Epistola 201, quæ scripta est anno 375, Neocæsarienses incusat quod sibi jam totam fere hominis ætatem succenseant; quos tamen non ita pridem amicos habuerat; ac anno 568, Musonii morte afflictos litteris amicissimis consolatus fuerat. Sæculum apud Latinos non semper stricte sumitur; velut cum ait Hieronymus in Epist. 27 ad Marcellum, in Christi verbis explicandis per tanta jam sæcula tantorum ingenia sudasse; vel cum auctor*

VIII. The man who in a rage has taken up a hatchet against his own wife is a murderer. But it is what I should have expected from your intelligence that you should very properly remind me to speak on these points more fully, because a wide distinction must be drawn between cases where there is and where there is not intent. A case of an act purely unintentional, and widely removed from the purpose of the agent, is that of a man who throws a stone at a dog or a tree, and hits a man. The object was to drive off the beast or to shake down the fruit. The chance comer falls fortuitously in the way of the blow, and the act is unintentional. Unintentional too is the act of any one who strikes another with a strap or a flexible stick, for the purpose of chastising him, and the man who is being beaten dies. In this case it must be taken into consideration that the object was not to kill, but to improve, the offender. Further, among unintentional acts must be reckoned the case of a man in a fight who when warding off an enemy's attack with cudgel or hand, hits him without mercy in some vital part, so as to injure him, though not quite to kill him. This, however, comes very near to the intentional; for the man who employs such a weapon in self-defense, or who strikes without mercy, evidently does not spare his opponent, because he is mastered by passion. In like-manner the case of any one who uses a heavy cudgel, or a stone too big for a man to stand, is reckoned among the unintentional, because he does not do what he meant: in his rage he deals such a blow as to kill his victim, yet all he had in his mind was to give him a thrashing, not to do him to death. If, however, a man uses a sword, or anything of the kind, he has no excuse: certainly none if he throws his hatchet. For he does not strike with the hand, so that the force of the blow may be within his own control, but throws, so that from the weight and edge of the iron, and the force of the throw, the wound cannot fail to be fatal.

On the other hand, acts done in the attacks of war or robbery are

---

libri De rebaptismate *in Cyprianum tacito nomine invehitur, quod* adversus prisca consulta post tot sæculorum tantam seriem nunc primum repente sine rationeinsurgat, *p. 357. De hoc ergo triginta annorum numero non paucos deducendos esse crediderim.*

distinctly intentional, and admit of no doubt. Robbers kill for greed, and to avoid conviction. Soldiers who inflict death in war do so with the obvious purpose not of fighting, nor chastising, but of killing their opponents. And if anyone has concocted some magic philter for some other reason, and then causes death, I count this as intentional. Women frequently endeavor to draw men to love them by incantations and magic knots, and give them drugs which dull their intelligence. Such women, when they cause death, though the result of their action may not be what they intended, are nevertheless, on account of their proceedings being magical and prohibited, to be reckoned among intentional homicides. Women also who administer drugs to cause abortion, as well as those who take poisons to destroy unborn children, are murderesses. So much on this subject.

IX. The sentence of the Lord that it is unlawful to withdraw from wedlock, save on account of fornication,[44] applies, according to the argument, to men and women alike. Custom, however, does not so obtain. Yet, in relation with women, very strict expressions are to be found; as, for instance, the words of the apostle "He which is joined to a harlot is one body"[45] and of Jeremiah, If a wife "become another man's shall he return unto her again? shall not that land be greatly polluted?"[46] And again, "He that hath an adulteress is a fool and impious."[47] Yet custom ordains that men who commit adultery and are in fornication be retained by their wives. Consequently, I do not know if the woman who lives with the man who has been dismissed can properly be called an adulteress; the charge in this case attaches to the woman who has put away her husband, and depends upon the cause for which she withdrew from wedlock.[48] In the case of her being

---

[44] Matt. 5:32.
[45] 1 Cor. 6:16.
[46] Jer. 3:1.
[47] Prov. 18:22 (LXX).
[48] The Ben. note is, *Sequitur in hoc canone Basilius Romanas leges, quas tamen fatetur cum evangelio minus consentire. Lex Constantini jubet in repudio mittendo a femina hæc sola crimina inquiri, si homicidam, vel medicamentarium, vel sepulcrorum dissolutorem maritum suum esse probaverit. At eadem lege viris conceditur, ut adulteras uxores dimittant. Aliud discrimen hoc in canone uxores inter et maritos ponitur, quod*

beaten, and refusing to submit, it would be better for her to endure than to be separated from her husband; in the case of her objecting to pecuniary loss, even here she would not have sufficient ground. If her reason is his living in fornication we do not find this in the custom of the church; but from an unbelieving husband a wife is commanded not to depart, but to remain, on account of the uncertainty of the issue. "For what knowest thou, O wife, whether thou shalt save thy husband?"[49] Here then the wife, if she leaves her husband and goes to another, is an adulteress. But the man who has been abandoned is pardonable, and the woman who lives with such a man is not condemned. But if the man who has deserted his wife goes to another, he is himself an adulterer because he makes her commit adultery; and the woman who lives with him is an adulteress, because she has caused another woman's husband to come over to her.

x. Those who swear that they will not receive ordination, declining orders upon oath, must not be driven to perjure themselves, although there does seem to be a canon making concessions to such persons. Yet I have found by experience that perjurers never turn out well.[50] Account must however be taken of the form of the oath, its terms, the frame of mind in which it was taken, and the minutest additions made to the terms, since, if no ground of relief can anywhere be found, such persons must be dismissed. The case, however, of Severus, I mean of the presbyter ordained by him, does seem to me to allow of relief of this kind, if you will permit it. Give directions for the district placed under Mestia, to which the man was appointed, to be reckoned under Vasoda. Thus he will not forswear himself by not

---

uxor injuste dimissa, si ab alia ducatur, adulterii notam non effugiat; dimissus autem injuste maritus nec adulter sit, si aliam ducat, nec quæ ab eo ducitur, adultera. Cæterum Basilius ante episcopatum eodem jure uxorem ac maritum esse censebat. Nam in Moral. reg. 73 statuit virum ab uxore, aut uxorem a viro non debere separari, nisi quis deprehendatur in adulterio. Utrique pariter interdicit novis nuptiis, sive repudient, sive repudientur.

[49] 1 Cor. 7:16.

[50] The Ben. note refers to the case of Dracontius, who had sworn that he would escape if he were ordained bishop, and so did; but was urged by Athanasius to discharge the duties of his diocese, notwithstanding his oath.

departing from the place, and Longinus, having Cyriacus with him, will not leave the Church unprovided for, nor himself be guilty of neglect of work.[51] I moreover shall not be held guilty of taking action in contravention of any canons by making a concession to Cyriacus who had sworn that he would remain at Mindana and yet accepted the transfer. His return will be in accordance with his oath, and his obedience to the arrangement will not be reckoned against him as perjury, because it was not added to his oath that he would not go, even a short time, from Mindana, but would remain there for the future. Severus, who pleads forgetfulness, I shall pardon, only telling him that One who knows what is secret will not overlook the ravaging of His Church by a man of such a character; a man who originally appoints uncanonically, then imposes oaths in violation of the Gospel, then tells a man to perjure himself in the matter of his transfer, and last of all lies in pretended forgetfulness. I am no judge of hearts; I only judge by what I hear; let us leave vengeance to the Lord, and ourselves pardon the common human error of forgetfulness, and receive the man without question.

XI. The man who is guilty of unintentional homicide has given sufficient satisfaction in eleven years. We shall, without doubt, observe what is laid down by Moses in the case of wounded men, and shall not hold a murder to have been committed in the case of a man who lies down after he has been struck, and walks again leaning on his staff.[52] If, however, he does not rise again after he has been struck,

---

[51] On this obscure passage the Ben. note is: *Longinus presbyter erat in agro Mestiæ subjecto. Sed cum is depositus essit ob aliquod delictum, ac forte honorem sacerdotii retineret, ut nonnumquam fiebat, Severus episcopus in ejus locum transtulit Cyriacum, quem antea Mindanis ordinaverat, ac jurare coegerat se Mindanis mansurum. Nihil hac in re statui posse videbatur, quod non in magnam aliquam diffcultatem incurreret. Nam si in agro Mestiæ subjecto Cyriacus remaneret, perjurii culpam sustinebat. Si rediret Mindana, ager Mestiæ subjectus presbytero carebat, atque hujus incommodi culpa redundabat in caput Longini, qui ob delictum depositus fuerat. Quid igitur Basilius? Utrique occurrit incommodo; jubet agrum, qui Mastiæ subjectus erat Vasodis subjici, id est loco, cui subjecta erant Mindana. Hoc ex remedio duo consequebatur Basilius, ut et ager ille presbytero non careret, et Cyriacus ibi remanens Mindana tamen redire censeretur, cum jam hic locus eidem ac Mindana chorepiscopo pareret.*

[52] Exod. 21:19.

nevertheless, from there being no intent to kill, the striker is a homicide, but an unintentional homicide.

XII. The canon absolutely excludes digamists from the ministry.[53]

XIII. Homicide in war is not reckoned by our Fathers as homicide; I presume from their wish to make concession to men fighting on behalf of chastity and true religion. Perhaps, however, it is well to counsel that those whose hands are not clean only abstain from communion for three years.[54]

XIV. A taker of usury, if he consent to spend his unjust gain on the poor, and to be rid for the future of the plague of covetousness, may be received into the ministry.[55]

XV. I am astonished at your requiring exactitude in Scripture, and arguing that there is something forced in the diction of the interpre-

---

[53] *Ap.* Can. xiii. 14: "It is clear from the *Philosophumena* of Hippolytus (ix. 12) that by the beginning of the 3d century the rule of monogamy for the clergy was well established, since he complains that in the days of Callistus 'digamist and trigamist bishops, and priests and deacons, *began* to be admitted into the clergy.' Tertullian recognises the rule as to the clergy. Thus in his *De Exhortatione Castitatis* (c. 7) he asks scornfully; 'Being a digamist, dost thou baptize? Dost thou make the offering?'" *Dict. C. A.* i. 552.
Vide also Canon Bright, *Notes on the Canons of the first four General Councils.* On Can. Nic. viii. p. 27.

[54] The Ben. note quotes Balsamon, Zonaras, and Alexius Aristenus as remarking on this that Basil gives advice, not direction, and regards the hands, not the hearts, of soldiers as defiled; and as recalling that this canon was quoted in opposition to the Emperor Phocas when he wished to reckon soldiers as martyrs. The canon was little regarded, as being contrary to general Christian sentiment.
Cf. Athan. *Ep.* xlviii. p. 557 of this edition: "In war it is lawful and praiseworthy to destroy the enemy; accordingly not only are they who have distinguished themselves in the field held worthy of great honors, but monuments are put up proclaiming their achievements."

[55] Cf. Can. Nic. xvii. Canon Bright (*On the Canons*, etc., p. 56) remarks: "It must be remembered that interest, called τόκος and *fenus*, as the product of the principal, was associated in the early stages of society—in Greece and Rome as well as in Palestine—with the notion of undue profit extorted by a rich lender from the needy borrower (see Grote, *Hist. Gr.* ii. 311 H.; Arnold, *Hist. Rome* i. 282; Mommsen, *Hist. R.* i. 291). Hence Tacitus says, '*sane vetus urbi fenebre malcum, et seditionum discordiarumque creberrima causa*' (*Ann.* vi. 16), and Gibbon calls usury 'the inveterate grievance of the city, abolished by the clamours of the people, revived by their wants and idleness.'" (v. 314.)

tation which gives the meaning of the original, but does not exactly render what is meant by the Hebrew word. Yet I must not carelessly pass by the question started by an enquiring mind. At the creation of the world, birds of the air and the fishes of the sea had the same origin;[56] for both kinds were produced from the water.[57] The reason is that both have the same characteristics. The latter swim in the water, the former in the air. They are therefore mentioned together. The form of expression is not used without distinction, but of all that lives in the water it is used very properly. The birds of the air and the fishes of the sea are subject to man; and not they alone, but all that passes through the paths of the sea. For every water-creature is not a fish, as for instance the sea monsters, whales, sharks, dolphins, seals, even sea-horses, sea-dogs, saw-fish, sword-fish, and sea-cows; and, if you like, sea nettles, cockles and all hard-shelled creatures of whom none are fish, and all pass through the paths of the sea; so that there are three kinds, birds of the air, fishes of the sea, and all water-creatures which are distinct from fish, and pass through the paths of the sea.

XVI. Naaman was not a great man with the Lord, but with his lord; that is, he was one of the chief princes of the King of the Syrians.[58] Read your Bible carefully, and you will find the answer to your question there.

Letter 199[59]

TO AMPHILOCHIUS, CONCERNING THE CANONS

I WROTE SOME TIME AGO in reply to the questions of your reverence, but I did not send the letter, partly because from my long and dangerous illness I had not time to do so; partly because I had no one to send with it. I have but few men with me who are experienced in travelling and fit for service of this kind. When you thus learn the causes of my delay, forgive me. I have been quite astonished

---

[56] Ps. 8:8.
[57] Gen. 1:20, 21.
[58] 2 Kings 5:1.
[59] Placed in 375.

at your readiness to learn and at your humility. You are entrusted with the office of a teacher, and yet you condescend to learn, and to learn of me, who pretend to no great knowledge. Nevertheless, since you consent, on account of your fear of God, to do what another man might hesitate to do, I am bound for my part to go even beyond my strength in aiding your readiness and righteous zeal.

XVII. You asked me about the presbyter Bianor—can he be admitted among the clergy, because of his oath? I know that I have already given the clergy of Antioch a general sentence in the case of all those who had sworn with him; namely, that they should abstain from the public congregations, but might perform priestly functions in private.[60] Moreover, he has the further liberty for the performance of his ministerial functions, from the fact that his sacred duties lie not at Antioch, but at Iconium; for, as you have written to me yourself, he has chosen to live rather at the latter than at the former place. The man in question may, therefore, be received; but your reverence must

---

[60] The Ben. Ed. note: "*Sæpe vituperantur apud sanctos Patres, qui sacra in privatis ædibus sive domesticis oratoriis celebrant. Hinc Irenæus, lib. iv. cap. 26, oportere ait eos, qui abistunt a principali successione et quocunque loco colligunt, suspectos habere, vel quasi hæreticos et malæ sententiæ, vel quasi scindentes et elatos et sibi placentes; aut rursus ut hypocritas quæstus gratia et vanæ gloriæ hoc operantes. Basilius, in Psalm xxvii. n. 3: Non igitur extra sanctam hanc aulam adorare oporet, sed intra ipsam, etc. Similia habet Eusebius in eundem psalmum, p. 313. Sic etiam Cyrillus Alexandrinus in libro adversus Anthropomorphitas, cap. 12, et in libro decimo De adorat., p. 356. Sed his in locis perspicuum est hæreticorum aut schismaticorum synagogas notari, vel quas vocat Basilius, can. 1. παρασυναγωγάς, sive illicitos conventus a presbyteris aut episcopis rebellibus habitos, aut a populis disciplinæ expertibus. At interdum graves causæ suberant, cur sacra in privatis ædibus impermissa non essent. Ipsa persecutio necessitatem hujus rei sæpe afferebat, cum catholici episcoporum hæreticorum communionem fugerent, ut Sebastiæ ecclesiarum aditu prohiberentur. Minime ergo mirum, si presbyteris Antiochenis eam sacerdotii perfunctionem Basilius reliquit, quæ et ad jurisjurandi religionem et ad temporum molestias accommodata videbatur. Synodus Laodicena vetat, can. 58, in domibus fieri oblationem ab episcopis vel presbyteris. Canon 31. Trullanus id clericis non interdicit, modo accedat episcopi consensus. Non inusitata fuisse ejusmodi sacra in domesticis oratoriis confirmat canon Basilii 27, ubi vetatur, ne presbyter illicitis nuptiis implicantus privatim aut publice sacerdotii munere fungatur. Eustathius Sebastenus Ancyræ cum Arianis in domibus communicavit, ut ex pluribus Basilii epistolis discimus, cum apertam ab eis communionem impetrare non posset.*"

require him to show repentance for the rash readiness of the oath which he took before the unbeliever,[61] being unable to bear the trouble of that small peril.

XVIII. Concerning fallen virgins, who, after professing a chaste life before the Lord, make their vows vain, because they have fallen under the lusts of the flesh, our fathers, tenderly[62] and meekly making allowance for the infirmities of them that fall, laid down that they might be received after a year, ranking them with the digamists. Since, however, by God's grace the Church grows mightier as she advances, and the order of virgins is becoming more numerous, it is my judgment that careful heed should be given both to the act as it appears upon consideration, and to the mind of Scripture, which may be discovered from the context. Widowhood is inferior to virginity; consequently, the sin of the widows comes far behind that of the virgins. Let us see what Paul writes to Timothy. "The young widows refuse: for when they have begun to wax wanton against Christ, they will marry; having damnation because they have cast off their first faith."[63] If, therefore, a widow lies under a very heavy charge, as setting at naught her faith in Christ, what must we think of the virgin, who is the bride of Christ, and a chosen vessel dedicated to the Lord? It is a grave fault even on the part of a slave to give herself away in secret wedlock and fill the house with impurity, and, by her wicked life, to wrong her owner; but it is forsooth far more shocking for the bride to become an adulteress, and, dishonoring her union with the bridegroom, to yield herself to unchaste indulgence. The widow, as being a corrupted slave, is indeed condemned; but the virgin comes under the charge of adultery. We call the man who lives with another man's wife an adulterer, and do not receive him into communion until he has ceased from his sin; and so we shall ordain in the case of him who has the virgin. One point, however, must be determined beforehand,

---

[61] *Videtur infidelis ille vir unus aliquis fuisse ex potentioribus Arianis ejusque furor idcirco in presbyteros Antiochenos incitatus quod hi ecclesiam absente Meletio regerent, ac maximam civium partem in illius fide et communione retinerent.*

[62] ἀπαλῶς, with four mss., *al.* ἁπλῶς.

[63] 1 Tim. 5:11, 12.

that the name *virgin* is given to a woman who voluntarily devotes herself to the Lord, renounces marriage, and embraces a life of holiness. And we admit professions dating from the age of full intelligence.[64] For it is not right in such cases to admit the words of mere children. But a girl of sixteen or seventeen years of age, in full possession of her faculties, who has been submitted to strict examination, and is then constant, and persists in her entreaty to be admitted, may then be ranked among the virgins, her profession ratified, and its violation rigorously punished. Many girls are brought forward by their parents and brothers, and other kinsfolk, before they are of full age, and have no inner impulse towards a celibate life. The object of the friends is simply to provide for themselves. Such women as these must not be readily received, before we have made public investigation of their own sentiments.

XIX. I do not recognize the profession of men, except in the case of those who have enrolled themselves in the order of monks, and seem to have secretly adopted the celibate life. Yet in their case I think it becoming that there should be a previous examination, and that a distinct profession should be received from them, so that whenever they may revert to the life of the pleasures of the flesh, they may be subjected to the punishment of fornicators.

XX. I do not think that any condemnation ought to be passed on women who professed virginity while in heresy, and then afterwards preferred marriage. "What things so ever the law saith, it saith to them who are under the law."[65] Those who have not yet put on Christ's yoke do not recognize the laws of the Lord. They are therefore to be received in the church, as having remission in the case of these sins too, as of all, from their faith in Christ. As a general rule, all sins formerly committed in the catechumenical state are not taken into account.[66] The Church does not receive these persons without baptism;

---

[64] "*Hoc Basilii decretum de professionis ætate citatur in canone quadragesimo synodi in Trullo*" (a.d.691) "*et decem et septem anni quos Basilius requirit, ad decem rediguntur.*"

[65] Rom. 3:19.

[66] "*Male Angli in Pandectis et alit interpretes reddunt, quæ* in catechumenica vita

and it is very necessary that in such cases the birthrights should be observed.

XXI. If a man living with a wife is not satisfied with his marriage and falls into fornication, I account him a fornicator, and prolong his period of punishment. Nevertheless, we have no canon subjecting him to the charge of adultery, if the sin be committed against an unmarried woman. For the adulteress, it is said, "being polluted shall be polluted,"[67] and she shall not return to her husband: and "He that keepeth an adulteress is a fool and impious."[68] He, however, who has committed fornication is not to be cut off from the society of his own wife. So the wife will receive the husband on his return from fornication, but the husband will expel the polluted woman from his house. The argument here is not easy, but the custom has so obtained.[69]

XXII. Men who keep women carried off by violence, if they carried them off when betrothed to other men, must not be received before removal of the women and their restoration to those to whom they were first contracted, whether they wish to receive them, or to separate from them. In the case of a girl who has been taken when not betrothed, she ought first to be removed, and restored to her own people, and handed over to the will of her own people whether parents, or brothers, or anyone having authority over her. If they choose

---

fiunt. *Non enim dicit Basilius ea non puniri quæ in hoc statu peccantur, sed tantum peccata ante baptismum commissa baptismo expiari, nec jam esse judicio ecclesiastico obnoxia. Hinc observat Zonaras non pugnare hunc canonem cum canone quinto Neocæsariensi, in quo pœnæ catechumenis peccantibus decernuntur.*"

[67] Jer. 3:1.

[68] Prov. 18:22 (LXX).

[69] "*Non solus Basilius hanc consuetudinem secutus. Auctor* constitutionum apostolicarum *sic loquitur lib.* vi. *cap.* 14: Qui corruptam retinet, naturæ legem violat: quando quidem *qui retinet adulteram, stultus est et impius. Abscinde enim eam,* inquit, *a carnibus tuis.* Nam adjutrix non est, sed insidiatrix, quæ mentem ad alium declinarit. *Canon 8, Neocæsariensis laicis, quorum uxores adulterii convictæ, aditum ad ministerium ecclesiasticum claudit; clericis depositionis pœnam irrogat, si adulteram nolint dimittere. Canon 65 Eliberitanus sic habet:* Si cujus clerici uxor fuerit mæchata, et scierit eam maritus suus mæchari, et non eam statim projecerit, nec in fine accipiat communionem. *Hermas lib.* i, *c.* 2, *adulteram ejici jubet, sed tamen pœnitentem recipi. S. Augustinus adulterium legitimam esse dimittendi causam pronuntiat, sed non necessariam, lib.* ii. *De Adulter. nuptiis, cap.* 5, *n.* 13."

to give her up, the cohabitation may stand; but, if they refuse, no violence should be used. In the case of a man having a wife by seduction, be it secret or by violence, he must be held guilty of fornication. The punishment of fornicators is fixed at four years. In the first year, they must be expelled from prayer, and weep at the door of the church; in the second they may be received to sermon; in the third to penance; in the fourth to standing with the people, while they are withheld from the oblation. Finally, they may be admitted to the communion of the good gift.

XXIII. Concerning men who marry two sisters, or women who marry two brothers a short letter of mine has been published, of which I have sent a copy to your reverence.[70] The man who has taken his own brother's wife is not to be received until he have separated from her.

XXIV. A widow whose name is in the list of widows, that is, who is supported[71] by the Church, is ordered by the Apostle to be supported no longer when she marries.[72]

There is no special rule for a widower. The punishment appointed for digamy may suffice. If a widow who is sixty years of age chooses again to live with a husband, she shall be held unworthy of the communion of the good gift until she be moved no longer by her impure desire. If we reckon her before sixty years, the blame rests with us, and not with the woman.

XXV. The man who retains as his wife the woman whom he has violated, shall be liable to the penalty of rape, but it shall be lawful for him to have her to wife.

XXVI. Fornication is not wedlock, nor yet the beginning of wedlock. Wherefore it is best, if possible, to put asunder those who are united in fornication. If they are set on cohabitation, let them admit the penalty of fornication. Let them be allowed to live together, lest a worse thing happen.

---

[70] Probably *Letter* clx. to Diodorus is referred to.

[71] Διακονουμένην. So the Ben. Ed. Another possible rendering is "received into the order of deaconesses."

[72] 1 Tim. 5:11, 12.

XXVII. As to the priest ignorantly involved in an illegal marriage,[73] I have made the fitting regulation, that he may hold his seat, but must abstain from other functions. For such a case pardon is enough. It is unreasonable that the man who has to treat his own wounds should be blessing another, for benediction is the imparting of holiness. How can he who through his fault, committed in ignorance, is without holiness, impart it to another? Let him bless neither in public nor in private, nor distribute the body of Christ to others, nor perform any other sacred function, but, content with his seat of honor, let him beseech the Lord with weeping, that his sin, committed in ignorance, may be forgiven.

XXVIII. It has seemed to me ridiculous that any one should make a vow to abstain from swine's flesh. Be so good as to teach men to abstain from foolish vows and promises. Represent the use to be quite indifferent. No creature of God, received with thanksgiving, is to be rejected.[74] The vow is ridiculous; the abstinence unnecessary.

XXIX. It is especially desirable that attention should be given to the case of persons in power who threaten on oath to do some hurt to those under their authority. The remedy is twofold. In the first place, let them be taught not to take oaths at random: secondly, not to persist in their wicked determinations. Anyone who is arrested in the design of fulfilling an oath to injure another ought to show repentance for the rashness of his oath, and must not confirm his wickedness under the pretext of piety. Herod was none the better for fulfilling his oath, when, of course only to save himself from perjury, he became the prophet's murderer.[75] Swearing is absolutely forbidden,[76] and it is only reasonable that the oath which tends to evil should be condemned. The swearer must therefore change his mind, and not persist in confirming his impiety. Consider the absurdity of the thing a little further. Suppose a man to swear that he will put his brother's eyes out: is it well for him to carry his oath into action?

---

[73] "Ἀθέσμῳ γάμῳ." *Illicitas nuptias*.

[74] 1 Tim. 4:4.

[75] Matt. 14:10.

[76] Matt. 5:34.

Or to commit murder? or to break any other commandment? "I have sworn, and I will perform it,"[77] not to sin, but to "keep thy righteous judgments." It is no less our duty to undo and destroy sin, than it is to confirm the commandment by immutable counsels.

XXX. As to those guilty of abduction we have no ancient rule, but I have expressed my own judgment. The period is three years;[78] the culprits and their accomplices to be excluded from service. The act committed without violence is not liable to punishment, whenever it has not been preceded by violation or robbery. The widow is independent, and to follow or not is in her own power. We must, therefore, pay no heed to excuses.

XXXI. A woman whose husband has gone away and disappeared, and who marries another, before she has evidence of his death, commits adultery. Clerics who are guilty of the sin unto death[79] are degraded from their order, but not excluded from the communion of the laity. Thou shalt not punish twice for the same fault.[80]

XXXIII. Let an indictment for murder be preferred against the woman who gives birth to a child on the road and pays no attention to it.

XXXIV. Women who had committed adultery, and confessed their fault through piety, or were in any way convicted, were not allowed by our fathers to be publicly exposed, that we might not cause their death after conviction. But they ordered that they should be excluded from communion till they had fulfilled their term of penance.

XXXV. In the case of a man deserted by his wife, the cause of the desertion must be taken into account. If she appears to have aban-

---

[77] Ps. 118:106.

[78] The Ben. Ed. point out that in Canon xxii. four years is the allotted period, as in the case of fornicators.

[79] St. Basil on Isaiah 4 calls sins willfully committed after full knowledge "sins unto death." But in the same commentary he applies the same designation to sins which lead to hell. The sense to be applied to the phrase in Canon xxxii. is to be learnt, according to the Ben. note, from Canons lxix. and lxx., where a less punishment is assigned to mere willful sins unto death than in Canon xxxii.

[80] Nahum 1:9 (LXX).

doned him without reason, he is deserving of pardon, but the wife of punishment. Pardon will be given to him that he may communicate with the Church.

XXXVI. Soldiers' wives who have married in their husbands' absence will come under the same principle as wives who, when their husbands have been on a journey, have not waited their return. Their case, however, does admit of some concession on the ground of there being greater reason to suspect death.

XXXVII. The man who marries after abducting another man's wife will incur the charge of adultery for the first case; but for the second will go free.

XXXVIII. Girls who follow against their fathers' will commit fornication; but if their fathers are reconciled to them, the act seems to admit of a remedy. They are not however immediately restored to communion, but are to be punished for three years.

XXXIX. The woman who lives with an adulterer is an adulteress the whole time.[81]

XL. The woman who yields to a man against her master's will commits fornication; but if afterwards she accepts free marriage, she marries. The former case is fornication; the latter marriage. The covenants of persons who are not independent have no validity.

XLI. The woman in widowhood, who is independent, may dwell with a husband without blame, if there is no one to prevent their cohabitation; for the Apostle says; "but if her husband be dead, she is at liberty to be married to whom she will; only in the Lord."[82]

XLII. Marriages contracted without the permission of those in authority, are fornication. If neither father nor master be living the contracting parties are free from blame; just as if the authorities assented to the cohabitation, it assumes the fixity of marriage.

XLIII. He who smites his neighbor to death is a murderer, whether he struck first or in self-defense.

XLIV. The deaconess who commits fornication with a heathen may be received into repentance and will be admitted to the oblation in

---

[81] Or, according to another reading, in every way.
[82] 1 Cor. 7:39.

the seventh year; of course, if she be living in chastity. The heathen who, after he has believed, takes to idolatry, returns to his vomit. We do not, however, give up the body of the deaconess to the use of the flesh, as being consecrated.

XLV. If anyone, after taking the name of Christianity, insults Christ, he gets no good from the name.

XLVI. The woman who unwillingly marries a man deserted at the time by his wife, and is afterwards repudiated, because of the return of the former to him, commits fornication, but involuntarily. She will, therefore, not be prohibited from marriage; but it is better if she remains as she is.[83]

XLVII. Encratitæ,[84] Saccophori,[85] and Apotactitæ[86] are not regarded in the same manner as Novatians, since in their case a canon has been pronounced, although different; while of the former nothing has been said. All these I re-baptize on the same principle. If among you their re-baptism is forbidden, for the sake of some arrangement, nevertheless let my principle prevail. Their heresy is, as it were, an offshoot of the Marcionites, abominating, as they do, marriage, refusing wine, and calling God's creature polluted. We do not therefore receive them into the Church, unless they be baptized into our baptism. Let them not say that they have been baptized into Father, Son and Holy Ghost, inasmuch as they make God the author of evil, after the example of Marcion and the rest of the heresies. Wherefore, if this be determined on, more bishops ought to meet together in one place and publish the canon in these terms, that action may be taken without peril, and authority given to answers to questions of this kind.

XLVIII. The woman who has been abandoned by her husband, ought, in my judgment, to remain as she is. The Lord said, "If any-

---

[83] This is Can. xciii. of the Council in Trullo.

[84] Generally reckoned rather as Manichæans than as here by Basil as Marcionites, but dualism was common to both systems.

[85] A Manichæan sect, who led a solitary life. Death is threatened against them in a law of Theodosius dated a.d. 322 (*Cod. Theod. lib.* xvi. *tit.* 5, *leg.* 9), identified by the Ben. Ed. with the Hydroparastatæ.

[86] A Manichæan sect. Cf. Epiphanius ii. 18. In the work of Macarius Magnes, published in Paris 1876, they are identified with the Encratites.

one leaves[87] his wife, saving for the cause of fornication, he causeth her to commit adultery;"[88] thus, by calling her adulteress, He excludes her from intercourse with another man. For how can the man being guilty, as having caused adultery, and the woman, go without blame, when she is called adulteress by the Lord for having intercourse with another man?

XLIX. Suffering violation should not be a cause of condemnation. So the slave girl, if she has been forced by her own master, is free from blame.

L. There is no law as to trigamy: a third marriage is not contracted by law. We look upon such things as the defilements of the Church. But we do not subject them to public condemnation, as being better than unrestrained fornication.[89]

Letter 200[90]
TO AMPHILOCHIUS, BISHOP OF ICONIUM

I AM ATTACKED BY sickness after sickness, and all the work given me, not only by the affairs of the Church, but by those who are troubling the Church, has detained me during the whole winter, and up to the present time. It has been therefore quite impossible for me to send any one to you or to pay you a visit. I conjecture that you are similarly situated; not, indeed, as to sickness, God forbid; may the Lord grant you continued health for carrying out His commandments. But I know that the care of the Churches gives you the same distress as it does me. I was now about to send someone to get me accurate information about your condition. But when my well-beloved son Meletius, who is moving the newly enlisted troops, reminded me of the opportunity of my saluting you by him, I gladly accepted the occasion to write and had recourse to the kind services

---

[87] καταλίπῃ for ἀπολύσῃ.

[88] Matt. 5:22.

[89] Cf. however Canon iv., where trigamy is called polygamy or at best a limited fornication, and those guilty of it subjected to exclusion from the Eucharist.

[90] Placed in 375.

of the conveyor of my letter. He is one who may himself serve instead of a letter, both because of his amiable disposition, and of his being well acquainted with all which concerns me. By him, then, I beseech your reverence especially, to pray for me, that the Lord may grant to me a riddance from this troublesome body of mine; to His Churches, peace; and to you, rest; and, whenever you have settled the affairs of Lycaonia in apostolic fashion, as you have begun, an opportunity to visit also this place. Whether I be sojourning in the flesh, or shall have been already bidden to take my departure to the Lord, I hope that you will interest yourself in our part of the world, as your own, as indeed it is, strengthening all that is weak, rousing all that is slothful and, by the help of the Spirit Which abides in you, transforming everything into a condition well pleasing to the Lord. My very honorable sons, Meletius and Melitius, whom you have known for some time, and know to be devoted to yourself, keep in your good care and pray for them. This is enough to keep them in safety. Salute in my name, I beg you, all who are with your holiness, both all the clergy, and all the laity under your pastoral care, and my very religious brothers and fellow ministers. Bear in mind the memory of the blessed martyr Eupsychius, and do not wait for me to mention him again. Do not take pains to come on the exact day, but anticipate it, and so give me joy, if I be yet living on this earth. Till then may you, by the grace of the Holy One, be preserved for me and for God's Churches, enjoying health and wealth in the Lord, and praying for me.

Letter 201[91]

TO AMPHILOCHIUS, BISHOP OF ICONIUM

I LONG TO MEET YOU for many reasons, that I may have the benefit of your advice in the matters I had in hand, and that on beholding you after a long interval I may have some comfort for your absence. But since both of us are prevented by the same reasons, you by the illness which has befallen you, and I by the malady of lon-

---

[91] Placed in 375.

ger standing which has not yet left me, let us, if you will, each forgive the other, that both may free ourselves from blame.

Letter 202[92]
TO AMPHILOCHIUS, BISHOP OF ICONIUM

UNDER OTHER CIRCUMSTANCES I should think it a special privilege to meet with your reverence, but above all now, when the business which brings us together is of such great importance. But so much of my illness as still clings to me is enough to prevent my stirring ever so short a distance. I tried to drive as far as the martyrs[93] and had a relapse almost into my old state. You must therefore forgive me. If the matter can be put off for a few days, I will, by God's grace join you, and share your anxieties. If the business presses, do, by God's help, what has to be done; but reckon me as present with you and as participating in your worthy deeds. May you, by the grace of the Holy One, be preserved to God's Church, strong and joyous in the Lord, and praying for me.

Letter 217
TO AMPHILOCHIUS, THE CANONS[94]

ON MY RETURN FROM a long journey (for I have been into Pontus on ecclesiastical business, and to visit my relations) with my body weak and ill, and my spirits considerably bro-

---

[92] Placed in 375.

[93] Tillemont conjectures that the drive was to St. Eupsychius, but the day of St. Eupsychius fell in September, which the Ben. note thinks too late for the date of this letter. The memorials of St. Julitta and St. Gordius were also near Cæsarea, but their days fell in January, which the same note thinks too early. Gregory of Nyssa (Migne iii. p. 653) says that there were more altars in Cappadocia than in all the world, so that we need have no difficulty in supposing some saint whose date would synchronize with the letter. Basil, however, may have tried to drive to the shrine of some martyr on some other day than the anniversary of his death.

[94] The third canonical letter, written on Basil's return from Pontus, in 375.

ken, I took your reverence's letter into my hand. No sooner did I receive the tokens of that voice which to me is of all voices the sweetest, and of that hand that I love so well, than I forgot all my troubles. And if I was made so much more cheerful by the receipt of your letter, you ought to be able to conjecture at what value I price your actual presence. May this be granted me by the Holy One, whenever it may be convenient to you and you yourself send me an invitation. And if you were to come to the house at Euphemias it would indeed be pleasant for me to meet you, escaping from my vexations here, and hastening to your unfeigned affection. Possibly also for other reasons I may be compelled to go as far as Nazianzus by the sudden departure of the very God-beloved bishop Gregory. How or why this has come to pass, so far, I have no information.[95] The man about whom I had spoken to your excellency, and whom you expected to be ready by this time, has, you must know, fallen ill of a lingering disease, and is moreover now suffering from an affection of the eyes, arising from his old complaint and from the illness which has now befallen him, and he is quite unfit to do any work. I have no one else with me. It is consequently better, although the matter was left by them to me, for someone to be put forward by them. And indeed, one cannot but think that the expressions were used merely as a necessary form, and that what they really wished was what they originally requested, that the person selected for the leadership should be one of themselves. If there is any one of the lately baptized,[96] whether Macedonius approve or not, let him be appointed. You will instruct him in his duties, the Lord, Who in all things cooperates with you, granting you His grace for this work also.

---

[95] This is the sudden disappearance of Gregory from Nazianzus at the end of 375, which was due at once to his craving for retirement and his anxiety not to complicate the appointment of a successor to his father (who died early in 374) in the see of Nazianzus. He found a refuge in the monastery of Thecla at the Isaurian Seleucia. (*Carm.* xi. 549.)

[96] The Ben. note appositely points out that any astonishment, such as expressed by Tillemont, at the consecration of a neophyte, is quite out of place, in view of the exigencies of the times and the practice of postponing baptism. St. Ambrose at Milan and Nectarius at Constantinople were not even "neophytes,"

LI. As to the clergy, the Canons have enjoined without making any distinction that one penalty is assigned for the lapsed—ejection from the ministry, whether they be in orders[97] or remain in the ministry which is conferred without imposition of hands.

LII. The woman who has given birth to a child and abandoned it in the road, if she was able to save it and neglected it, or thought by this means to hide her sin, or was moved by some brutal and inhuman motive, is to be judged as in a case of murder. If, on the other hand, she was unable to provide for it. and the child perish from exposure and want of the necessities of life, the mother is to be pardoned.

LIII. The widowed slave is not guilty of a serious fall if she adopts a second marriage under color of rape. She is not on this ground open to accusation. It is rather the object than the pretext which must be taken into account, but it is clear that she is exposed to the punishment of digamy.[98]

LIV. I know that I have already written to your reverence, so far as I can, on the distinctions to be observed in cases of involuntary homicide,[99] and on this point I can say no more. It rests with your intelligence to increase or lessen the severity of the punishment as each individual case may require.

LV. Assailants of robbers, if they are outside, are prohibited from the communion of the good thing.[100] If they are clerics they are de-

---

but were actually unbaptized at the time of their appointment to their respective sees. "If there is any one among the lately baptized," argues the Ben. note, is tantamount to saying "If there is any one fit to be bishop."

[97] εἴτε ἐν βαθυῷ. This is understood by Balsamon and Zonaras to include Presbyters, Deacons, and sub-deacons; while the ministry conferred without imposition of hands refers to Readers, Singers, Sacristans, and the like. Alexius Aristenus ranks Singers and Readers with the higher orders, and understands by the lower, keepers of the sacred vessels, candle-lighters, and chancel door keepers. The Ben. note inclines to the latter view on the ground that the word "remain" indicates a category where there was no advance to a higher grade, as was the case with Readers and Singers.

[98] Cf. Can. xxx. p. 239.

[99] i.e. in Canon viii. p. 226 and Canon xi. p. 228.

[100] Here reading, punctuation, and sense are obscure. The Ben. Ed. have ἔξω μὲν ὄντες, τῆς κοινωνίας εἴργονται, and render "Si sint quidem laici, a boni communione arcentur." But ἔξω ὄντες, standing alone, more naturally means non-Chris-

graded from their orders. For, it is said, "All they that take the sword shall perish with the sword."[101]

LVI. The intentional homicide, who has afterwards repented, will be excommunicated from the sacrament[102] for twenty years. The twenty years will be appointed for him as follows: for four he ought to weep, standing outside the door of the house of prayer, beseeching the faithful as they enter in to offer prayer in his behalf, and confessing his own sin. After four years he will be admitted among the hearers, and during five years will go out with them. During seven years he will go out with the kneelers,[103] praying. During four years he will only stand with the faithful, and will not take part in the oblation. On the completion of this period he will be admitted to participation of the sacrament.

LVII. The unintentional homicide will be excluded for ten years from the sacrament. The ten years will be arranged as follows: For two years he will weep, for three years he will continue among the hearers; for four he will be a kneeler; and for one he will only stand. Then he will be admitted to the holy rites.

LVIII. The adulterer will be excluded from the sacrament for fif-

---

tians. Balsamon and Zonaras in Pandects have ἔξω μὲν ὄντες τῆς Ἐκκλησίας εἴργονται τῆς κοινωνίας τοῦ ἀγαθοῦ.

[101] Matt. 26:52.

[102] ἁγιάσμασι. The Ben. Ed. render *Sacramento*. In the Sept. (*e.g.* Amos 7:13) the word=sanctuary. In patristic usage both S. and P. are found for the Lord's Supper, or the consecrated elements; *e.g.* ἁγίασμα in Greg. Nyss., *Ep. Canon. Can*. v. The plural as in this place "*frequentius*." (Suicer *s.v.*)

[103] μετὰ τῶν ἐν ὑποπτώσει. The ὑποπίπτοντεςor *substrati* constituted the third and chief station in the oriental system of penance, the first and second being the προσκλαίοντες, *flentes* or *weepers*, and the ἀκροώμενος, *audientes*, or *hearers*. In the Western Church it is the substrati who are commonly referred to as being in penitence, and the Latin versions of the Canons of Ancyra by Dionysius Exiguus and Martin of Braga render ὑποπίπτοντεςand ὑποπτῶσις by *pœnitentis* and *pœnitentia*. In Basil's Canon xxii. p. 238, this station is specially styled μετάνοια. Cf. *D.C.A.* ii. 1593. "Μετάνοιαnotat *pœnitentiam eorum qui ob delicta sua in ecclesia* ἐπιτιμίοις ἐσωφρονίζοντο (Zonaras, *Ad. Can*. v. *Conc. Antioch*, p. 327), *quique dicebantur* οἱ ἐν μετανοια ὄντες. Chrysostom, *Hom.* iii. *in Epist. ad Eph. in S. Cœnæ communione clamabat* κήρυξ, ὅσοι ἐν μετανοία ἀπέλθετε πάντες." Suicers.*v.*

teen years. During four he will be a weeper, and during five a hearer, during four a kneeler, and for two a slander without communion.

LIX. The fornicator will not be admitted to participation in the sacrament for seven years;[104] weeping two, hearing two, kneeling two, and standing one: in the eighth he will be received into communion.

LX. The woman who has professed virginity and broken her promise will complete the time appointed in the case of adultery in her continence.[105] The same rule will be observed in the case of men who have professed a solitary life and who lapse.

LXI. The thief, if he has repented of his own accord and charged himself, shall only be prohibited from partaking of the sacrament for a year; if he be convicted, for two years. The period shall be divided between kneeling and standing. Then let him be held worthy of communion.

LXII. He who is guilty of unseemliness with males will be under discipline for the same time as adulterers.

---

[104] Cf. Can. xxii. p. 228. The Ben. note is "*Laborant Balsamon et Zonaras in hoc canone conciliando cum vicesimo secundo, atque id causæ afferunt, cur in vicesimo secundo quatuor anni, septem in altero decernantur, quod Basilius in vicesimo secundo antiqua Patrum placita sequatur, suam in altero propriam sententiam exponat. Eundem hunc canonem Alexius Aristenus, ut clarum et perspicuum, negat explicatione indigere. Videbat nimirum doctissimus scriptor duplicem a Basilio distingui fornicationem, leviorem alteram, alteram graviorem levior dicitur, quæ inter personas matrimonio solutas committitur: gravior, cum conjugati hominis libido in mulierem solutam erumpit. Priori anni quatuor, septem alteri imponuntur. Manifesta res est ex canone 21, ubi conjugati peccatum cum soluta fornicationem appellat Basilius, ac longioribus pœnis coerceri, non tamen instar adulterii, testatur. In canone autem 77 eum qui legitiman uxorem dimittit, et aliam ducit, adulterum quidem esse ex Domini sententia testatur, sed tamen ex canonibus Patrum annos septem decernit, non quindecim, ut in adulterio cum aliena uxore commisso. Secum ergo non pugnat cum fornicationi nunc annos quatuor, nunc septem, adulterio nunc septem, nunc quindecim indicit. Eamdem in sententiam videtur accipiendus canon quartus epistolæ Sancti Gregorii Nysseni ad Letoium. Nam cum fornicationi novem annos, adulterio decem et octo imponit, gravior illa intelligenda fornicatio, quam conjugatur cum soluta committit. Hinc ilium adulterium videri fatetur his qui accuratius examinant.*

[105] Cf. Can. xviii. Augustine (*De Bono Viduitatis*, n. 14) represents breaches of the vows of chastity as graver offenses than breaches of the vows of wedlock. The rendering of τῇ οἰκονομίᾳ τῆς καθ' ἑαυτὴν ζωῆς by *continency* is illustrated in the Ben. note by Hermas ii. 4 as well as by Basil, Canon xiv and xlv.

LXIII. He who confesses his iniquity in the case of brutes shall observe the same time in penance.

LXIV. Perjurers shall be excommunicated for ten years; weeping for two, hearing for three, kneeling for four, and standing only during one year; then they shall be held worthy of communion.

LXV. He who confesses magic or sorcery shall do penance for the time of murder, and shall be treated in the same manner as he who convicts himself of this sin.

LXVI. The tomb breaker shall be excommunicated for ten years, weeping for two, hearing for three, kneeling for four, standing for one, then he shall be admitted.

LXVII. Incest with a sister shall incur penance for the same time as murder.

LXVIII. The union of kindred within the prohibited degrees of marriage, if detected as having taken place in acts of sin, shall receive the punishment of adultery.[106]

LXIX. The Reader who has intercourse with his betrothed before marriage, shall be allowed to read after a year's suspension, remaining without advancement. If he has had secret intercourse without betrothal, he shall be deposed from his ministry. So too the minister.[107]

LXX. The deacon who has been polluted in lips, and has confessed his commission of this sin, shall be removed from his ministry. But he shall be permitted to partake of the sacrament together with the deacons. The same holds good in the case of a priest. If anyone be detected in a more serious sin, whatever be his degree, he shall be deposed.[108]

---

[106] This Canon is thus interpreted by Aristenus, *Matrimonium cum propinqua legibus prohibitum eadem ac adulterium pœna castigatur: et cum diversæ sint adulterorum pœnæ sic etiam pro ratione propinquitatis tota res temperabitur. Hinc duas sorores ducenti vii. anni pœnitentiæ irrogantur, ut in adulterio cum muliere libera commisso. non xv. ut in graviore adulterio,* or does it mean that incestuous fornication shall be treated as adultery?

[107] By minister Balsamon and Zonaras understand the subdeacon. Aristenus understands all the clergy appointed without imposition of hands. The Ben. ed. approve the latter. Cf. n. on Canon li. p. 256, and *Letter* liv. p. 157.

[108] On the earlier part of the canon the Ben. note says: "*Balsamon, Zonaras, et*

LXXI. Whoever is aware of the commission of any one of the aforementioned sins, and is convicted without having confessed, shall be under punishment for the same space of time as the actual perpetrator.

Aristenus varia commentantur in hunc canonem, sed a mente Basilii multum abludentia. Liquet enim hoc labiorum peccatum, cui remissior pœna infligitur ipsa actione, quam Basilius minime ignoscendam esse judicat, levius existimari debere. Simili ratione sanctus Pater in cap. vi. Isaiæ n. 185, p. 516, labiorum peccata actionibus, ut leviora, opponit, ac prophetæ delecta non ad actionem et operationem erupisse, sed labiis tenus constitisse observat. In eodem commentarion. 170, p. 501, impuritatis peccatum variis gradibus constare demonstrat, inter quos enumerat ῥήματα φθοροποιά, *verba ad corruptelam apta,* ὁμιλίας μαχράς, *longas confabulationes, quibus ad stuprum pervenitur. Ex his perspici arbitror peccatum aliquod in hoc canone designari, quod ipsa actione levius sit: nedum ea suspicari liceat, quæ Basilii interpretibus in mentem venerunt. Sed tamen cum dico Basilium in puniendis labiorum peccatis leniorem esse, non quodlibet turpium sermonum genus, non immunda colloquia (quomodo enim presbyteris hoc vitio pollutis honorem cathedræ reliquisset?), sed ejusmodi intelligenda est peccandi voluntas, quæ foras quidem aliquo sermone prodit, sed tamen quominus in actum erumpat, subeunte meliori cogitatione, reprimitur. Quemadmodum enim peccata, quæ sola cogitatione committuntur, idcirca leviora esse pronuntiat Basilius, comment. in Isaiamn. 115, p. 459, et n. 243, p. 564, qui repressa est actionis turpitudo; ita hoc loco non quælibet labiorum peccata; non calumnias, non blasphemias, sed ea tantum lenius tractat, quæ adeo gravia non erant, vel etiam ob declinatam actionis turpitudinem, ut patet ex his verbis,* seque eo usque peccasse confessus est, *aliquid indulgentiæ merere videbantur.*"
On the word καθαιρεθήσεται it is remarked: "*In his canonibus quos de clericorum peccatis edidit Basilius, duo videntur silentio prætermissa. Quæri enim possit 1° cur suspensionis pœnam soli lectori ac ministro, sive subdiacono, imponat, diaconis autem et presbyteris depositionem absque ulla prorsus exceptione infligat, nisi quod eis communionem cum diaconis et presbyteris relinquit, si peccatum non ita grave fuerit. Erat tamen suspensionis pœna in ipsos presbyteros non inusitata, ut patet ex plurimis apostolicis canonibus, in quibus presbyteri ac etiam ipsi episcopi segregantur, ac postea, si sese non emendaverint, deponuntur. Forte hæc reliquit Basilius episcopo dijudicanda quemadmodum ejusdem arbitrio permittet in canonibus 74 et 84, ut pœnitentiæ tempus imminuat, si bonus evasint is qui peccavit. 2° Hæc etiam possit institui quæstio, utrumne in gravissimis quidem criminibus pœnitentiam publicam depositioni adjercerit. Adhibita ratio in Canone 3, cur aliquid discriminis clericos inter et laicos ponendum sit, non solum ad gravia peccata, sed etiam ad gravissima pertinet. Ait enim æquum esse ut, cum laici post pœnitentiam in eumdem locum restituantur, clerici vero non restituantur, liberalius et mitius cum clericis agatur. Nolebat ergo clericos lapsos quadruplicem pœnitentiæ gradum percurrere. Sed quemadmodum lapso in fornicationem diacono non statim communionem reddit, sed ejus conversionem et morum emendationem probandam esse censit, ut ad eumdem canonem tertium observavimus, ita dubium esse non potest quin ad criminis magnitudinem probandi modum et tempus accommodaverit.*

LXXII. He who has entrusted himself[109] to soothsayers, or any such persons, shall be under discipline for the same time as the homicide.

LXXIII. He who has denied Christ, and sinned against the mystery of salvation, ought to weep all his life long, and is bound to remain in penitence, being deemed worthy of the sacrament in the hour of death, through faith in the mercy of God.

LXXIV. If, however, each man who has committed the former sins is made good, through penitence,[110] he to whom is committed by the loving-kindness of God the power of loosing and binding[111] will not be deserving of condemnation, if he becomes less severe, as he beholds the exceeding greatness of the penitence of the sinner, so as to lessen the period of punishment, for the history in the Scriptures informs us that all who exercise penitence[112] with greater zeal quickly receive the loving-kindness of God.[113]

LXXV. The man who has been polluted with his own sister, either on the father's or the mother's side, must not be allowed to enter the house of prayer, until he has given up his iniquitous and unlawful conduct. And, after he has come to a sense of that fearful sin, let him

---

[109] The Ben. ed. suppose for the purpose of learning sorcery. Cf. Can. lxxxiii., where a lighter punishment is assigned to consulters of wizards.

[110] ἐξομολογούμενος. "The verb in St. Matt. 11:25 expresses thanksgiving and praise, and in this sense was used by many Christian writers (Suicer,*s.v.*). But more generally in the early Fathers it signifies the whole course of penitential discipline, the outward act and performance of penance. From this it came to mean that public acknowledgment of sin which formed so important a part of penitence. Irenæus (*c. Hær.* i. 13, § 5) speaks of an adulterer who, having been converted, passed her whole life in a state of penitence (ἐξομολογουμένη, in exomologesi); and (*ib.* iii. 4) of Cerdon often coming into the church and confessing his errors (ἐξομολογούμενος)." *D.C.A.* i. 644.

[111] Here we see "binding and loosing" passing from the Scriptural sense of declaring what acts are forbidden and committed (Matt. 16:19 and 23:4. See note of Rev. A. Carr in *Cambridge Bible for Schools*) into the later ecclesiastical sense of imposing and remitting penalties for sin. The first regards rather moral obligation, and, as is implied in the force of the tenses alike in the passages of St. Matthew cited and in St. John 20:23, the recognition and announcement of the divine judgment already passed on sins and sinners; the later regards the imposition of disciplinary penalties.

[112] τοὺς ἐξομολογουμένους.

[113] *e.g.* according to the Ben. note, Manasseh and Hezekiah.

weep for three years standing at the door of the house of prayer, and entreating the people as they go in to prayer that each and all will mercifully offer on his behalf their prayers with earnestness to the Lord. After this let him be received for another period of three years to hearing alone, and while hearing the Scriptures and the instruction, let him be expelled and not be admitted to prayer. Afterwards, if he has asked it with tears and has fallen before the Lord with contrition of heart and great humiliation, let kneeling be accorded to him during other three years. Thus, when he shall have worthily shown the fruits of repentance, let him be received in the tenth year to the prayer of the faithful without oblation; and after standing with the faithful in prayer for two years, then, and not till then, let him be held worthy of the communion of the good thing.

LXXVI. The same rule applies to those who take their own daughters in law.

LXXVII. He who abandons the wife, lawfully united to him, is subject by the sentence of the Lord to the penalty of adultery. But it has been laid down as a canon by our Fathers that such sinners should weep for a year, be hearers for two years, in kneeling for three years, stand with the faithful in the seventh; and thus be deemed worthy of the oblation, if they have repented with tears.[114]

LXXVIII. Let the same rule hold good in the case of those who marry two sisters, although at different times.[115]

---

[114] The Ben. note points out the St. Basil refers to the repudiation of a lawful wife from some other cause than adultery. It remarks that though Basil does not order it to be punished as severely as adultery there is no doubt that he would not allow communion before the dismissal of the unlawful wife. It proceeds "*illud autem difficilius est statuere, quid de matrimonio post ejectam uxorem adulteram contracto senserit. Ratum a Basilio habitum fuisse ejusmodi matrimonium pronuntiat Aristentus. Atque id quidem Basilius, conceptis verbis non declarat; sed tamen videtur hac in re a saniori ac meliori sententia discessisse. Nam 1° maritum injuste dimissum ab alio matrimonio non excludit, ut vidimus in canonibus 9 et 35. Porro non videtur jure dimittenti denegasse, quod injuste dimisso concedebat. 2° Cum jubeat uxorem adulteram ejici, vix dubium est quin matrimonium adulterio uxoris fuisset mariti, ac multo durior, quam uxoris conditio, si nec adulteram retinere, necaliam ducere integrum fuisset.*

[115] Cf. *Letter* clx. p. 212.

LXXIX. Men who rage after their stepmothers are subject to the same canon as those who rage after their sisters.[116]

LXXX. On polygamy the Fathers are silent, as being brutish and altogether inhuman. The sin seems to me worse than fornication. It is therefore reasonable that such sinners should be subject to the canons; namely a year's weeping, three years kneeling and then reception.[117]

LXXXI. During the invasion of the barbarians many men have sworn heathen oaths, tasted things unlawfully offered them in magic temples and so have broken their faith in God. Let regulations be made in the case of these men in accordance with the canons laid down by our Fathers.[118] Those who have endured grievous tortures

---

[116] The Ben. note is *Prima specie non omnino perspicuum est utrum sorores ex utroque parente intelligat, an tantum ex alterutro. Nam cum in canone 79 eos qui suas nurus accipiunt non severius puniat, quam cui cum sorore ex matre vel ex patre rem habent, forte videri posset idem statuere de iis qui in novercas insaniunt. Sed tamen multo probabilius est eamdem illis pœnam imponi, ac iis qui cum sorore ex utroque parente contaminantur. Non enim distinctione utitur Basilius ut in canone 75; nec mirum si peccatum cum noverca gravius quam cum nuru, ob factam patri injuriam, judicavit.*

[117] *i.e.* probably only into the place of standers. Zonaras and Balsamon understand by polygamy a fourth marriage; trigamy being permitted (Cf. Canon l. p. 240) though discouraged. The Ben. annotator dissents, pointing out that in Canon iv. Basil calls trigamy, polygamy, and quoting Gregory of Nazianzus (*Orat.* 31) as calling a third marriage παρανομία. Maran confirms this opinion by the comparison of the imposition on polygamy of the same number of years of penance as are assigned to trigamy in Canon iv. "Theodore of Canterbury a.d. 687 imposes a penance of seven years on trigamists but pronounces the marriages valid (*Penitential, lib.* 1. c. xiv. § 3). Nicephorus of Constantinople, a.d. 814, suspends trigamists for five years. (*Hard. Concil. tom.* iv. p. 1052.) Herard of Tours, a.d. 858 declares any greater number of wives than two to be unlawful (*Cap* cxi. *ibid. tom.*v. p. 557). Leo the Wise, Emperor of Constantinople, was allowed to marry three wives without public remonstrance, but was suspended from communion by the patriarch Nicholas when he married a fourth. This led to a council being held at Constantinople, a.d. 920, which finally settled the Greek discipline on the subject of third and fourth marriages. It ruled that the penalty for a fourth marriage was to be excommunication and exclusion from the church; for a third marriage, if a man were forty years old, suspension for five years, and admission to communion thereafter only on Easter day. If he were thirty years old, suspension for four years, and admission to communion thereafter only three times a year." *Dict. Christ. Ant.*ii. p. 1104.

[118] The Ben. n. thinks that the Fathers of Ancyra are meant, whose authority seems to have been great in Cappadocia and the adjacent provinces.

and have been forced to denial, through inability to sustain the anguish, may be excluded for three years, hearers for two, kneelers for three, and so be received into communion. Those who have abandoned their faith in God, laying hands on the tables of the demons and swearing heathen oaths, without under going great violence, should be excluded for three years, hearers for two. When they have prayed for three years as kneelers, and have stood other three with the faithful in supplication, then let them be received into the communion of the good thing.

LXXXII. As to perjurers, if they have broken their oaths under violent compulsion, they are under lighter penalties and may therefore be received after six years. If they break their faith without compulsion, let them be weepers for two years, hearers for three, pray as kneelers for five, during two be received into the communion of prayer, without oblation, and so at last, after giving proof of due repentance, they shall be restored to the communion of the body of Christ.

LXXXIII. Consulters of soothsayers and they who follow heathen customs, or bring persons into their houses to discover remedies and to effect purification, should fall under the canon of six years. After weeping a year, hearing a year, kneeling for three years and standing with the faithful for a year so let them be received.

LXXXIV. I write all this with a view to testing the fruits of repentance.[119] I do not decide such matters absolutely by time, but I give heed to the manner of penance. If men are in a state in which they find it hard to be weaned from their own ways and choose rather to serve the pleasures of the flesh than to serve the Lord, and refuse to accept the Gospel life, there is no common ground between me and them. In the midst of a disobedient and gainsaying people I have been taught to hear the words "Save thy own soul."[120] Do not then let us consent to perish together with such sinners. Let us fear the awful judgment. Let us keep before our eyes the terrible day of the retribution of the Lord. Let us not consent to perish in other men's sins,

---

[119] μετανοίας. Here the word seems to include both repentance and penance.
[120] Gen. 19:17 (LXX)

for if the terrors of the Lord have not taught us, if so great calamities have not brought us to feel that it is because of our iniquity that the Lord has abandoned us, and given us into the hands of barbarians, that the people have been led captive before our foes and given over to dispersion, because the bearers of Christ's name have dared such deeds; if they have not known nor understood that it is for these reasons that the wrath of God has come upon us, what common ground of argument have I with them?

But we ought to testify to them day and night, alike in public and in private. Let us not consent to be drawn away with them in their wickedness. Let us above all pray that we may do them good, and rescue them from the snare of the evil one. If we cannot do this, let us at all events do our best to save our own souls from everlasting damnation.

Letter 218[121]

TO AMPHILOCHIUS, BISHOP OF ICONIUM

BROTHER ÆLIANUS HAS HIMSELF COMPLETED the business concerning which he came, and has stood in need of no aid from me. I owe him, however, double thanks, both for bringing me a letter from your reverence and for affording me an opportunity of writing to you. By him, therefore, I salute your true and unfeigned love, and beseech you to pray for me more than ever now, when I stand in such need of the aid of your prayers. My health has suffered terribly from the journey to Pontus and my sickness is unendurable. One thing I have long been anxious to make known to you. I do not mean to say that I have been so affected by any other cause as to forget it, but now I wish to put you in mind to send some good man into Lycia, to enquire who are of the right faith, for peradventure they ought not to be neglected, if indeed the report is true, which has been brought to me by a pious traveler from thence, that they have become altogether alienated from the opinion of the

---

[121] Placed in 375.

Asiani[122] and wish to embrace communion with us. If anyone is to go let him enquire at Corydala[123] for Alexander, the late monk, the bishop; at Limyra[124] for Diotimus, and at Myra[125] for Tatianus, Polemo,[126] and Macarius presbyters; at Patara[127] for Eudemus,[128] the bishop; at Telmessus[129] for Hilarius, the bishop; at Phelus for Lallianus, the bishop. Of these and of more besides I have been informed that they are sound in the faith, and I have been grateful to God that even any in the Asian region should be clear of the heretic's pest. If, then, it be possible, let us in the meanwhile make personal enquiry about them. When we have obtained information, I am for writing a letter, and am anxious to invite one of them to meet me. God grant that all may go well with that Church at Iconium, which is so dear to me. Through you I salute all the honorable clergy and all who are associated with your reverence.

Letter 231[130]
TO AMPHILOCHIUS, BISHOP OF ICONIUM

I FIND FEW OPPORTUNITIES of writing to your reverence, and this causes me no little trouble. It is just the same as if, when it was in my power to see you and enjoy your society very often, I did so but seldom. But it is impossible for me to write to you because so few travel hence to you, otherwise there is no reason why my letter should not be a kind of journal of my life, to tell you, my dear friend,

---

[122] i.e. the inhabitants of the Roman province of Asia. Cf. Acts 20:4. Ασιανοὶ δὲ Τυχικὸς καὶ Τρόφιμος.

[123] Corydalla, now Hadginella, is on the road between Lystra and Patara. There are ruins of a theatre. Cf. Plin. v. 25.

[124] Now Phineka.

[125] So the Ben. ed. Other readings are ἐν Κύροις and ἐν Νύροις On Myra Cf. Acts 27:5, on which Conybeare and Howson refer to Fellows' *Asia Minor*, p. 194 and Spratt and Forbes's *Lycia*.

[126] Afterwards bishop of Myra, and as such at Constantinople 381, Labbe 1, 665.

[127] Cf. Acts 21:1.

[128] At Constantinople in 381.

[129] Now Macri, where the ruins are remarkable.

[130] Placed in 375.

everything that happens to me day by day. It is a comfort to me to tell you my affairs, and I know that you care for nothing more than for what concerns me. Now, however, Elpidius[131] is going home to his own master, to refute the calumnies falsely got up against him by certain enemies, and he has asked me for a letter. I therefore salute your reverence by him and commend to you a man who deserves your protection, at once for the sake of justice and for my own sake. Although I could say nothing else in his favor, yet, because he has made it of very great importance to be the bearer of my letter, reckon him among our friends, and remember me and pray for the Church.

You must know that my very God-beloved brother is in exile, for he could not endure the annoyance caused him by shameless persons.[132] Doara[133] is in a state of agitation, for the fat sea monster[134] is throwing everything into confusion. My enemies, as I am informed by those who know, are plotting against me at court. But hitherto the hand of the Lord has been over me. Only pray that I be not abandoned in the end. My brother is taking things quietly. Doara has received the old muleteer.[135] She can do no more. The Lord will scatter the counsels of my enemies. The one cure for all my troubles present and to come is to set eyes on you. If you possibly can, while I am still alive, do come to see me. The book on the Spirit has been written by me, and is finished, as you know. My brethren here have prevented me from sending it to you written on paper, and have told me that they had Your Excellency's orders to engross it on parchment.[136] Not, then, to appear to do anything against your injunctions, I have delayed

---

[131] It is doubtful whether this Elpidius is to be identified with any other of the same name mentioned in the letters.

[132] On the withdrawal of Gregory of Nyssa.

[133] Doara was one of the bishoprics in Cappadocia Secunda under Tyana; now Hadji Bektash. Ramsay, *Hist. Geog. Asia Minor*, p. 287.

[134] *i.e.* Demosthenes. Such language may seem inconsistent with the tone of *Letter* ccxxv., but that, it will be remembered, was an official and formal document, while the present letter is addressed to an intimate friend.

[135] Possibly another hit at Demosthenes. The name might be thought to fit Anthimus, but with him Basil had made peace. Cf. *Letter* ccx.

[136] ἐν σωματίῳ, *i.e.* in a volume, not on leaves of papyrus, but in book form, as *e.g.* the *Cod. Alexandrinus* in the B.M.

now, but I will send it a little later, if only I find any suitable person to convey it. May you be granted to me and to God's Church by the kindness of the Holy One, in all health and happiness, and praying for me to the Lord.

Letter 232[137]
TO AMPHILOCHIUS, BISHOP OF ICONIUM

EVERY DAY THAT BRINGS me a letter from you is a feast day, the very greatest of feast days. And when symbols of the feast are brought, what can I call it but a feast of feasts, as the old law used to speak of Sabbath of Sabbaths? I thank the Lord that you are quite well, and that you have celebrated the commemoration of the economy of salvation[138] in a Church at peace. I have been disturbed by some troubles; and have not been without distress from the fact of my God-beloved brother being in exile. Pray for him that God may one day grant him to see his Church healed from the wounds of heretical bites. Do come to see me while I am yet upon this earth. Act in accordance with your own wishes and with my most earnest prayers. I may be allowed to be astonished at the meaning of your blessings, inasmuch as you have mysteriously wished me a vigorous old age. By your lamps[139] you rouse me to nightly toil; and by your sweet meats you seem to pledge yourself securely that all my body is in good case. But there is no munching for me at my time of life, for my teeth have

---

[137] Placed in 375. Maran, *Vit. Bas.* xxxv., thinks that this letter is to be placed either in the last days of 375, if the Nativity was celebrated on December 25, or in the beginning of 376, if it followed after the Epiphany. The Oriental usage up to the end of the fourth century, was to celebrate the Nativity and Baptism on January 6. St. Chrysostom, in the homily on the birthday of our Savior, delivered c. 386, speaks of the separation of the celebration of the Nativity from that of the Epiphany as comparatively recent. Cf. *D.C.A.*, 1, pp. 361, 617.

[138] *i.e.* the incarnation. Cf. pp. 7 and 12, n.

[139] The reading of the Ben. ed. is λαμπηνῶν. The only meaning of λαμπήνη in Class. Greek is a kind of *covered carriage*, and the cognate adj. λαμπήνικος is used for the *covered* waggons of Numb. 7:3 in the LXX. But the context necessitates some such meaning as *lamp* or candle. Ducange *s.v.* quotes John de Janua "*Lampenæ sunt stellæ fulgentes.*" Cf. Italian *Lampana*, *i.e.* lamp.

long ago been worn away by time and bad health. As to what you have asked me there are some replies in the document I send you, written to the best of my ability, and as opportunity has allowed.

Letter 233[140]
TO AMPHILOCHIUS, IN REPLY TO CERTAIN QUESTIONS

I KNOW THAT I have myself heard of this, and I am aware of the constitution of mankind. What shall I say? The mind is a wonderful thing, and therein we possess that which is after the image of the Creator. And the operation of the mind is wonderful; in that, in its perpetual motion, it frequently forms imaginations about things non-existent as though they were existent, and is frequently carried straight to the truth. But there are in it two faculties; in accordance with the view of us who believe in God, the one evil, that of the demons which draws us on to their own apostasy; and the divine and the good, which brings us to the likeness of God. When, therefore, the mind remains alone and unaided, it contemplates small things, commensurate with itself. When it yields to those who deceive it, it nullifies its proper judgment, and is concerned with monstrous fancies. Then it considers wood to be no longer wood, but a god; then it looks on gold no longer as money, but as an object of worship.[141] If on the other hand it assents to its diviner part, and accepts the boons of the Spirit, then, so far as its nature admits, it becomes perceptive of the divine. There are, as it were, three conditions of life, and three operations of the mind. Our ways may be wicked, and the movements of our mind wicked; such as adulteries, thefts, idolatries, slanders, strife, passion, sedition, vain-glory, and all that the apostle Paul enumerates among the works of the flesh.[142] Or the soul's operation is, as it were, in a mean, and has nothing about it either damnable or laud-

---

[140] Placed in 376.
[141] St. Basil's word may point either at the worshippers of a golden image in a shrine in the ordinary sense, or at the state of things where, as A. H. Clough has it, "no golden images may be worshipped except the currency."
[142] Cf. Gal. 5:19, 20, 21.

able, as the perception of such mechanical crafts as we commonly speak of as indifferent, and, of their own character, inclining neither towards virtue nor towards vice. For what vice is there in the craft of the helmsman or the physician? Neither are these operations in themselves virtues, but they incline in one direction or the other in accordance with the will of those who use them. But the mind which is impregnated with the Godhead of the Spirit is at once capable of viewing great objects; it beholds the divine beauty, though only so far as grace imparts and its nature receives.

Let them dismiss, therefore, these questions of dialectics and examine the truth, not with mischievous exactness but with reverence. The judgment of our mind is given us for the understanding of the truth. Now our God is the very truth.[143] So the primary function of our mind is to know one God, but to know Him so far as the infinitely great can be known by the very small. When our eyes are first brought to the perception of visible objects, all visible objects are not at once brought into sight. The hemisphere of heaven is not beheld with one glance, but we are surrounded by a certain appearance, though in reality many things, not to say all things, in it are unperceived—the nature of the stars, their greatness, their distances, their movements, their conjunctions, their intervals, their other conditions, the actual essence of the firmament, the distance of depth from the concave circumference to the convex surface. Nevertheless, no one would allege the heaven to be invisible because of what is unknown; it would be said to be visible on account of our limited perception of it. It is just the same in the case of God. If the mind has been injured by devils it will be guilty of idolatry, or will be perverted to some other form of impiety. But if it has yielded to the aid of the Spirit, it will have understanding of the truth, and will know God. But it will know Him, as the Apostle says, in part; and in the life to come more perfectly. For "when that which is perfect is come, then that which is in part shall be done away."[144] The judgment of the mind is, therefore, good and given us for a good end—the perception of God; but it operates only so far as it can.

---

[143] ἡ αὐτοαλήθεια.
[144] 1 Cor. 13:10.

Letter 234[145]
TO THE SAME, IN ANSWER TO ANOTHER QUESTION

DO YOU WORSHIP WHAT you know or what you do not know? If I answer, I worship what I know, they immediately reply, What is the essence of the object of worship? Then, if I confess that I am ignorant of the essence, they turn on me again and say, So you worship you know not what. I answer that the word *to know* has many meanings. We say that we know the greatness of God, His power, His wisdom, His goodness, His providence over us, and the justness of His judgment; but not His very essence. The question is, therefore, only put for the sake of dispute. For he who denies that he knows the essence does not confess himself to be ignorant of God, because our idea of God is gathered from all the attributes which I have enumerated. But God, he says, is simple, and whatever attribute of Him you have reckoned as knowable is of His essence. But the absurdities involved in this sophism are innumerable. When all these high attributes have been enumerated, are they all names of one essence? And is there the same mutual force in His awfulness and His loving-kindness, His justice and His creative power, His providence and His foreknowledge, and His bestowal of rewards and punishments, His majesty and His providence? In mentioning any one of these do we declare His essence? If they say, yes, let them not ask if we know the essence of God, but let them enquire of us whether we know God to be awful, or just, or merciful. These we confess that we know. If they say that essence is something distinct, let them not put us in the wrong on the score of simplicity. For they confess themselves that there is a distinction between the essence and each one of the attributes enumerated. The operations are various, and the essence simple, but we say that we know our God from His operations, but do not undertake to approach near to His essence. His operations come down to us, but His essence remains beyond our reach.

---

[145] Placed in 376.

But, it is replied, if you are ignorant of the essence, you are ignorant of Himself. Retort, If you say that you know His essence, you are ignorant of Himself. A man who has been bitten by a mad dog, and sees a dog in a dish, does not really see any more than is seen by people in good health; he is to be pitied because he thinks he sees what he does not see. Do not then admire him for his announcement, but pity him for his insanity. Recognize that the voice is the voice of mockers, when they say, if you are ignorant of the essence of God, you worship what you do not know. I do know that He exists; what His essence is, I look at as beyond intelligence. How then am I saved? Through faith. It is faith sufficient to know that God exists, without knowing what He is; and "He is a rewarder of them that seek Him."[146] So knowledge of the divine essence involves perception of His incomprehensibility, and the object of our worship is not that of which we comprehend the essence, but of which we comprehend that the essence exists.

And the following counter question may also be put to them. "No man hath seen God at any time, the Only-begotten which is in the bosom hath declared him."[147] What of the Father did the Only-begotten Son declare? His essence or His power? If His power, we know so much as He declared to us. If His essence, tell me where He said that His essence was the being unbegotten?[148] When did Abraham worship? Was it not when he believed? And when did he believe? Was it not when he was called? Where in this place is there any testimony in Scripture to Abraham's comprehending? When did the disciples worship Him? Was it not when they saw creation subject to Him? It was from the obedience of sea and winds to Him that they recognized His Godhead. Therefore, the knowledge came from the operations, and the worship from the knowledge. "Believest thou that I am able to do this?" "I believe, Lord;"[149] and he worshipped Him. So, worship follows faith, and faith is confirmed by power. But if you say that the believer also knows, he knows from what he believes; and vice versa

---

[146] Heb. 11:6.
[147] John 1:18.
[148] ἀγεννησία. Cf. Prolegomena on the Books against Eunomius, and p. 39 n.
[149] Cf. Matt. 9:28.

he believes from what he knows. We know God from His power. We, therefore, believe in Him who is known, and we worship Him who is believed in.

Letter 235[150]
TO THE SAME, IN ANSWER TO ANOTHER QUESTION

WHICH IS FIRST IN order, knowledge or faith? I reply that generally, in the case of disciples, faith precedes knowledge. But, in our teaching, if anyone asserts knowledge to come before faith, I make no objection; understanding knowledge so far as is within the bounds of human comprehension. In our lessons, we must first believe that the letter *a* is said to us; then we learn the characters and their pronunciation, and last of all we get the distinct idea of the force of the letter. But in our belief about God, first comes the idea that God is. This we gather from His works. For, as we perceive His wisdom, His goodness, and all His invisible things from the creation of the world,[151] so we know Him. So, too, we accept Him as our Lord. For since God is the Creator of the whole world, and we are a part of the world, God is our Creator. This knowledge is followed by faith, and this faith by worship.

But the word knowledge has many meanings, and so those who make sport of simpler minds, and like to make themselves remarkable by astounding statements (just like jugglers who get the balls out of sight before men's very eyes), hastily included everything in their general enquiry. Knowledge, I say, has a very wide application, and knowledge may be got of what a thing is, by number, by bulk, by force, by its mode of existence, by the period of its generation, by its essence. When then our opponents include the whole in their question, if they catch us in the confession that we know, they straightway demand from us knowledge of the essence; if, on the contrary, they see us cautious as to making any assertion on the subject, they affix on us the stigma of impiety. I, however, confess that I know what is

---
[150] Placed in 376.
[151] Cf. Rom. 1:20.

knowable of God, and that I know what it is which is beyond my comprehension.[152] So if you ask me if I know what sand is, and I reply that I do, you will obviously be slandering me, if you straightway ask me the number of the sand; inasmuch as your first enquiry bore only on the form of sand, while your second unfair objection bore upon its number. The quibble is just as though any one were to say, Do you know Timothy? Oh, if you know Timothy you know his nature. Since you have acknowledged that you know Timothy, give me an account of Timothy's nature. Yes; but I at the same time both know and do not know Timothy, though not in the same way and in the same degree. It is not that I do not know in the same way in which I do know; but I know in one way and am ignorant in one way. I know him according to his form and other properties; but I am ignorant of his essence. Indeed, in this way too, I both know, and am ignorant of, myself. I know indeed who I am, but, so far as I am ignorant of my essence I do not know myself.

Let them tell me in what sense Paul says, "Now we know in part";[153] do we know His essence in part, as knowing parts of His essence? No. This is absurd; for God is without parts. But do we know the whole essence? How then "When that which is perfect is come, then that which is in part shall be done away."[154] Why are idolaters found fault with? Is it not because they knew God and did not honor Him as God? Why are the "foolish Galatians"[155] reproached by Paul in the words, "After that ye have known God, or rather are known of God, how turn ye again to the weak and beggarly elements?"[156] How was God known in Jewry? Was it because in Jewry it was known what His essence is? "The ox," it is said, "knoweth his owner."[157] According to your argument the ox knows his lord's essence. "And the ass his

---

[152] A various reading gives the sense "but do not know what is beyond my comprehension."
[153] 1 Cor. 13:9.
[154] 1 Cor. 13:10.
[155] Gal. 3:1.
[156] Gal. 4:9.
[157] Is. 1:3.

master's crib."[158] So the ass knows the essence of the crib, but "Israel doth not know me." So, according to you, Israel is found fault with for not knowing what the essence of God is. "Pour out thy wrath upon the heathen that have not known thee,"[159] that is, who have not comprehended thy essence. But, I repeat, knowledge is manifold—it involves perception of our Creator, recognition of His wonderful works, observance of His commandments and intimate communion with Him. All this they thrust on one side and force knowledge into one single meaning, the contemplation of God's essence. Thou shalt put them, it is said, before the testimony and I shall be known of thee thence.[160] Is the term, "I shall be known of thee," instead of, "I will reveal my essence"? "The Lord knoweth them that are his."[161] Does He know the essence of them that are His, but is ignorant of the essence of those who disobey Him? "Adam knew his wife."[162] Did he know her essence? It is said of Rebekah "She was a virgin, neither had any man known her,"[163] and "How shall this be seeing I know not a man?"[164] Did no man know Rebekah's essence? Does Mary mean "I do not know the essence of any man"? Is it not the custom of Scripture to use the word "know" of nuptial embraces? The statement that God shall be known from the mercy seat means that He will be known to His worshippers. And the Lord knoweth them that are His, means that on account of their good works He receives them into intimate communion with Him.

---

[158] Is. 1:3.
[159] Ps. 78:6 (LXX).
[160] Referred by the Ben. Ed. to Ex. 25:21 and 22. The first clause is apparently introduced from Ex. 16:34.
[161] 2 Tim. 2:19.
[162] Gen. 4:1.
[163] Gen. 24:16.
[164] Luke 1:34.

Letter 236[165]
TO THE SAME AMPHILOCHIUS

ENQUIRY HAS ALREADY FREQUENTLY been made concerning the saying of the gospels as to our Lord Jesus Christ's ignorance of the day and of the hour of the end;[166] an objection constantly put forward by the Anomœans to the destruction of the glory of the Only-Begotten, in order to show Him to be unlike in essence and subordinate in dignity; inasmuch as, if He know not all things, He cannot possess the same nature nor be regarded as of one likeness with Him, who by His own prescience and faculty of forecasting the future has knowledge coextensive with the universe. This question has now been proposed to me by your intelligence as a new one. I can give in reply the answer which I heard from our fathers when I was a boy, and which on account of my love for what is good, I have received without question. I do not expect that it can undo the shamelessness of them that fight against Christ, for where is the reasoning strong enough to stand their attack? It may, however, suffice to convince all that love the Lord, and in whom the previous assurance supplied them by faith is stronger than any demonstration of reason.

Now "no man" seems to be a general expression, so that not even one person is excepted by it, but this is not its use in Scripture, as I have observed in the passage "there is none good but one, that is, God."[167] For even in this passage the Son does not so speak to the exclusion of Himself from the good nature. But, since the Father is the first good, we believe the words "no man" to have been uttered with the understood addition of "first."[168] So with the passage "No man

---

[165] This letter is also dated in 376, and treats of further subjects not immediately raised by the *De Spiritu Sancto*: How Christ can be said to be ignorant of the day and the hour; Of the prediction of Jeremiah concerning Jeconiah; Of an objection of the Encratites; Of fate; Of emerging in baptism; Of the accentuation of the word φάγος; Of essence and hypostasis; Of the ordaining of things neutral and indifferent.

[166] Mark 13:32.

[167] Mark 10:18. *i.e.* in *Adv. Eumon.* iv. *vide* Proleg.

[168] The manuscripts at this point are corrupt and divergent.

knoweth the Son but the Father;"[169] even here there is no charge of ignorance against the Spirit, but only a testimony that knowledge of His own nature naturally belongs to the Father first. Thus also we understand "No man knoweth,"[170] to refer to the Father the first knowledge of things, both present and to be, and generally to exhibit to men the first cause. Otherwise how can this passage fall in with the rest of the evidence of Scripture, or agree with the common notions of us who believe that the Only-Begotten is the image of the invisible God, and image not of the bodily figure, but of the very Godhead and of the mighty qualities attributed to the essence of God, image of power, image of wisdom, as Christ is called "the power of God and the wisdom of God"?[171] Now of wisdom knowledge is plainly a part; and if in any part He falls short, He is not an image of the whole; and how can we understand the Father not to have shown that day and that hour—the smallest portion of the ages—to Him through Whom He made the ages? How can the Creator of the universe fall short of the knowledge of the smallest portion of the things created by Him? How can He who says, when the end is near, that such and such signs shall appear in heaven and in earth, be ignorant of the end itself? When He says, "The end is not yet."[172] He makes a definite statement, as though with knowledge and not in doubt. Then further, it is plain to the fair enquirer that our Lord says many things to men, in the character of man; as for instance, "give me to drink"[173] is a saying of our Lord, expressive of His bodily necessity; and yet the asker was not soulless flesh, but Godhead using flesh endued with soul.[174] So in the present instance no one will be carried beyond the bounds of the interpretation of true religion, who understands the ignorance of him who had received all things according to the œconomy,[175] and

---

[169] Matt. 11:27.
[170] Matt. 24:36.
[171] 1 Cor. 1:24.
[172] Matt. 24:6.
[173] John 4:7.
[174] Cf. *Ep.* cclxi. 2. The reference is to the system of Apollinarius, which denied to the Son a ψυχὴ λογική or reasonable soul.
[175] οἰκονομικῶς, *i.e.* according to the œconomy of the incarnation.

was advancing with God and man in favor and wisdom.[176]

It would be worthy of your diligence to set the phrases of the Gospel side by side, and compare together those of Matthew and those of Mark, for these two alone are found in concurrence in this passage. The wording of Matthew is "of that day and hour knoweth no man, no, not the angels of heaven, but my Father only."[177] That of Mark runs, "But of that day and that hour knoweth no man, no, not the angels which are in heaven, neither the Son, but the Father."[178] What is noticeable in these passages is this; that Matthew says nothing about the ignorance of the Son, and seems to agree with Mark as to sense in saying "but my Father only." Now I understand the word "only" to have been used in contradistinction to the angels, but that the Son is not included with His own servants in ignorance.

He could not say what is false Who said "All things that the Father hath are Mine,"[179] but one of the things which the Father hath is knowledge of that day and of that hour. In the passage in Matthew, then, the Lord made no mention of His own Person, as a matter beyond controversy, and said that the angels knew not and that His Father alone knew, tacitly asserting the knowledge of His Father to be His own knowledge too, because of what He had said elsewhere, "as the Father knoweth me even so know I the Father,"[180] and if the Father has complete knowledge of the Son, nothing excepted, so that He knows all knowledge to dwell in Him, He will clearly be known as fully by the Son with all His inherent wisdom and all His knowledge of things to come. This modification, I think, may be given to the words of Matthew, "but my Father only." Now as to the words of Mark, who appears distinctly to exclude the Son from the knowledge, my opinion is this. No man knoweth, neither the angels of God;

---

[176] Cf. Luke 2:52.

[177] Matt. 24.36. R.V. in this passage inserts "Neither the Son," on the authority of ℵ, B. D. Plainly St. Basil knew no such difference of reading. On the general view taken by the Fathers on the self-limitation of the Savior, Cf. C. Gore's *Bampton Lectures* (vi. p. 163, and notes 48 and 49, p. 267).

[178] Mark 13:32.

[179] John 16:15.

[180] John 10:15.

nor yet the Son would have known unless the Father had known: that is, the cause of the Son's knowing comes from the Father. To a fair hearer there is no violence in this interpretation, because the word "only" is not added as it is in Matthew. Mark's sense, then, is as follows: of that day and of that hour knoweth no man, nor the angels of God; but even the Son would not have known if the Father had not known, for the knowledge naturally His was given by the Father. This is very decorous and becoming the divine nature to say of the Son, because He has, His knowledge and His being, beheld in all the wisdom and glory which become His Godhead, from Him with Whom He is consubstantial.

As to Jeconias, whom the prophet Jeremiah declares in these words to have been rejected from the land of Judah, "Jeconias was dishonoured like a vessel for which there is no more use; and because he was cast out he and his seed; and none shall rise from his seed sitting upon the throne of David and ruling in Judah,"[181] the matter is plain and clear. On the destruction of Jerusalem by Nebuchadnezzar, the kingdom had been destroyed, and there was no longer a hereditary succession of reigns as before. Nevertheless, at that time, the deposed descendants of David were living in captivity. On the return of Salathiel and Zerubbabel the supreme government rested to a greater degree with the people, and the sovereignty was afterwards transferred to the priesthood, on account of the intermingling of the priestly and royal tribes; whence the Lord, in things pertaining to God, is both King and High Priest. Moreover, the royal tribe did not fail until the coming of the Christ; nevertheless, the seed of Jeconias sat no longer upon the throne of David. Plainly it is the royal dignity which is described by the term "throne." You remember the history, how all Judæa, Idumæa, Moab, both the neighboring regions of Syria and the further countries up to Mesopotamia, and the country on the other side as far as the river of Egypt, were all tributary to David. If then none of his descendants appeared with a sovereignty so wide, how is not the word of the prophet true that no one of the seed of

---

[181] Jer. 22:28–30 (LXX).

Jeconias should any longer sit upon the throne of David, for none of his descendants appears to have attained this dignity. Nevertheless, the tribe of Judah did not fail, until He for whom it was destined came. But even He did not sit upon the material throne. The kingdom of Judæa was transferred to Herod, the son of Antipater the Ascalonite, and his sons who divided Judæa into four principalities, when Pilate was Procurator and Tiberius was Master of the Roman Empire. It is the indestructible kingdom which he calls the throne of David on which the Lord sat. He is the expectation of the Gentiles[182] and not of the smallest division of the world, for it is written, "In that day there shall be a root of Jesse which shall stand for an ensign of the people; to it shall the Gentiles seek."[183] "I have called thee...for a covenant of the people for a light of the Gentiles";[184] and thus then God remained a priest although He did not receive the sceptre of Judah, and King of all the earth; so the blessing of Jacob was fulfilled, and in Him[185] "shall all the nations of the earth be blessed," and all the nations shall call the Christ blessed.

And as to the tremendous question put by the facetious Encratites, why we do not eat everything? Let this answer be given, that we turn with disgust from our excrements. As far as dignity goes, to us flesh is grass; but as to distinction between what is and what is not serviceable, just as in vegetables, we separate the unwholesome from the wholesome, so in flesh we distinguish between that which is good and that which is bad for food. Hemlock is a vegetable, just as vulture's flesh is flesh; yet no one in his senses would eat henbane nor dog's flesh unless he were in very great straits. If he did, however, he would not sin.

Next as to those who maintain that human affairs are governed by fate, do not ask information from me, but stab them with their own shafts of rhetoric. The question is too long for my present infirmity. With regard to emerging in baptism—I do not know how it came into

---

[182] Gen. 49:10 (LXX).
[183] Is. 11:10. The LXX is καὶ ὁ ἀνιστάμενος ἄρχειν ἐθνῶν.
[184] Is. 42:6, and 2 Kings 7:13.
[185] Gen. 22:18.

your mind to ask such a question, if indeed you understood immersion to fulfil the figure of the three days. It is impossible for anyone to be immersed three times, without emerging three times. We write the word φάγος paroxytone.[186]

The distinction between οὐσία and ὑπόστασις is the same as that between the general and the particular; as, for instance, between the animal and the particular man. Wherefore, in the case of the Godhead, we confess one essence or substance so as not to give a variant definition of existence, but we confess a particular hypostasis, in order that our conception of Father, Son and Holy Spirit may be without confusion and clear.[187] If we have no distinct perception of the separate characteristics, namely, fatherhood, son-ship, and sanctification, but form our conception of God from the general idea of existence, we cannot possibly give a sound account of our faith. We must, therefore, confess the faith by adding the particular to the common. The Godhead is common; the fatherhood particular. We must therefore combine the two and say, "I believe in God the Father." The like course must be pursued in the confession of the Son; we must combine the particular with the common and say "I believe in God the Son," so in the case of the Holy Ghost we must make our utterance conform to the appellation and say "in God[188] the Holy Ghost." Hence it results that there is a satisfactory preservation of the unity by the confession of the one Godhead, while in the distinction of the indi-

---

[186] Amphilochius's doubt may have arisen from the fact that φαγός, the Doric form of φηγός, the esculent oak of Homer, is oxytone.

[187] "ἀσύγχυτος," *unconfounded, or without confusion*, is the title of *Dialogue II.* of Theodoret. Cf. p. 195. n.

[188] The Benedictine note is *Videtur in Harlæano codice scriptum prima manu* εἰς τὸν θεόν. Their reading is εἰς τὸ θεῖον πνεῦμα τὸ ἅγιον. Cf. *Ep.* viii., § 2, where no variation of MSS. is noted and *Ep.* cxli, both written before he was bishop. Cf. Proleg. Gregory of Nazianzus, *Or.* xliii., explains the rationale of St. Basil's use of the word "God," of the Holy Ghost; alike in his public and private teaching he never shrank from using it, whenever he could with impunity, and his opinions were perfectly well known, but he sought to avoid the sentence of exile at the hands of the Arians by its unnecessary obtrusion. He never uses it in his homily *De Fide*, and the whole treatise *De Spiritu Sancto*, while it exhaustively vindicates the doctrine, ingeniously steers clear of the phrase.

vidual properties regarded in each there is the confession of the peculiar properties of the Persons. On the other hand those who identify essence or substance and hypostasis are compelled to confess only three Persons,[189] and, in their hesitation to speak of three hypostases, are convicted of failure to avoid the error of Sabellius, for even Sabellius himself, who in many places confuses the conception, yet, by asserting that the same hypostasis changed its form[190] to meet the needs of the moment, does endeavor to distinguish persons.

Lastly as to your enquiry in what manner things neutral and indifferent are ordained for us, whether by some chance working by its own accord, or by the righteous providence of God, my answer is this: Health and sickness, riches and poverty, credit and discredit, inasmuch as they do not render their possessors good, are not in the category of things naturally good, but, in so far as in any way they make life's current flow more easily, in each case the former is to be preferred to its contrary, and has a certain kind of value. To some men these things are given by God for stewardship's sake,[191] as for instance to Abraham, to Job and such like. To inferior characters they are a chal-

---

[189] πρόσωπα.

[190] The Ben. Edd. note "*Existimat Combefisius verbum* μετασχηματίζεσθαι *sic reddendum esse,*in various formas mutari. *Sed id non dicebat Sabellius. Hoc tantum dicebat, ut legimus in Epist.* ccxiv. Unum quidem hypostasi Deum esse, sed sub diversis personis a Scripturare præsentari. According to Dante the minds of the heresiarchs were to Scripture as bad mirrors, reflecting distorted images; and, in this sense, μετασχηματίζειν might be applied rather to them.

"Si fe Sabellio ed Arrio e quegli stolti,
Che furon come spade alle scritture
In render torti li diritti volti."
Par. xiii. 123 (see Cary's note).

[191] ἐξ οἰκονομίας. In *Ep.* xxxi. Basil begins a letter to Eusebius of Samosata: "The dearth has not yet left us, we are therefore compelled still to remain in the town, either for stewardship's sake or for sympathy with the afflicted." Here the Benedictines' note is *Sæpe apud Basilium* οἰκονομία *dicitur id quod pauperibus distribuitur. Vituperat in Comment. in Isa.* præsules qui male partam pecuniam accipiunt vel ad suos usus, ἡ ἐπὶ λόγῳ τῆς τῶν πτωχευόντων ἐν τῇ Ἐκκλησίᾳ οἰκονομίας, *vel per causam distribuendi pauperibus Ecclesiæ. In Epistola 92 Orientales inter mala Ecclesiæ illud etiam deplorant quod ambitiosi præsules* οἰκονομ *as* πτωχῶν, *pecunias pauperibus destinatas in suos usus convertant.*

lenge to improvement. For the man who persists in unrighteousness, after so goodly a token of love from God, subjects himself to condemnation without defense. The good man, however, neither turns his heart to wealth when he has it, nor seeks after it if he has it not. He treats what is given him as given him not for his selfish enjoyment, but for wise administration. No one in his senses runs after the trouble of distributing other people's property, unless he is trying to get the praise of the world, which admires and envies anybody in authority.

Good men take sickness as athletes take their contest, waiting for the crowns that are to reward their endurance. To ascribe the dispensation of these things to anyone else is as inconsistent with true religion as it is with common sense.

Letter 248[192]

TO AMPHILOCHIUS, BISHOP OF ICONIUM

SO FAR AS MY own wishes are concerned I am grieved at living at such a distance from your reverence. But, as regards the peace of your own life, I thank the Lord Who has kept you out of this conflagration which has specially ravaged my diocese. For the just Judge has sent me, in accordance with my works, a messenger of Satan,[193] who is buffeting me[194] severely enough, and is vigorously defending the heresy. Indeed, to such a pitch has he carried the war against us, that he does not shrink even from shedding the blood of those who trust in God. You cannot fail to have heard that a man of the name of Asclepius,[195] because he would not consent to communion with Doeg,[196] has died under the blows inflicted on him by them, or rather, by their blows has been translated into life. You may sup-

---

[192] Placed in 376.

[193] Cf. 2 Cor. 12:7.

[194] The word κατακονδυλίζω here used (it occurs in Æschines) is a synonym, slightly strengthened, for the κολαφίζω of St. Paul. St. Basil seems plainly to have the passage quoted in his mind.

[195] I have failed to find further mention of this Asclepius. An Asclepius of Cologne is commemorated on June 30.

[196] Cf. 1 Sam. 21:18.

pose that the rest of their doings are of a piece with this; the persecutions of presbyters and teachers, and all that might be expected to be done by men abusing the imperial authority at their own caprice. But, in answer to your prayers, the Lord will give us release from these things, and patience to bear the weight of our trials worthily of our hope in Him. Pray write frequently to me of all that concerns yourself. If you find anyone who can be trusted to carry you the book that I have finished, be so kind as to send for it, that so, when I have been cheered by your approval, I may send it on to others also. By the grace of the Holy One may you be granted to me and to the Church of the Lord in good health rejoicing in the Lord, and praying for me.

ⲁ☦ⲱ

Made in the USA
Las Vegas, NV
27 August 2022